Creating Shareholder Value

Creating Shareholder Value

The New Standard for Business Performance

ALFRED RAPPAPORT

THE FREE PRESS
A Division of Macmillan, Inc.
NEW YORK

Maxwell Macmillan Canada
TORONTO

Maxwell Macmillan International
NEW YORK OXFORD SINGAPORE SYDNEY

The Free Press
A Division of Macmillan, Inc.
866 Third Avenue, New York, N.Y. 10022

Maxwell Macmillan Canada, Inc.
1200 Eglinton Avenue East
Suite 200
Don Mills, Ontario M3C 3N1

Macmillan, Inc. is part of the Maxwell Communication Group of Companies.

Printed in the United States of America

printing number

15 16 17 18 19 20

Library of Congress Cataloging-in-Pulication Data

Rappaport, Alfred.
Creating shareholder value.

Bibliography: p.
Includes index.
1. Corporations—Valuation. 2. Stocks—Prices.
3. Corporate profits. 4. Investments—Accounting.
I. Title. II. Title: Shareholder value.
HG4028.V3R36 1986 658.1'55 86-18336
ISBN 0-02-925720-4

To Sharon

Contents

List of Illustrations

Preface

THE IDEA THAT BUSINESS STRATEGIES should be judged by the economic value they create for shareholders is well accepted in the business community. After all, to suggest that companies be operated in the best interests of its owners is hardly controversial. Nonetheless, based on surveys of practice and my own experience with a cross section of large, publicly held companies, there is great uncertainty about how to evaluate strategies and subsequent performance with measures that are reliably linked to the objective of providing maximum returns to shareholders. Some companies emphasize short-term measures while others employ longer-term measures. Even within the same company, some investments are evaluated with accounting criteria such as earnings or return on investment while others are often assessed using the discounted cash flow approach.

The current climate for a fundamental reassessment of the measurement of business performance could not be better. Despite impressive double-digit earnings-per-share growth, returns to shareholders were minimal or negative during much of the 1970s due to inflation and lagging productivity. The growing recognition that traditional accounting measures such as earnings per share are not reliably linked to increasing the value of the company's stock price has made top management more receptive than ever to considering alternative measures. Couple this with the pervasive threat of corporate takeover for which incumbent management's best defense is a higher stock price, and it comes as no surprise that increasing shareholder value has become the driving force for the current corporate restructuring movement.

This book presents major applications of the shareholder value approach to management planning and performance evaluation. Not only is the rationale for the shareholder value approach presented, but the tools needed to implement it as the new standard for business performance are provided as well. The shareholder value approach can be used to analyze publicly traded or privately held corporations, as well as business units, strategies, or product lines. Throughout the book an effort is made to integrate operating and financial analysis. In particular, the direct linkage between competitive strategy and shareholder value analysis is demonstrated by translating business strategies into the dollars of value they create. What is most encouraging is that the shareholder value applications presented here have recently been introduced and successfully implemented by an ever-increasing number of companies.

The book is intended for a broad audience and is directed to senior management with operating, planning, or financial responsibilities who wish to develop value-creating business strategies and to security analysts who wish to develop improved insights about the potential economic attractiveness of companies and industries. The book also provides a useful foundation for management consultants, investment bankers, commercial bankers, public accountants, and others offering professional services to companies. Finally, the book's integration of strategic planning concepts with modern finance theory is compatible with the leading textbooks currently used in business school classrooms.

There are a number of people whom I would like to acknowledge and thank for their contributions to the book. First, my thanks go to Donald P. Jacobs, Dean of the Kellogg Graduate School of Management at Northwestern University, who has not only been a source of encouragement for many years, but whose leadership has fostered an extraordinarily stimulating environment for research and teaching. I have also benefited from a number of my colleagues at Kellogg who offered constructive challenges at earlier stages when some of the ideas in the book were far less developed.

More recently, I have benefited greatly from my association with The Alcar Group. The following Alcar people provided insightful comments on the entire manuscript: Kevin Dages, Andrew Garrett, Susan L. Hall, Jeffrey Miller, John C. Miller, Jerald I. Moskowitz, William Roper, Jr., Robert C. Statius Muller, and Charles H. Zent. Philip J. Eynon, Elizabeth Friskey, and Thomas W. Swann not only contributed substantive comments, but also helped make the book eminently more readable than it might otherwise have been. Others who have offered useful comments include Thomas F. Barnum, Michael A. Bell (Monitor Company), Professor William H. Beaver (Stanford), Professor Bruce D. Henderson (Vanderbilt and former chairman of The Boston Consulting Group), Professor Roger Ibbotson (Yale), Raymond D. Oddi (Baxter Travenol), Professor Michael E. Porter (Harvard), Professor Stephen A. Ross (Yale), Wolf Weinhold, and Jeffrey R. Williams (Carnegie-Mellon).

I owe a special debt of gratitude to a valued friend, Carl M. Noble, Jr., who as a former colleague at Kellogg and now as president of The Alcar Group has been a constant source of encouragement and an active partner in the mission to make shareholder value the standard for measuring business performance. I am particularly grateful to Robert Wallace, my editor at The Free Press, who persuaded me that it was time to do "the book" and has been extraordinarily supportive throughout the process. Finally, I would like to thank Elaine Zimmerman and Gary Lewis, both of Kellogg, for their care and expertise in typing several drafts of the manuscript.

Creating Shareholder Value

Chapter 1

Shareholder Value and Corporate Purpose

CORPORATE MISSION STATEMENTS proclaiming that the primary responsibility of management is to maximize shareholders' total return via dividends and increases in the market price of the company's shares abound. While the principle that the fundamental objective of the business corporation is to increase the value of its shareholders' investment is widely accepted, there is substantially less agreement about *how* this is accomplished.

On the cover of its 1984 annual report Coca-Cola states that "to increase shareholder value over time is the objective driving this enterprise." On the very next page the company goes on to say that to accomplish its objective "growth in annual earnings per share and increased return on equity are still the names of the game." In contrast, Hillenbrand Industries, a producer of caskets and hospital equipment, also declares its intention to provide a superior return to its shareholders, but to accomplish that objective management is focusing not on earnings but rather on creating "shareholder value," which, it explains in the 1984 annual report, "is created when a company generates free cash flow in excess of the shareholders' investment in the business."

Both Coca-Cola and Hillenbrand Industries acknowledge their responsibility to maximize return to their respective shareholders.

(For the ten-year period ending December 31, 1985, Coca-Cola achieved a 10 percent total return to shareholders and Hillenbrand Industries achieved a 21.5 percent return. They ranked 314 and 122, respectively, among the Fortune 500 companies in this category.) However, Coca-Cola emphasizes accounting indicators, earnings-per-share growth, and return on equity, while Hillenbrand Industries emphasizes the cash-flow based shareholder value approach to achieve shareholder returns. There are material differences between these two approaches to assessing a company's investment opportunities. These differences and the superiority of the shareholder value approach over the accounting approach will be presented in Chapters 2 and 3. At this point, it is enough to state that maximizing earnings-per-share growth or other accounting numbers may not necessarily lead to maximizing return for shareholders.

The Growing Interest

Numerous surveys indicate that a majority of the largest industrial companies have employed the shareholder value approach in capital budgeting for some time. Capital budgeting applications deal with investment projects such as capacity additions rather than total investment at the business level. Thus, we sometimes see a situation where capital projects regularly exceed the minimum acceptable rate of return, while the business unit itself is a "problem" and creates little or no value for shareholders. This situation can arise because capital expenditures typically represent only a small percentage of total company outlays. For example, capital expenditures amount to about 10 percent of total outlays at General Motors, a particularly capital intensive company.

During the past ten years, the shareholder value approach has been frequently applied not only to internal investments such as capacity additions, but also to opportunities for external growth such as mergers and acquisitions. Recently a number of major companies such as American Hospital Supply, Combustion Engineering, Hillenbrand Industries, Libbey-Owens-Ford, Marriott, and Westinghouse have found that the shareholder value approach can be productively extended from individual projects to the entire strategic plan. A strategic business unit (SBU) is commonly defined as the smallest organizational unit for which integrated strategic planning, related to a distinct product that serves a well-defined market, is feasible. A strategy for an SBU may then be seen as a collection of product-market related investments and the company itself may be characterized as a portfolio of these investment-requiring strategies. By estimating the future cash flows associated with each strategy, a company can assess the economic value to shareholders of alternative strategies at the business unit and corporate levels.

The interest in shareholder value is gaining momentum as a result of several recent developments.[1]

- The threat of corporate takeovers by those seeking undervalued, undermanaged assets
- Impressive endorsements by corporate leaders who have adopted the approach
- The growing recognition that traditional accounting measures such as EPS and ROI are not reliably linked to increasing the value of the company's shares
- Reporting of returns to shareholders along with other measures of performance in the business press such as Fortune's annual ranking of the 500 leading industrial firms
- A growing recognition that executives' long-term compensation needs to be more closely tied to returns to shareholders

Endorsements of the shareholder value approach can be found in an increasing number of annual reports and other corporate publications. One of the more thoughtful statements appears in Libbey-Owens-Ford's 1983 annual report and is reproduced as Table 1–1. Combustion Engineering's vice president for finance states that "a primary financial objective for Combustion Engineering is to create shareholder value by earning superior returns on capital invested in the business. This serves as a clear guide for management action and is the conceptual framework on which CE's financial objectives and goals are based."[2]

Whether or not executives agree with the well-publicized tactics of raiders such as Carl Icahn and T. Boone Pickens, they recognize that the raiders characterize themselves as champions of the shareholders. The raiders attack on two fronts. First, they are constantly searching for poorly managed companies, where aggressive changes in strategic directions could dramatically improve the value of the stock. Second, they identify undervalued assets that can be redeployed to boost the stock price. As a result, many executives rec-

Table 1–1 Libbey-Owens-Ford

A GREATER EMPHASIS ON SHAREHOLDER VALUE

Libbey-Owens-Ford's mission statement specifies that its primary responsibility is to its shareholders, and that the company has a continuing requirement to increase the value of our shareholders' investment in LOF. This is not just a contemporary business phrase, but the basis for a long-term company strategy. It evaluates business strategies and plans in terms of value to our shareholders, not just on the incremental income that the results will contribute to the bottom line. It requires a greater emphasis on developing strategies and plans that will increase shareholder value as measured by the market appreciation of our stock and dividends.

TRADITIONAL ACCOUNTING MEASURES MAY NOT TELL THE ENTIRE STORY

Traditionally, the most popular way to determine whether a company is performing well is through such accounting measurements as earnings per share (EPS) and return on investment. These measures do, of course, give an indication of a company's performance, but they can be misleading in that often they do not measure the increase or decrease in shareholder value. Sustained growth as measured by EPS does not necessarily reflect an increase in stock value.

This occurs because earnings do not reflect changes in risk and inflation, nor do they take into account the cost of added capital that may have been invested in the business to finance its growth. Yet these are critical considerations when you are striving to increase the value of the shareholders' investment.

CASH FLOW ANALYSIS IS EMPHASIZED

LOF stresses the importance of cash flow measurement and performance. Individual operating companies must analyze the cash flow effects of running their businesses. Where cash comes from and what cash is used for must be simply and clearly set forth. LOF's cash and short-term investments increased $46.3 million during 1983.

THE SHAREHOLDER VALUE APPROACH

The shareholder value approach taken by LOF emphasizes economic cash flow analysis in evaluating individual projects and in determining the economic value of the overall strategy of each business unit and the corporation as a whole. Management looks at the business units and the corporation and determines the minimum operating return necessary to create value. It then reviews the possible contribution of alternative strategies and evaluates the financial feasibility of the strategic plan, based on the company's cost of capital, return on assets, the cash flow stream and other important measurements.

This disciplined process allows LOF to objectively evaluate all its corporate investments, including internal projects and acquisitions, in light of our primary goal to increase shareholder value.

Libbey-Owens-Ford Company
1983 Annual Report

ognize a new and compelling reason to be concerned with the performance of their company's stock.

Executives have also become increasingly aware that many accrual-based accounting measures do not provide a dependable picture of the current and future performance of an organization. Numerous companies have sustained double-digit EPS growth while providing minimal or even *negative* returns to shareholders. Hillenbrand Industries, for example, points out in its 1984 annual report (p. 4) that "public companies that focus on achieving short-term earnings to meet external expectations sometimes jeopardize their ability to create long-term value."

Considerable attention has focused recently on the problems associated with rewarding executives on the basis of short-term accounting-based indicators. As a reflection of the increasing scrutiny under which executive compensation has come, business publications such as *Fortune* and *Business Week* have begun to publish compensation surveys that examine the correlation between the executives' pay and how well their companies have performed based on several measures—including returns to shareholders. For example, *Business Week*'s executive compensation scoreboard now includes a "pay-performance index" for 255 companies in 36 industries. The index shows how well the top two executives in each company were paid relative to how shareholders fared. The index is the ratio of the executive's three-year total pay as a percent of the industry average to the shareholders' total three-year return as a percent of the industry average. If an executive's pay and shareholders' return are both at the industry average, the index is 100. The lower the index, the better shareholders fared. The broad range in the pay-performance index, even within industries, has further fueled the interest in achieving shareholder value. For the 1982–1984 period, for example, *Business Week* reported a pay-performance index of 59 for Roger Smith, CEO of General Motors, and an index of 160 for Phillip Caldwell, CEO of Ford Motor.[3]

When the shareholder value approach first gained attention toward the end of the 1970s, even the executives who found the concept an intriguing notion tended to think that the approach would be very difficult to implement. The task of educating managers seemed substantial, and they were also not eager to develop a new planning system if it might involve upheaval in the corporate information system. Recent advances in technology have put impressive analytical potential at management's disposal. Managers' decisions are now greatly facilitated by microcomputer software. New approaches thus can more readily be incorporated without displacing existing information systems.

Management Versus Shareholder Objectives

It is important to recognize that the objectives of management may in some situations differ from those of the company's shareholders. Managers, like other people, act in their self-interest. The theory of a market economy is, after all, based on individuals promoting their self-interests via market transactions to bring about an efficient allocation of resources. In a world in which principals (e.g., stockholders) have imperfect control over their agents (e.g., managers), these agents may not always engage in transactions solely in the best interests of the principals. Agents have their own objectives and it may sometimes pay them to sacrifice the principals' interests. The problem is exacerbated in large corporations where it is difficult to identify the interests of a diverse set of stockholders ranging from institutional investors to individuals with small holdings.

Critics of large corporations often allege that corporate managers have too much power and that they act in ways to benefit themselves at the expense of shareholders and other corporate constituencies. The argument is generally developed along the following lines.[4] Responsibility for administering companies or "control" is vested in the hands of professional managers and thereby has been separated from "ownership." Since the ownership of shares in large corporations tends to be diffused, individual shareholders are said to have neither influence on nor interest in corporate governance issues such as the election of board members. Therefore, boards are largely responsive to management which, in turn, can ignore shareholders and run companies as they see fit.

The foregoing "separation of ownership and control" argument advanced by Berle and Means[5] in 1932 has been a persistent theme of corporate critics during the intervening years. There are, however, a number of factors that induce management to act in the best interests of shareholders. These factors derive from the fundamental premise that the greater the expected unfavorable consequences to the manager who decreases the wealth of shareholders, the less likely it is that the manager will, in fact, act against the interests of shareholders.

Consistent with the above premise, at least four major factors will induce management to adopt a shareholder orientation: (1) a relatively large ownership position, (2) compensation tied to shareholder return performance, (3) threat of takeover by another organization, and (4) competitive labor markets for corporate executives.

Economic rationality dictates that stock ownership by management motivates executives to identify more closely with the shareholders' economic interests. Indeed, we would expect that the greater the proportion of personal wealth invested in company stock or tied to stock options, the greater would be management's shareholder orientation. While the top executives in many companies often have relatively large percentages of their wealth invested in company stock, this is much less often the case for divisional and business unit managers. And it is at the divisional and business unit levels that most resource allocation decisions are made in decentralized organizations.

Even when corporate executives own shares in their company, their viewpoint on the acceptance of risk may differ from that of shareholders. It is reasonable to expect that many corporate executives have a lower tolerance for risk. If the company invests in a risky project, stockholders can always balance this risk against other risks in their presumably diversified portfolios. The manager, however, can balance a project failure only against the other activities of the division or the company. Thus, managers are hurt by the failure more than shareholders.

The second factor likely to influence management to adopt a shareholder orientation is compensation tied to shareholder return performance. The most direct means of linking top management's interests with those of shareholders is to base compensation, and particularly the incentive portion, on market returns realized by shareholders. Exclusive reliance on shareholder returns, however, has its own limitations. First, movements in a company's stock price may well be greatly influenced by factors beyond management control such as the overall state of the economy and stock market. Second, shareholder returns may be materially influenced by what management believes to be unduly optimistic or pessimistic market expectations at the beginning or end of the performance measurement period. And third, divisional and business unit performance cannot be directly linked to stock price.

Rather than linking incentive compensation directly to the

market returns earned by shareholders, most Fortune 500 companies tie annual bonuses and long-term performance plans to internal financial goals such as earnings or accounting return on investment. As will be demonstrated in Chapter 2, these accounting criteria can often conflict with the way corporate shares are valued by the market. If incentives were largely based on earnings, for example, management might well be motivated to pursue economically unsound strategies when viewed from the perspective of shareholders. In such a situation what is economically irrational from the shareholder viewpoint may be a perfectly rational course of action for the decision-making executives.

The third factor affecting management behavior is the threat of takeover by another company. Tender offers have become a commonly employed means of transferring corporate control. Moreover the size of the targets continues to become larger. During the 1979–1985 period, seventy-seven acquisitions each in excess of $1 billion were completed. The threat of takeover is an essential means of constraining corporate managers who might choose to pursue personal goals at the expense of shareholders. Any significant exploitation of shareholders should be reflected in a lower stock price. This lower price, relative to what it might be with more efficient management, offers an attractive takeover opportunity for another company which in many cases will replace incumbent management. An active market for corporate control places limits on the divergence of interests between management and shareholders and thereby serves as an important counterargument to the "separation of ownership and control" criticisms.

The fourth and final factor influencing management's shareholder orientation is the labor market for corporate executives. Managerial labor markets are an essential mechanism for motivating management to function in the best interests of shareholders. Managers compete for positions both within and outside of the firm. The increasing number of executive recruiting firms and the length of the "Who's News" column in the *Wall Street Journal* are evidence that the managerial labor market is very active. What is less obvious is how managers are evaluated in this market. Within the firm, performance evaluation and incentive schemes are the basic mechanisms for monitoring managerial performance. As seen earlier, the question here is whether these measures are reliably linked to the market price of the company's shares.

How managers communicate their value to the labor market outside of their individual firms is less apparent. While the performance of top-level corporate officers can be gleaned from annual reports and other publicly available corporate communications, this is not generally the case for divisional managers. For corporate level executives, the question is whether performance for shareholders is the dominant criterion in assessing their value in the executive labor market. The question in the case of division managers is, first, how does the labor market monitor and gain insights about their performance and second, what is the basis for valuing their services.

"Excellence" and Restructuring

Two of the most visible business phenomena of the first half of the 1980s have been the publication of Peters and Waterman's *In Search of Excellence*[6] and the unprecedented surge in the restructuring of companies. The "excellence phenomenon" certainly provided no obvious encouragement for management to link its decisions more closely with the objective of maximizing returns to shareholders. In contrast, the more recent restructuring movement is clearly a manifestation of top management's growing concern with its company's share price and shareholder returns.

As U.S. corporations began the 1980s, saddled with a decade of inflation and lagging productivity, nothing could have come as better news than the idea that not all excellent companies are Japanese. It was in this climate that *In Search of Excellence*, published in 1982, became an absolute sensation. Its longevity on the top of the best-seller list along with its wide coverage in the business press provided an extraordinary platform for the authors' ideas.

The basic purpose of *In Search of Excellence* was to identify key attributes of corporate excellence that are common among successful American corporations. To choose the "excellent" companies, Peters and Waterman began by assembling a list of sixty-two U.S. companies that were considered "successful" by business leaders, consultants, members of the business press, and business school professors. From that list they selected thirty-six "excellent" companies based on superior performance for such financial measures as return on total capital, return on equity, return on sales, and asset growth. Eight attributes of corporate excellence were identified—a bias for action; staying close to the customer; autonomy and entrepreneurship; productivity through people; hands-on, value-driven management; sticking to the knitting; simple organization form and lean staff; and simultaneous loose-tight properties.

Even though the "excellent" firms exhibited superior *financial* (accounting) performance over the 1960–1980 period, they did not provide consistently superior returns to shareholder via dividends plus share price appreciation.[7] The excellent companies did not perform significantly better than the market. Indeed, they did not consistently outperform their respective industry groups or closest competitors. These results once again raise questions about the use of *accounting* measures to gauge the *economic* performance of corporations. Since the eight attributes of corporate excellence are not associated with systematically superior returns to shareholders, efforts to emulate these attributes may be ill-advised.

While *In Search of Excellence* became "must reading" in many organizations during 1982 and 1983, a certain degree of disenchantment set in during the following two years as a number of "excellent" companies experienced strategic setbacks. Atari, Avon Products, Caterpillar Tractor, Digital Equipment, Hewlett-Packard, Levi Strauss, and Texas Instruments serve as examples.

But if emulating excellent companies has lost some of its luster, a new focal point of interest has captured the imagination of management during the past couple of years—restructuring. Hardly a day passes without some company announcing a major restructuring of its businesses or capital structure. Restructuring involves diverse activities such as divestiture of underperforming businesses or businesses that do not "fit," spinoffs directly to shareholders, acquisitions paid with "excess cash," stock repurchases, debt swaps, and liquidation of overfunded pension funds. In many cases, these restructurings are motivated by a desire to foil a takeover bid by so-called "raiders" who look for undermanaged companies where changes in strategic direction could dramatically increase the value of the stock, and for companies with high liquidation values relative to their current share price. There is, of course, no better means of avoiding a takeover than increasing the price of the stock. Thus, increasing share price has become the fundamental purpose of corporate restructuring.

In contrast to the earlier euphoria over emulating excellent companies, the current restructuring movement is solidly based on shareholder value creation principles.[8] In 1985, the Standard &

Poor's 500 appreciated 26 percent in price. Goldman Sachs estimates that corporate restructuring accounted for about 30 percent of that price change. However, the early stage of the restructuring movement, which I call "Phase I restructuring," is largely based on one-time transactions such as those listed above rather than changes in day-to-day management of the business.

The necessary agenda for the second half of the 1980s seems clear. Companies need to move from Phase I restructuring to Phase II restructuring. In Phase II, the shareholder value approach is employed not only when buying and selling businesses or changing the company's capital structure, but also in the planning and performance monitoring of all business strategies on an ongoing basis. Frequently, the most difficult issue in this area is how to go about estimating the impact of strategies on shareholder value. Fortunately, relatively straightforward approaches do exist for estimating the shareholder value created by a business strategy, and an increasing number of major companies have begun to use them.

Most companies already use the same discounted cash-flow techniques used in the shareholder value approach to assess the attractiveness of capital investment projects and to value prospective acquisition targets. As will be shown, this approach can be extended to estimate the value creation potential of individual business units and the strategic plan for the entire company.

In Phase II restructuring it will also become increasingly important that executive compensation be tied closely to the shareholder value driven plans so that management will be strongly motivated to make decisions consistent with creating maximum returns to shareholders. A successful implementation of Phase II restructuring not only ensures that management has met its fiduciary responsibility to develop corporate performance evaluation systems consistent with the parameters investors use to value the company, but also minimizes the Phase I concern that a takeover of an undermanaged company is imminent.

Rationale for Shareholder Value Approach

Business strategies should be judged by the economic returns they generate for shareholders, as measured by dividends plus the increase in the company's share price. As management considers alternative strategies, those expected to develop the greatest sustainable competitive advantage will be those that will also create the greatest value for shareholders. The "shareholder value approach" estimates the economic value of an investment (e.g., the shares of a company, strategies, mergers and acquisitions, capital expenditures) by discounting forecasted cash flows by the cost of capital. These cash flows, in turn, serve as the foundation for shareholder returns from dividends and share-price appreciation. A more detailed description of the shareholder value approach will be presented in Chapter 3. For now, I will provide a brief rationale for the approach.

The case for why management should pursue this objective is comparatively straightforward. Management is often characterized as balancing the interests of various corporate constituencies such as employees, customers, suppliers, debtholders, and stockholders. As Treynor[9] points out, the company's continued existence depends upon a financial relationship with each of these parties. Employees want competitive wages. Customers want high quality at a competitive price. Suppliers and debtholders each have financial claims that must be satisfied with cash when they fall due. Stockholders as residual claimants of the firm look for cash dividends and the prospect of future dividends which is reflected in the market price of the stock.

If the company does not satisfy the financial claims of its constituents, it will cease to be a viable organization. Employees, customers, and suppliers will simply withdraw their support. Thus, a going concern must strive to enhance its cash-generating ability. The ability of a company to distribute cash to its various constituencies depends on its ability to generate cash from operating its businesses and on its ability to obtain any additional funds needed from external sources.

Debt and equity financing are the two basic external sources. The company's ability to borrow today is based on projections of how much cash will be generated in the future. Borrowing power and the market value of the shares both depend on a company's cash-generating ability. The market value of the shares directly impacts the second source of financing, that is, equity financing. For a given level of funds required, the higher the share price, the less dilution will be borne by current shareholders. Therefore, management's financial power to deal effectively with corporate claimants also comes from increasing the value of the shares. Treynor, a former editor of the *Financial Analysts Journal*, summarizes this line of thinking best.

> Those who criticize the goal of share value maximization are forgetting that stockholders are not merely the beneficiaries of the corporation's financial success, but also the referees who determine management's financial power.[10]

> Any management—no matter how powerful and independent—that flouts the financial objective of maximizing share value does so at its own peril.[11]

Overview of the Book

Creating Shareholder Value presents a comprehensive application of the shareholder value approach to the management planning and performance evaluation process. It not only provides the rationale for why creating shareholder value must emerge as the new standard for business performance but provides managers with the framework needed to implement the standard. While ultimately the value-creating potential of strategies is judged in financial terms, the focus of the book is directed toward managers from the business unit to the corporate level who have an interest in product-market strategies.

The book is organized into three parts. Part I examines and contrasts business performance measurement under the conventional accounting approach with the shareholder value approach. Part II provides the linkage between competitive strategy analysis and shareholder value analysis and goes on to show its usefulness for formulating and selecting value-creating business strategies. Part III addresses additional shareholder value applications including performance evaluation, executive compensation, and mergers and acquisitions.

Chapter 2 demonstrates the shortcomings of accounting numbers such as earnings per share (EPS), return on investment (ROI), and return on equity (ROE). EPS growth, for example, does not necessarily lead to an increase in the market value of a company's shares. The chapter concludes with a perspective on the role of accounting and a proposal for a data-base approach to corporate financial reporting.

Chapter 3 provides an introduction to the shareholder value approach. Specifically, the estimation of shareholder value and shareholder value creation is demonstrated. Threshold margin, the minimum operating profit margin a business needs to maintain shareholder value, is developed as a particularly useful concept in value creation analysis.

Chapter 4 describes some important new advances in strategy formulation and then links this analysis with the shareholder value approach to valuing business strategies. The strategy formulation process which assesses industry attractiveness, competitive position within the industry, and sources of competitive advantage is based on the competitive strategy framework developed by Michael E. Porter. This chapter presents the link between competitive strategy analysis using value chains and the cash flows underlying the shareholder value approach as well as other relationships between the Porter framework and the shareholder value approach.

Chapter 5 illustrates the application of the concepts developed in Chapter 4. After differentiating between business unit and corporate level strategies, the chapter demonstrates the approach for developing value-creating business strategies with the help of three case illustrations. The chapter concludes with the important, and sometimes overlooked, issue of strategy implementation.

Chapter 6 addresses the financial feasibility or fundability of proposed strategies. The popular "sustainable growth" model is shown to be neither reliably linked to value creation nor an accurate measure of the fundable rate of growth. The affordable sales growth approach is presented as a superior alternative for assessing the financial feasibility of proposed strategies.

Chapter 7 focuses on what the price of the shares tells us about the market's expectations about a company's future performance. The analysis in this chapter shows that even if a company creates shareholder value by investing at above the cost of capital rate, shareholders will not necessarily earn a rate of return exceeding the cost of capital. Shareholder returns depend on not only corporate investment plans but also on the market's assessment of these plans as reflected in the current stock price.

Chapter 8 reviews some of the major shortcomings in existing performance evaluation and executive compensation plans. Performance standards based on stock market versus corporate financial measures and relative versus absolute standards are evaluated. The discussion concludes with a shareholder value oriented approach to linking strategy and performance.

Chapter 9 presents a comprehensive value creation framework for analyzing mergers and acquisitions. Care is taken to differentiate between value created by an acquisition and the value created for the buyer's shareholders. The chapter examines the operating, financial, and tax benefits that can materialize in a merger. After outlining the five essential stages of the acquisition process, the process is illustrated with a detailed analysis of the recent acquisition of Stokely–Van Camp by Quaker Oats.

PART **I**

Measuring Business Performance

Chapter 2

Shortcomings of Accounting Numbers

In both corporate reports and the financial press, there is an obsessive fixation on earnings per share (EPS) as the scorecard of corporate performance. Quarterly and annual earnings are reported in the *Wall Street Journal* and other leading financial publications. Analyses of corporate strategies by *Business Week*, *Fortune*, and *Forbes* are replete with references to EPS growth rates and price-earnings multiples. The broad dissemination of accounting earnings figures fuels the business community's belief that stock prices are strongly influenced, if not totally determined, by reported earnings. It is commonly assumed that if a company produces "satisfactory" growth in EPS, then the market value of its shares will increase. But EPS growth does not necessarily lead to an increase in the market value of the stock. As will be shown in the next two sections, this conclusion is supported by simple economic reasoning and can be convincingly demonstrated empirically as well. This discussion will be followed by an enumeration of the shortcomings of the accounting return on investment (ROI) as a standard for measuring business performance. The chapter concludes with a brief overview of the role of accounting in external versus internal performance evaluation of the firm and a proposal for a data-base approach to corporate financial reporting.

Earnings—An Unreliable Bottom Line

In Chapter 1 providing maximum return for shareholders was established as the fundamental objective of the business corporation. It was further established that shareholder return is generated by dividends and increases in share price. The issue to be addressed now is whether accounting earnings as a standard for assessing alternative strategies and measuring subsequent performance is consistent with the shareholder return objective. Stated more concretely, the issue is whether earnings can reliably measure the change in the present value of the firm.

There are several important reasons why earnings fail to measure changes in the economic value of the firm:

- Alternative accounting methods may be employed.
- Risk is excluded.
- Investment requirements are excluded.
- Dividend policy is not considered.
- The time value of money is ignored.

Alternative Accounting Methods Employed

The earnings number may be computed using alternative and equally acceptable accounting methods. Prominent examples are the differences that arise from last-in, first-out (LIFO) and first-in, first-out (FIFO) approaches to computing cost of sales, various methods of computing depreciation, and purchase versus pooling-of-interests accounting for mergers and acquisitions. Bear in mind that a change in accounting method for financial reporting purposes, whether mandated by the Financial Accounting Standards Board (FASB) or simply dictated by management choice, does not alter the company's cash flows and therefore should not affect its economic value.[1] Yet a new financial accounting standard, such as one dealing with foreign currency translation, can materially impact reported earnings. In some instances such changes can turn reported net income into a reported loss or vice versa.

The accountant's earnings figure results from attempts to match costs against revenues. This process involves allocating costs of assets, for example by depreciation, over their estimated useful life. Accounting allocations often differ among companies and for a particular company over time. Depreciation methods include the straight-line approach and accelerated depreciation methods such as sum-of-the-years digits and double declining balance. In any event, these allocations are arbitrary because there is no sound basis for choosing one method over alternative methods. But then, it is important to emphasize that conventional income determination by the matching process does not, nor do accountants purport it to, measure changes in the value of the firm.

Risk Excluded

Risk is a parameter of central importance in establishing the economic value of any asset. The level of risk is determined both by the nature of the firm's operations and by the relative proportions of debt and equity used to finance its investments. These two types of risk are commonly referred to as "business risk" and "financial risk," respectively. Earnings figures do not incorporate consideration of risk.

To illustrate, consider a business evaluating two competing strategies for its five-year plan. Management's earnings growth projections and probability estimates associated with each outcome are shown below.

Strategy A		Strategy B	
Probability	*Earnings Growth Rate (%)*	*Probability*	*Earnings Growth Rate (%)*
.10	6	.05	8
.25	8	.25	9
.30	10	.40	10
.25	12	.25	11
.10	14	.05	12

The expected value or mean for each strategy is an earnings growth rate of 10 percent[2] The most likely value is also 10 percent in each case. The riskiness of the strategies is a function of the variability of the possible outcomes. The tighter the probability distribution, the less risky is the strategy. In this respect the two strategies are quite different. Note that the range of outcomes for Strategy A (6 to 14 percent) is wider than the range for Strategy B (8 to 12 percent). Further, the probabilities associated with the lowest and highest outcomes are higher for Strategy A, thereby contributing to even greater variability. One summary measure of the dispersion of the probability distribution is the standard deviation. The standard deviation for Strategy A is 2.28 percent and for Strategy B it is 0.90 percent.[3] Strategy A with a higher standard deviation would be considered more risky than Strategy B. Using an earnings growth standard, management would be indifferent between these two strategies since the most likely forecast is a 10 percent rate in each case. Once risk is introduced into the analysis, Strategy B with its lower risk would be preferred over Strategy A.

When debt is introduced into the firm's capital structure, the rate of return required by investors incorporates not only a premium for business risk, but a premium for financial risk as well. As financial leverage is increased, the risk associated with shareholders likewise increases.

To illustrate, consider a firm evaluating two alternative strategies for its initial capital structure—leverage and no leverage. The company requires $10 million in capital and the initial price per share of common stock is $10. The leverage strategy calls for selling 500,000 shares and obtaining an equal amount of capital, $5 million, via debt at an after-tax cost of 8 percent or $400,000. The no-leverage strategy simply involves the sale of one million shares at $10 per share. Optimistic, most likely, and pessimistic scenarios for earnings levels are shown below:

	OPTIMISTIC	MOST LIKELY	PESSIMISTIC
No-leverage strategy			
Operating earnings after taxes	$1,000,000	$ 800,000	$ 400,000
Shares outstanding	1,000,000	1,000,000	1,000,000
Earnings per share	1.00	0.80	0.40
Leverage strategy			
Operating earnings after taxes	1,000,000	800,000	400,000
Interest expense after taxes	400,000	400,000	400,000
Net income after taxes	600,000	400,000	0
Shares outstanding	500,000	500,000	500,000
Earnings per share	1.20	0.80	0.00

For the no-leverage strategy the percent increase or decrease in operating earnings and EPS is identical, while for the leverage case the change in EPS is greater than the change in operating earnings. In the above example a 25 percent increase in operating earnings, from $800,000 in the most likely case to $1 million in the optimistic case, results in an increase of 50 percent in EPS (from $0.80 to $1.20). The EPS range for the no-leverage case is $0.40–$1.00, while for the leverage strategy the range increases to $0.00–$1.20. The increased variability and the greater danger of insolvency due to the introduction of leverage increases the financial risk to shareholders who will, in turn, demand higher rates of return as compensation. As long as the incremental earnings generated by debt financing exceed interest expense, debt financing will increase net income. But since debt also increases risk, the increase in earnings may not necessarily lead to an increase in economic value.[4]

Investment Requirements Excluded

The relationship between the change in economic value and earnings is further obscured by the fact that investments in working capital and fixed capital needed to sustain the firm are excluded from the earnings calculation. Consider the case of working capital. As a business grows, normally there will be an associated growth in its level of accounts receivable, inventory, and accounts payable. An increase in receivables between the beginning and end of the year means that the cash flow from sales is less than the revenue figure reflected in the income statement. To illustrate, assume current year's sales are $10 million, receivables at the beginning of the year, $1 million, and year-end receivables are $1.2 million. Cash flow from sales for the year is calculated as follows:

Beginning receivables	$ 1,000,000
Sales	10,000,000
Cash flow potential	11,000,000
Ending receivables	1,200,000
Cash flow realized	$ 9,800,000

What is important to recognize is that the $10 million sales figure does not represent the current period's cash generated. Instead, cash flow from sales is total sales *less* the $200,000 increase in accounts receivable. The $200,000 is not available to meet current cash commitments. For accounting purposes revenue is recognized at the time goods or services are delivered. For purposes of economic valuation, recognition must await the receipt of cash. In brief, cash is received after revenue is recognized. Thus for companies with expanding receivables the sales figure on the income statement will overstate the current period's cash flow generated from sales.

Inventory investment is another important component of working capital that contributes to differences between earnings and the cash flow valuation approach. An increase in the level of inventory clearly involves cash payments for materials, labor, and overhead. For accrual accounting purposes the investment in additional inventory is, however, reflected as an asset on the balance sheet and is not included in the cost of sales figure appearing in the income statement. Therefore for companies with expanding inventory levels, the cost of sales figure will understate the current period's cash outflow for inventory expenditures. In brief, for expanding firms, increases in accounts receivable and inventories will cause the earnings figure to be greater than cash flow.

The third major component of working capital, payables, acts as a countervailing force. Accounts payable and accrued liabilities represent unpaid bills for items already included as expenses in the income statement or for increases in inventory reflected on the balance sheet. Thus, the cost of sales and selling, general, and administrative expense accounts in the income statement overstate the cash outflow by the amount of the related increase in payables. In other words, cash is disbursed after the expense is recognized.

A reconciliation of earnings and cash flows for assumed changes in accounts receivable, inventory, and accounts payable and accruals is presented in Table 2–1. In brief, to arrive at cash flow the earnings figure must be adjusted by $440,000. This amount represents the net cash requirements due to the increases in the three major categories of working capital—receivables, inventory, and payables.

We now turn from working capital to investment in fixed assets. Depreciable assets such as property, plant, and equipment are initially recorded at cost and included in the fixed asset section of the balance sheet. Accountants then allocate this cost over the estimated useful life of the asset through depreciation. They often stress

Table 2–1 Reconciliation of Earnings and Cash Flow

	Earnings	Adjustment	Cash Flow
Sales	$10,000,000		
– Increase in accounts receivable		$200,000	
			$9,800,000
Cost of Sales	8,000,000		
+ Increase in inventories		300,000	
– Increase in payables and accruals		50,000	
			8,250,000
Selling, General, and Administrative Expenses	1,000,000		
– Increase in payables and accruals		10,000	
			990,000
Net increase in working capital		$440,000	
Depreciation Expense	100,000		
+ Depreciation expense		100,000	
– Capital expenditures		150,000	150,000
Income Before Income Taxes	900,000		
Income tax expense	400,000		
– Increase in deferred income taxes		30,000	
			370,000
CASH FLOW			$ 40,000
NET INCOME	$500,000		

that depreciation is a process of allocating original cost and not a process of valuation. Depreciation on fixed assets purchased during the current year as well as on those purchased in prior years is a deduction to arrive at net income. But while depreciation is an expense, it does not involve an outlay of cash. On the other hand, the earnings number will not include the capital expenditures made during the year. Thus, to move from earnings to cash flow, two adjustments are needed. First, the depreciation must be added back to earnings and second, capital expenditures must be deducted from earnings.

Incorporating the adjustments discussed in this section cash flow from operations may be calculated as follows:

Cash flow from operations = Sales – Operating expenses including taxes + Depreciation and other noncash items – Incremental working capital investment – Capital expenditures

Returning to Table 2–1, which is a summary illustration of the concepts developed in this section, the earnings to cash flow reconciliations for capital investment and deferred taxes appear below the working capital accounts. While the firm reported net income of $500,000, the cash flow generated was only $40,000. This difference is due to the fact that outflows of $440,000 for increased working capital and $150,000 for capital expenditures need to be deducted from earnings, and depreciation of $100,000 and an increase in deferred taxes of $30,000, both noncash items, need to be added back to earnings.

Dividend Policy Not Considered

The conflict between earnings and economic value can also be seen in the area of dividend policy. If the objective were to maximize earnings, one could argue persuasively that the company should never pay any dividends as long as it expected to achieve a positive return on new investment. But we know that if the company invested shareholders' funds at below the minimum acceptable market rate, the value of the company would decrease.

For example, suppose a company had an opportunity today to invest $1 million in additional inventory and thereby provide better service to its customers. The resulting increase in net cash flow over the next five years is estimated to be $206,040 annually. For simplicity, assume that the annual earnings increase over the next five years was also projected to be $206,040. If the investment were made, this year's dividend to shareholders would be decreased from its planned level by $1 million.[5]

From an earnings viewpoint, the dividend decrease looks very favorable since earnings would increase by $206,040 for each of the next five years. From an economic value standpoint, a very different conclusion emerges. The discounted cash flow rate of return on this investment is a modest 1 percent.[6] Assume investors could invest in opportunities with similar risk at a yield of 15 percent. As soon as the market learns of management's intention to invest funds at substantially below the 15 percent opportunity investment rate, the market value of the stock can be expected to drop.

Time Value of Money Ignored

Another important reason why earnings fail to measure changes in economic value is that the earnings calculation ignores the time value of money. Recall that the economic value of an investment is the discounted values of the anticipated cash flows. Economic value calculations explicitly incorporate the idea that a dollar of cash received today is worth more than a dollar to be received a year from now, because today's dollar can be invested to earn a return over the next year. The discount rate used to estimate economic value includes not only compensation for bearing risk but also compensation for expected rates of inflation.

EPS Growth and Shareholder Returns

In the last section some fundamental differences between the calculation of accounting earnings and economic value were presented. Now we turn to the uncertain relationship between earnings growth and returns to shareholders that results from these differences.

More specifically, *earnings growth does not necessarily lead to the creation of economic value for shareholders*. A company's shares will increase in value only if management can be expected to earn a rate of return on new investments greater than the rate investors can expect to earn by investing in alternative, identically risky securities. Earnings growth, however, can be achieved not only when management is investing at or above the market discount rate, but also when it is investing below the discount rate and thereby decreasing the value of the common shares. To illustrate, consider the example of Gamma Inc. For ease of exposition, assume that Gamma has no debt and requires only additional working capital to expand its sales. Gamma's income statement for the most recent year appears below:

	($ IN MILLIONS)
Sales	$200
Operating expenses	170
Earnings before income taxes	$ 30
Income taxes (40%)	12
Earnings (and cash flow) after taxes	$ 18

Suppose the company pays its entire earnings as dividends. It also expects to maintain its present sales level and margins for the foreseeable future. Assuming an 18 percent cost of equity capital, the value of Gamma equity is $18/.18 or $100 million.[7] If Gamma invested $10 million now it could expect to expand its sales by 10 percent while maintaining the pretax margin on sales at 15 percent. Gamma's projected income statement for next year and subsequent years follows:

	($ IN MILLIONS)
Sales	$220.00
Operating expenses	187.00
Earnings before income taxes	$ 33.00
Income taxes (40%)	13.20
Earnings (and cash flow) after taxes	$ 19.80

The value of Gamma now is $19.8/.18 or $110 million less the $10 million investment or $100 million. Despite 10 percent earnings growth, Gamma's present value is unchanged. This is the case because for its $10 million investment Gamma is increasing its annual after-tax cash flow by $1.8 million which, when discounted at 18 percent, is also valued at $10 million. In brief, when the present value of incremental cash inflow is identical to the present value of investment or cash outflow, value is unchanged.

A decrease in shareholder value can take place despite earnings growth whenever a firm is operating below the market discount rate. Assume that Gamma's sales growth next year will be 20 percent, but its return on incremental sales will be 10 percent rather than the 15 percent rate projected earlier.

The new income statement follows:

	($ IN MILLIONS)
Sales	$240.00
Operating expenses	206.00
Earnings before taxes	$ 34.00
Taxes (40%)	13.60
Earnings (and cash flow) after taxes	$ 20.40

While earnings are growing from $18 million to $20.4 million or 13.33 percent, the value of Gamma has declined $6.67 million from $100 million to $93.33 million, that is, ($20.4/.18) – $20.

In summary, an increase or decrease in earnings may not give rise to a corresponding increase or decrease in shareholder value because the earnings figure does not reflect the company's level of business and financial risk, nor does it take into account the working capital and fixed investment needed for anticipated growth. In addition, the earnings figure is affected by a wide variety of accounting conventions governing the assignment of costs to current and future time periods. Such accounting conventions do not ordinarily affect a firm's cash flow and hence should not affect the value of the firm.

The unreliable linkage between earnings growth and shareholder returns can be demonstrated not only on a theoretical level, but can be observed empirically as well. As can be seen in Table 2–2, the Standard & Poor's 500 index experienced impressive earnings-per-share growth during much of the 1970s while shareholder returns from stock price change plus dividends were modest. For example, while EPS grew during the 1973–1978 period at an annual rate of 8.6 percent, total shareholder returns were less than 1 percent for the same period. Undoubtedly, the increasing inflationary expectations which were incorporated in the market discount rate were a major cause of the disappointing results for shareholders. Earnings calculations, on the other hand, do not incorporate the discount rate. The strong stock market performance that began in 1982 appears to be largely attributable to declining inflation and interest rates rather than any major shift in EPS growth.

Additional evidence of the uncertain relationship between earnings growth and returns to shareholders is provided by another study focusing on the performance of the Standard & Poor's 400 in-

Table 2–2 Earnings Per Share and Shareholder Returns for Standard & Poor's 500 Index, 1973–1985

	Annual Growth Rate in EPS (%)	Total Shareholder Return (Dividends Plus Stock Price Change) (%)	Consumer Price Index: Inflation Rates (%)
1973	27.1	(14.7)	8.8
1974	9.0	(26.4)	12.2
1975	(10.5)	37.2	7.0
1976	24.5	23.8	4.8
1977	9.9	(7.2)	6.8
1978	13.2	6.6	9.0
1979	20.5	18.4	13.3
1980	(0.3)	32.4	12.4
1981	3.6	(4.9)	8.9
1982	(17.7)	21.4	3.9
1983	11.3	22.5	3.8
1984	18.9	6.3	4.0
1985	(12.5)	32.2	3.8
1973–1978	8.6	0.9	

SOURCES: *Analysts Handbook* (New York: Standard & Poor's Corporation, April 1986) and *Stocks, Bonds, Bills, and Inflation—1986 Yearbook* (Chicago: Ibbotson Associates, 1986).

dustrial companies during the 1970s.[8] The results are summarized in Table 2–3. Of the 400 companies, 172 achieved compounded EPS growth rates of 15 percent or better during 1974–1979. Stockholders realized *negative* rates of return from dividends plus capital losses in 27 (16 percent) of these EPS growth companies. For 60 (35 percent) of the 172 companies, shareholders' returns were inadequate to compensate them just for inflation. In other words, in inflation-adjusted or real terms shareholders' wealth decreased. Nor were shareholders provided with any compensation for risk.

Some analysts believe that EPS growth sustained over a longer duration, say ten years, assures shareholder returns. But this, too, is an ill-founded belief. A review of recent annual Fortune 500 surveys of the largest industrial corporations confirms that it is not uncommon for companies to achieve positive, ten-year EPS growth rates, while their shareholders realized negative rates of return.[9] Companies that have achieved double-digit EPS growth rates over recent ten-year periods while providing negative returns to shareholders include such established names as Anheuser-Busch, Coca-Cola, Corning Glass, Honeywell, Eli Lilly, Schering-Plough, Sperry, and Xerox.

Table 2–3 EPS Growth Rates Versus Rates of Return Earned by Shareholders for Standard & Poor's Industrial Companies

	1976–1979	1975–1979[b]	1974–1979
Companies achieving annual EPS growth rates of 15% or greater[a]	191 (100%)	205 (100%)	172 (100%)
Negative rates of return to shareholders	14 (7%)	2 (1%)	27 (16%)
Rates of return inadequate to compensate shareholder for inflation[c]	33 (17%)	20 (10%)	60 (35%)

[a]Restated primary EPS excluding extraordinary items and discontinued operations.

[b]The small number of companies with negative rates of return to shareholders for this period is due to low level of market at the end of 1974. The Standard & Poor's Stock Index at the close of 1973 was 109.14 and in subsequent years was: 76.47, 100.88, 119.46, 104.71, 107.21, and 121.02.

[c]The annual growth rates in the Consumers Price Index for the 1976–1979, 1975–1979 and 1974–1979 periods are 7.7%, 7.6%, and 8.0%, respectively.

The Trouble with Accounting Return on Investment (ROI)

The growing recognition that earnings increases are no guarantee of increases in shareholder value, particularly during inflationary periods, has led to the increasing popularity of accounting-based return on investment (ROI) and return on equity (ROE) as financial performance standards. A survey of the 1976 *Fortune* 1000 found ROI by far the most frequently used measure of a division's performance.[10] However, taking an unreliable numerator (i.e., earnings) and relating it to an investment denominator generated by the same accounting process does not solve the problem.

Reece and Cool, citing the advantages that may explain its wide use, state that "ROI, being a percentage-return measurement, is consistent with how companies measure the cost of capital."[11] Indeed, hurdle rates or minimum acceptable rates for ROI are often based on an estimate of the business unit's cost of capital or the corporate cost of capital. The assumption is that if ROI is greater than the cost of capital, then shareholder value will be created. The essential problem with this approach is that ROI is an accrual accounting return and is being compared to a cost of capital measure which is an economic return demanded by investors. Comparing one with the other is clearly an example of comparing apples with oranges.

The economic or discounted cash flow (DCF) one-year return for an investment is simply this year's cash flow plus the change in value over the year, divided by the value at the beginning of the year:

$$\text{DCF return} = \frac{\text{Cash flow} + (\text{Present value at end of year} - \text{Present value at beginning of year})}{\text{Present value at beginning of year}}$$

$$= \frac{\text{Cash flow} + \text{Change in present value}}{\text{Present value at beginning of year}}$$

The numerator of the DCF return (cash flow plus change in present value) is *economic income*. The change in the present value component of economic income is the net result of two factors. First, the present value one year from now excludes the current year's cash flow which will have already been received. Second, one year from now the cash flows for subsequent years will each be received one year sooner and thus increase in value. In brief, economic income for the year is derived by a comparison of cash flow projections at the beginning and at the end of the year.

Accounting or *book income*, in contrast, is calculated as follows:

$$\begin{aligned}\text{Book income} = {} & \text{Cash flow} - \text{Depreciation and other noncash charges} \\ & + \text{Incremental investments in working capital} \\ & + \text{Capital expenditures}\end{aligned}$$

Note that unlike economic income which depends strictly on cash flows, book income departs from cash flow since it does not incorporate current year's investment outlays for working capital or fixed capital. In addition, noncash items such as depreciation and deferred income taxes are deducted to arrive at book income. Accountants do not attempt nor do they claim to estimate changes in present value. Rather, depreciation represents the allocation of cost over the expected economic life of an asset. If depreciation and the change in present value differ, then book income will not be an accurate measure of economic income.

The accounting return on investment or ROI is computed by a wide variety of methods. For example, some companies include plant and equipment at gross book value while others use the net book value (i.e., gross book value minus accumulated depreciation) approach. Some companies include the capitalized value of leases as a part of assets employed while others do not. Computations most commonly found in practice include:

$$\text{ROI} = \frac{\text{Net income}}{\text{Book value of assets}} \qquad (1)$$

$$\text{ROI} = \frac{\text{Net income} + \text{Interest } (1 - \text{Tax rate})}{\text{Book value of assets}} \qquad (2)$$

Equation (1) will reflect a higher return if equity financing is substituted for debt financing. This is the case because less interest increases net income. To avoid this bias, and thereby separate operating decisions from financing decisions, equation (2) is often used as an ROI measure.

A couple of observations can be made at this point. First, ROI is a single period measurement. Income is computed for a specified year and then divided by the average book value of assets of the same year. Thus, ROI ignores events beyond the current period. Computing an average ROI for several periods would reduce, but certainly not eliminate this problem. In contrast, the DCF return for a given year explicitly considers estimates of cash flows over the entire forecast period. Second, both the numerator and the denominator for the ROI ratio are affected by arbitrary accounting allocations. For example, depreciation expense for the year is a deduction to arrive at net income, while the additional accumulated depreciation is deducted from the company's assets.

Ezra Solomon analyzed the divergences between ROI and the DCF rate of return (internal rate of return) both for individual projects and for collections of projects representative of an entire company. He, and others subsequently, concluded that *ROI is not an accurate or reliable estimate of the DCF return.* Furthermore, they found that there is no systematic pattern in the error that allows a correction to be made. For an assumed set of cash flows, and hence a known DCF return, ROI sometimes understates, but more often overstates, the DCF rate. The error potential ranges from modest in certain situations to very significant and misleading in others.

Solomon demonstrates that the extent to which ROI overstates the economic or DCF return is a complex function of four factors.[12]

- *Length of project life.* The longer the project life, the greater the overstatement.

- *Capitalization policy*. The smaller the fraction of total investment capitalized on the books, the greater will be the overstatement. At the limit, for investments that are expensed 100 percent, the book ROI will rise toward infinity.
- *The rate at which depreciation is taken on the books*. Depreciation procedures faster than straight-line basis will result in higher ROIs. At the limit, the most rapid method of depreciation is, of course, tantamount to 100 percent expensing of outlays and hence leads to the same result.
- *The lag between investment outlays and the recoupment of these outlays from cash inflows*. The greater the lag, the greater the degree of overstatement.

It is important to emphasize that capitalization and depreciation policies are strictly accounting decisions that have no effect (except, in some situations, on taxes) on the company's cash flow and hence its economic rate of return. Research and development expenditures, a form of capital investment, are customarily expensed in the current period. Consequently ROI comparisons between, for example, drug companies which are very R&D-intensive and other industrial companies with relatively low R&D-intensiveness can be seriously misleading. The exclusion of R&D investment from the ROI investment base increases ROI. Thus, while a drug company and a less R&D-intensive manufacturing company may be earning identical economic rates of return, the drug company will report higher ROIs. The problem is compounded by FASB-mandated changes in accounting standards, such as lease capitalization, foreign exchange gains and losses, and capitalization of pension liabilities, as well as changes in accounting procedures initiated by individual firms, such as a shift from first-in, first-out (FIFO) to last-in, first-out (LIFO) inventory costing.

In addition to the factors enumerated above, the growth rate of new investment is a key variable affecting the magnitude of ROI. Faster-growing companies or divisions will be more heavily weighted with more recent investment projects leading to higher book value denominators. Thus, their ROIs will be smaller than those for a nongrowth company investing at an identical economic rate of return. Inflation only adds to the sensitivity of ROIs to the average age of a company's depreciable assets.

ROI Versus DCF Return Illustrated

The management of Noble Restaurant Inc. (NRI) is considering the possibility of investing $1 million in a new restaurant. Management forecasts operating results for a five-year period only, because it believes that in five years the facility will require substantial remodeling and much of the equipment will need to be replaced. Thus, management will be faced with another investment decision in five years that in principle, will be much like today's decision of whether or not to open the restaurant. Projected cash flows for the next five years are $176,230, $250,000, $350,000, $400,000, and $400,000, respectively.

Assuming the cost of capital, which is reflected in the discount rate, is 15 percent, the net present value (NPV) of the investment is zero. That is, the present value of the cash flows discounted at 15 percent is equal to the $1 million investment:

$$NPV = -1{,}000{,}000 + \frac{176{,}230}{1.15} + \frac{250{,}000}{(1.15)^2} + \frac{350{,}000}{(1.15)^3} + \frac{400{,}000}{(1.15)^4} + \frac{400{,}000}{(1.15)^5} = 0$$

When the net present value of an investment is zero, the DCF rate of return is identical to the cost of capital or minimum acceptable rate of return.

A more detailed analysis of the DCF rate of return for the restaurant investment is presented as Table 2–4. The first row depicts the forecasted cash flows for each of the next five years. The present value at the beginning of the year is calculated by discounting the remaining cash flows at 15 percent. For example, the present value at the beginning of the first year is

$$\frac{176{,}230}{1.15} + \frac{250{,}000}{(1.15)^2} + \frac{350{,}000}{(1.15)^3} + \frac{400{,}000}{(1.15)^4} + \frac{400{,}000}{(1.15)^5} = \$1{,}000{,}000$$

The present value at the end of the first year is computed as the discounted cash flows for years 2 through 5, that is,

$$\frac{250{,}000}{1.15} + \frac{350{,}000}{(1.15)^2} + \frac{400{,}000}{(1.15)^3} + \frac{400{,}000}{(1.15)^4} = \$973{,}755$$

The decrease in present value for the first year is thus $26,245, that is, $1,000,000 minus $973,755. Economic income for year 1 is the sum of cash flow of $176,230 less the $26,245 decrease in present value, or $149,985. This amount represents a 15 percent return on the $1 million investment made at the beginning of the year. Similar analysis for years 2 through 5 yields a 15 percent DCF rate of return for each year.

While the restaurant investment is expected to yield an economic return of 15 percent, the ROI results are substantially different. Table 2–5 presents the expected ROI for each of the five years. ROI is computed as net income divided by average book value. ROI progresses from a negative figure in the first year to 200 percent in the fifth year when the restaurant facilities are almost fully depreciated. Thus, ROI materially understates the economic rate of return in the first two years and significantly overstates returns for the last three years. ROI for the entire five-year period can be computed as the sum of the five net income figures divided by the sum of the five average book value figures. This computation yields an ROI of approximately 29 percent or almost twice the 15 percent DCF rate of return. As the above example illustrates, accounting ROI typically understates rates of return during the early stage of an investment and overstates rates in later stages as the undepreciated asset base continues to decrease. Some might contend that these errors offset one another over time as the firm moves toward a balanced mix of old and new investments. Unfortunately, the errors are not ordinarily offsetting. Table 2–6 illustrates this problem.

One restaurant per year is opened during the first five years. Each restaurant's forecasted cash flows are identical to the investment discussed earlier. Therefore, each is expected to yield a 15 percent economic rate of return. After the fifth year, one new restaurant is opened annually to replace the restaurant that has come to the end of its five-year economic life. Thus, beginning in the fifth year NRI will find itself in a steady-state no-growth situation. As can be seen from Table 2–6, the steady-state ROI is 23 percent which seriously overstates the 15 percent economic return. This overstatement may well induce management to commit more capital to the restaurant business than might be economically justified.

Table 2–4 DCF Rate of Return on Restaurant Investment

	Year				
	1	2	3	4	5
(1) Cash flows	$ 176,230	$250,000	$350,000	$400,000	$400,000
(2) Present value at beginning of year	1,000,000	973,755	869,800	650,280	347,840
(3) Present value at end of year	973,755	869,800	650,280	347,840	0
(4) Change in value during year (3) – (2)	– 26,245	– 103,955	– 219,520	– 302,440	– 347,840
(5) Economic income (cash flow plus change in value) (1) + (4)	149,985	146,045	130,480	97,560	52,160
(6) DCF rate of return (5) ÷ (2)	15%	15%	15%	15%	15%

Table 2–5 ROI for One Restaurant Investment

	YEAR				
	1	*2*	*3*	*4*	*5*
Cash flows	$ 176,230	$250,000	$350,000	$400,000	$400,000
– Depreciation	200,000	200,000	200,000	200,000	200,000
Net income	$(23,770)	$ 50,000	$150,000	$200,000	$200,000
Book value, beginning of year	$1,000,000	800,000	600,000	400,000	200,000
– Depreciation	200,000	200,000	200,000	200,000	200,000
Book value, end of year	800,000	600,000	400,000	200,000	0
Average book value	$ 900,000	700,000	500,000	300,000	100,000
ROI	– 2.6%	7.1%	30.0%	66.7%	200%

Table 2–6 ROI for All Restaurant Investments

	Year					
	1	2	3	4	5	6
Net income for restaurant						
A	(23,770)	50,000	150,000	200,000	200,000	—
B		(23,770)	50,000	150,000	200,000	200,000
C			(23,770)	50,000	150,000	200,000
D				(23,770)	50,000	150,000
E					(23,770)	50,000
F						(23,770)
Total net income	(23,770)	26,230	176,230	376,230	576,230	576,230
Average book value for restaurant						
A	900,000	700,000	500,000	300,000	100,000	—
B		900,000	700,000	500,000	300,000	100,000
C			900,000	700,000	500,000	300,000
D				900,000	700,000	500,000
E					900,000	700,000
F						900,000
Total book value	900,000	1,600,000	2,100,000	2,400,000	2,500,000	2,500,000
ROI for all restaurants	– 2.6%	1.6%	8.4%	15.7%	23.0%	23.0%

The magnitude of the error in ROI is also affected by the growth rate in investment. If a company invests at an increasing rate, its mix will be more heavily weighted with new investments for which ROIs will be relatively low. Thus, the ROI of a growth company will be lower than that of a no-growth company even if both invest in identical projects yielding identical DCF rates of return.[13]

Additional Shortcomings of ROI

The use of ROI as a standard for evaluating strategies and performance at the business unit or corporate level can lead to a substantial misallocation of resources. There are three fundamental reasons for this beyond those already covered in this section. First, while the economic rate of return from a single project or an entire strategy depends solely on prospective cash flow, accounting ROI depends not only on prospective investment and cash flow, but also on undepreciated investments of past periods. Thus if two firms or business units have identical strategies and expectations, but one has a larger beginning investment base, then it will also have lower ROIs during the planning period. Such differences in ROI in the face of identical DCF returns are clearly countereconomic and can lead to serious executive misjudgments.

A second major shortcoming of using ROI for assessing strategies and performance is its neglect of the post-planning period residual value of the business unit or company. Only a small proportion of a company's market value can be reasonably attributed to its estimated cash flow for the next five or ten years. A simple calculation reveals that the present value of dividends over the next five years accounts for only a small fraction of current market price. Take the stock of IBM, which was priced during the summer of 1985 at about $120 a share. Its latest annual dividend was $3.80. If we assume that dividends will grow 13 percent annually, and we assume a market discount rate of 13 percent, then we can estimate the present value of dividends over the next five years to be $19, or 16 percent of market price. The proportion of the stock price assignable to dividends beyond five years is thus 84 percent.

Using Value Line dividend projections and stock prices for over 1200 companies and a broad cross-section of industries, I found a large clustering of companies whose expected dividends beyond the fifth year account for about 80 percent of their value. The lowest proportions, ranging 60 to 70 percent, were for the major public utilities—electric, natural gas, and telephone. The highest were for industries such as electronic components (93 percent), medical instruments (89 percent), retail drug stores (89 percent), radio-TV transmitting equipment (88 percent), and electronic computers (86 percent).[14]

A business attempting to increase its market share and competitive position will likely increase its new product development and marketing spending, price aggressively, and invest in expanded production capacity and working capital. While each of these activities is aimed at strengthening the organization's longer-term strategic position, ROI may well decline over the next several years even though such actions increase market value. In sharp contrast, a harvesting strategy allows erosion in market share, and thereby increases cash flow by minimizing investment in fixed capital and freeing up working capital. Harvesting is typically appropriate for products with relatively low market share in mature or declining markets. This strategy will generate better planning-period ROIs than the share-building strategy, but the residual value associated with harvesting is likely to be very small.

The economic return generated by a strategy depends on the estimated cash flow during the planning period and the estimated value of the business unit's strategic positioning at the end of the planning period. ROI performance during the planning period alone is not a reliable basis for estimating economic return. For example, increases in ROI during the planning period may be attributable to a business unit's ability to outperform competitors via successful implementation of cost leadership or differentiation strategies. Alternatively, ROI increase may result from a harvest strategy that culminates with a very modest residual value.

The third limitation in using ROI for financial planning and control involves the sometimes countereconomic effect of changes in financing policy on ROI. Suppose a company is operating at what it believes to be its optimal capital structure. In other words, its target proportions of debt and equity to finance the business are established so that the weighted average cost of capital is minimized. Any departure from this target financing would naturally increase the average cost of capital and, holding everything else constant, would reduce the value of the firm. The impact on ROI of employing more than or less than optimal debt is summarized on page 42.

If ROI is computed before interest, then it is unaffected by fi-

	SHAREHOLDER VALUE	ROI PREINTEREST	ROI AFTER INTEREST
More than optimal debt	Decrease	No change	Decrease
Less than optimal debt	Decrease	No change	Increase

nancing policy while the average cost of capital, and hence the value of the firm, is affected. When ROI is on an after-interest basis, ROI increases when the firm moves from optimal to less than optimal debt. The ROI increase takes place at the same time that the value of the company is decreasing.

Shortcomings of Return on Equity (ROE)

Until now the discussion in this section has focused on ROI. Another widely used measure of business performance is the accounting return on equity (ROE) ratio:

$$\text{ROE} = \frac{\text{Net income}}{\text{Book value of shareholders' equity}} \quad (3)$$

Whereas ROI relates net income to total assets, ROE employs shareholder equity as the denominator. ROI is the more commonly used measure at the business unit or divisional level, ROE is the more popular measure at the corporate level. One of the principal reasons that management focuses on ROI rather than ROE at the business unit level is its reluctance to allocate debt to the individual units. The focus on ROE at the corporate level is often explained on the grounds that it is a measure of primary concern to investors.

Because ROE is so similar to ROI, it necessarily shares all the shortcomings of ROI enumerated earlier. In addition, ROE is particularly sensitive to leverage. Assuming that proceeds from debt financing can be invested at a rate of return greater than the borrowing rate, ROE will increase with greater amounts of leverage. ROE will, in fact, increase as more than optimal debt is issued and the value of the company decreases due to the increase in financial risk. Thus, once again we observe that an accounting-based performance measurement can conflict with the shareholder value criterion.

Hergert[15] recently analyzed some of the pitfalls in relying on ROE as a measure of corporate performance. The ROE for the Standard & Poor's 400 industrial companies trended upward during the 1970s, a time when rates of return realized by shareholders oftentimes did not keep pace with inflation. To gain better insights into the factors responsible for the increase in ROE, Hergert decomposes the ratio into three ratios as follows:

$$\text{ROE} = \text{After-tax profit margin} \times \text{Asset turnover} \times \text{Asset leverage}$$

$$\text{ROE} = \frac{\text{Net income}}{\text{Sales}} \times \frac{\text{Sales}}{\text{Assets}} \times \frac{\text{Assets}}{\text{Common equity}}$$

The two factors contributing to the increase in ROE are an increase in asset turnover and an increase in leverage. At least a part of the increase in asset turnover is due to inflation. While current year's sales respond immediately to changes in inflation rates such as those experienced during the 1970s, the book value of assets which represents a mix of assets purchased at earlier dates and lower prices adapts much more slowly to changes in inflation. Thus, particularly for capital intensive companies such as steel companies, increases in asset turnover may be attributable to inflationary forces rather than simply better asset utilization.

During the 1970s the Standard & Poor's 400 companies increased their leverage substantially, thus generating an increase in ROE. The increase in ROE must, of course, be weighed against the increase in financial risk and consequent impact on the value of the companies. After-tax profit margins suffered a serious decline during the 1970s, thereby decreasing ROE. The decrease in margins, however, was more than offset by increases in asset turnover and leverage. In summary, the increase in ROE is largely attributable to inflation and leverage and was achieved despite deteriorating profit margins. The stock market apparently recognized the shortcomings of ROE as a reliable measure of corporate performance because despite the rise in ROE investors experienced a decade of generally dismal returns.

A Perspective on Accounting Numbers

The demonstration here that accounting-based numbers such as earnings per share and ROI are not reliable indicators of shareholder value should not be interpreted as a failure of accounting.

The problem lies not so much with accounting but rather its use by managers for unintended, inappropriate purposes. Accrual accounting conventions are governed by the objectives and institutional constraints of corporate financial reporting. Corporate reporting assesses a company's past performance and is designed primarily for nonmanagement groups. Performance for the most recent year cannot be properly evaluated without a recognition that the investments made by management during this and preceding years may not be recouped until subsequent years. Accounting copes with this lag and the uncertainty surrounding the amounts and timing of prospective cash flow by assigning the cost of certain investments such as R&D exclusively to the period in which the outlay takes place. For investments in fixed assets, the cost is assigned systematically, albeit arbitrarily, to a set of future time periods by the depreciation process.

Corporate financial reporting is an activity regulated by the Securities and Exchange Commission (SEC) and the FASB. The Securities Acts of 1933 and 1934 gave the SEC power to ensure "full and fair disclosure" by corporations issuing securities on an interstate basis.[16] Companies, on the other hand, have an incentive to limit the reported information, particularly information about prospects for the future. This is the case because financial reports are publicly available and information provided to shareholders is also available to competitors, suppliers, customers, employees, the government, and other constituents. Therefore, compared to the internal information available to management, accounting information communicated externally necessarily represents "second-best" information.

The use of the accrual accounting methodology that is designed for ex post external reporting as a basis for corporate planning is dysfunctional. Fortunately it is also unnecessary. Indeed, the role of top management is to assess the relationship between today's investments and the magnitude and timing of uncertain future cash flows and not to be influenced by arbitrary conventions that do not affect cash flow. Shareholder value is, after all, created by cash flow, not by accounting convention. A conceptual basis and operational means for implementing an economically based shareholder-value planning system does exist. By estimating the future cash flows associated with each strategy, management can assess the economic value to shareholders of alternate strategies at the business unit and corporate levels. The recommended approach presented in Chapter

3 requires virtually no data that are not already developed under existing financial planning systems.

Data-Base Approach to Corporate Financial Reporting[17]

As companies become increasingly value oriented and with the rapid advances in information technology, the role of accounting and corporate financial reporting will be affected as well. During the past decade we have seen an unparalleled growth in the number and complexity of corporate financial reporting requirements. Inflation, leasing, foreign currency translation, mergers, and pensions are just a few of the more controversial issues facing policy makers. A new financial accounting standard that can turn reported net income into a reported loss causes consternation in corporate boardrooms. These changes have also presented security analysts with the unenviable task of interpreting and productively using such financial data.

Yet from a technological perspective, financial reporting has not changed. At a time when information-communication technology is having staggering effects in other spheres, financial reporting still occurs largely as it has for the last fifty years. Annual and quarterly reports are mailed to shareholders, analysts, and others. The SEC reports are mailed to Washington and filed in the SEC reference room. Primary financial statements are based upon accrual accounting and are produced under a single set of methods chosen by management from generally accepted accounting principles.

Current technology has potentially revolutionary implications for the manner in which financial information could be disseminated to and processed by investors, analysts, and other users. An electronic capital market has already received much discussion and is in the process of being implemented.

The next step is electronic financial reporting. The SEC is currently taking its first steps toward an electronic filing and retrieval system that would permit users to employ computer terminals to access corporate reports filed with the commission. Although this proposal is a step toward acknowledging computer technology, it merely substitutes access via mail or a visit to the SEC's reference room with access via the computer. However, this step does not alter the basic information available, and therefore barely scratches the surface of what can be potentially achieved.

Information technology offers an unprecedented opportunity to effect a dramatic change in the nature, concept, and content of financial reporting. To appreciate the full potential of technology, consider the current state of corporate reporting.

The Financial Accounting Standards Board, the private sector organization that sets corporate financial reporting standards, has emphasized that the overriding objective of financial reporting is to provide information that is useful to investors, creditors, and other users. Consistent with this objective, the board has stated that since shareholder cash flows derived from dividends plus proceeds from sales of shares are related to the company's cash flows, financial reports should provide information to help investors assess the amounts, timing, and uncertainty of prospective company cash flows.

After establishing the importance of cash flow information, the board then declared that "the primary focus of financial reporting is information about earnings and its components." The FASB's renewed focus on income determination comes at a time that prices of shares often do not follow the pattern of reported earnings.

Enlightened security analysts and accountants alike would acknowledge that neither accountants nor conventional accounting measurements have a comparative advantage in assessing the value of a business. Both would agree that providing financial information to those who wish to estimate value is the more appropriate objective of corporate financial reporting. Microcomputer technology provides accounting policy makers at the FASB and the SEC an unprecedented opportunity to implement this objective more effectively and at less cost to users than ever before.

Financial statements result from masses of raw data involving individual corporate transactions that are classified into financial statement categories, aggregated, and quantified according to acceptable accounting alternatives (e.g., various depreciation and inventory costing methods). Today's general-purpose financial statements that "present fairly the financial position and the results of operations" are oriented toward providing *one* particular viewpoint of the company's performance.

As users of financial reports have become more sophisticated, they have the capacity to assess a firm's performance independently. Thus, for example, the accountant's transformation of raw cash flow data imposes costs on many Wall Street analysts who wish to estimate the company's cash flows *before* the application of accrual accounting procedures. In an increasingly institutionalized securities market, the accountant's contribution may appropriately shift from preparing highly structured financial statements based on raw data to identifying and providing input data for the market to incorporate in its analysis.

Information technology now makes it possible to accommodate this *data-base approach to corporate financial reporting*. An electronic financial data base containing the underlying data needed to produce conventional financial statements as well as alternative forms of analysis can be developed. Such a data base could be accessed by users in a manner that makes them less dependent upon the "official" financial statements. With a variety of software packages and the data base, users could compute any number of income figures, if they chose to, or none at all. Moreover, when the reporting company's data base is merged with industry and macro data bases, the potential quality of analysis is raised substantially.

A major concern in financial reporting by regulators, as well as users, is the issue of uniformity of accounting methods over time and across companies. This lack of consistency is perceived by regulators to have impaired the credibility of financial reporting. Under the data base approach, not only would users be able to choose the methods they prefer, but the issue of uniformity of accounting method would disappear. Users would be able to compute net income on a uniform basis, either across companies or over time.

The role of accounting standards would shift in emphasis. The basic issue would no longer be which inventory or depreciation method to permit. Instead the standards would be directed to disclosure issues such as: What should be stored in the data base? How can consistency be maintained in how data is entered across firms and over time?

These questions are not easily resolved. They are considerably different from the issues the FASB now devotes major time and effort to trying to resolve—such as trying to determine what accounting standard produces the "best" measure of net income. In brief, there would be less concern with how to calculate the "bottom line" and more concern with determining how many and which lines should be calculated. The task of developing standards for the design and maintenance of a user-friendly, low-cost data base for a broad cross-section of users poses a challenging opportunity that needs to be addressed by the accounting profession, management, and the financial community.

Thus far the costs of implementing this data-base approach have been ignored. In part, technological reasons have been invoked for minimizing the cost issue. However, recent research indicates that the stock market, as reflected in stock prices, acts as if it already is absorbing large amounts of publicly available information. Research indicates that prices do *not* myopically focus upon earnings but instead look beyond them to adjust for accounting method differences across companies and over time. Research also indicates reliance on a wide variety of qualitative information besides earnings, including announcements of dividends, litigation, franchise awards, contract awards, new product introduction, mineral discoveries, sale or spinoff of a division, among others.

Hence, earnings are viewed by the market as only one among many sources of information. The data-base concept is consonant with this view and may effectively reduce the cost to the market of developing better and more comprehensive analyses. Under a data-base system, users can still compute net income if they wish. Moreover, they may be able to do so at a lower cost to the extent that they currently spend resources reconstructing it. Finally, reported earnings are by no means a unique way to aggregate or combine the data. Prices may be responding to more primitive elements such as cash flow, and earnings may merely be correlated with those primitive elements. If so, future research would be able to determine if some alternative approach better explains stock prices than simply relying on earnings.

Under the data-base system, management's performance would be more easily judged by a variety of measures, rather than merely reported earnings. To a large extent, this is already the case. This fact may not always be fully recognized by management. However, if a variety of measures in addition to the "official" reported net income were readily available, it would become more difficult to justify myopic reliance upon a single number. Undue focus on reported earnings can lead to acceptance of strategies that reduce value and rejection of strategies that increase value.

The greatest potential benefit is the shift of management's focus from short-run reported earnings to longer-term shareholder value. To the extent that management focus is shifted to shareholder value, this should be reflected in more favorable market values. Hence, a major user of financial statements (shareholders) can potentially benefit in an indirect but significant way from the introduction of the data-base approach.

Obviously there are a number of unresolved issues such as the cost of implementation. However, it is likely that the major obstacle to electronic financial reporting will not be based upon technological or cost issues. Because the "let the user choose" approach proposed here will materially change the present corporate reporting system, it is likely to be vigorously debated. The intent here has not been to provide solutions, but rather to introduce an approach to electronic financial reporting that will require substantial research and debate before it can be effectively implemented. It is already technologically feasible. If it does not come to pass, the reason is more likely to be political than technological.

Chapter 3

Shareholder Value Approach

As discussed in Chapter 1, the "shareholder value approach" estimates the economic value of an investment by discounting forecasted cash flows by the cost of capital. These cash flows, in turn, serve as the foundation for shareholder returns from dividends and share-price appreciation. This chapter shows how the basic valuation parameters or *value drivers*—sales growth rate, operating profit margin, income tax rate, working capital investment, fixed capital investment, cost of capital, and forecast duration—are developed and incorporated in shareholder value calculations. The focus then shifts from estimating the value of a business to estimating the value created by its strategy during the forecast period. Throughout, the shareholder value approach is linked to parameters with which operating managers are familiar and comfortable.

Estimating Shareholder Value

The total economic value of an entity such as a company or business unit is the sum of the values of its debt and its equity. This value of the business is called "corporate value" and the value of the equity portion is called "shareholder value." In summary:

Corporate value = Debt + Shareholder value

The debt portion of corporate value includes the market value of debt, unfunded pension liabilities, and the market value of other claims such as preferred stock.[1] Rearranging the above equation to solve for shareholder value:

Shareholder value = Corporate value – Debt

In order to determine shareholder value, one must first determine the value of the total firm or business unit, that is, corporate value. Corporate value, in turn, consists of two basic components:

1. The present value of cash flow from operations during the forecast period
2. "Residual value," which represents the present value of the business attributable to the period beyond the forecast period.

For a more precise estimation of corporate value, a third component must also be included: the current value of marketable securities and other investments that can be converted to cash and are not essential to operating the business. Neither these investments nor the income from them is included in cash flows from operations. Nonetheless, these investments clearly have value, thus they need to be included in developing the corporate value estimate. Corporate value therefore has three components:

Corporate value = Present value of cash flow from operations during the forecast period + Residual value + Marketable securities

Cash Flow from Operations

Cash flow from operations represents the difference between operating cash inflows and outflows. These cash flows are relevant for estimating corporate value because they represent the cash available to compensate debtholders and shareholders. Once the cash flow from operations is estimated for each year in the forecast period, these flows are then discounted back to the present. The cash flows are discounted by the cost of capital or the weighted average of the costs of debt and equity capital.

To illustrate, consider the following three-year forecast for a firm with a 14 percent cost of capital.

YEAR	CASH FLOW	14% DISCOUNT FACTOR[a]	PRESENT VALUE OF CASH FLOW	CUMULATIVE PV OF CASH FLOWS
1	$100	.8772	$ 87.72	$ 87.72
2	150	.7695	115.43	203.15
3	200	.6750	135.00	338.15

[a]Discount factor $= \frac{1}{(1+.14)^n}$

The discounted cash flows arising during the forecast period (or more precisely, the "cumulative present value of cash flows") amount to $338.15.

Each year's cash flow is calculated as follows:

Cash flow = Cash inflow − Cash outflow
= [(Sales in prior year)(1 + Sales growth rate)(Operating profit margin)(1 − Cash income tax rate)] − (Incremental fixed plus working capital investment)

After each year's cash flow has been estimated, it is then discounted by the cost of capital to compute present value.

The above formula can be used to compute the forecasted cash flow of $100 for year 1. Assume:

Sales in prior year	$4000
Sales growth rate	15%
Operating profit margin	10%
Cash income tax rate	46%
Incremental fixed capital investment rate	15%
Incremental working capital investment rate	10%

Cash inflow:

Sales in year 1	= Sales in prior year (1 + Sales growth rate)	
	= $4000 (1 + .15)	
	= $4600	
Operating profit	= Sales (Operating profit margin)	
	= $4600 (.10)	$460
Less: Cash income taxes (46%)		210
Operating profit after taxes		$250

Cash outflow:

Incremental fixed capital investment	= Increase in sales (Incremental fixed capital investment rate)	
	= $600 (.15)	$ 90
Incremental working capital investment	= Increase in sales (Incremental working capital investment rate)	
	= $600 (.10)	60
Total investment		150
Cash flow from operations		$100

Before proceeding further, some brief comments about several of these value drivers are in order. *Operating profit margin* is the ratio of pre-interest, pretax operating profit to sales. To arrive at operating profit not only are cost of goods sold, selling and administrative expenses deducted, but so is depreciation expense which involves no cash outlay. The *incremental fixed capital investment* is defined as capital expenditures in excess of depreciation expense, that is:

Incremental fixed capital investment =
Capital expenditures − Depreciation expense

Thus, if depreciation were added back to operating profit (to convert it to a cash flow figure) and the same depreciation expense amount were added to the incremental fixed capital investment figure (to convert it to total capital expenditures), the cash flow from operations figure would remain the same.

When management is conducting analysis for its own business, it ordinarily has a long-term plan which includes capital expenditures estimates. In this case, these estimates of capital expenditures can be incorporated directly into the valuation. However, if the analysis concerns another company, say, a competitor, then typically only historical information is likely to be available. In such a situation, it is generally advantageous to forecast investment as a percentage of incremental sales.

$$\text{Incremental fixed capital investment rate (\%)} = \frac{\text{Capital expenditures} - \text{Depreciation expense}}{\text{Incremental sales}}(100)$$

$$= \frac{\text{Incremental fixed capital investment}}{\text{Incremental sales}}(100)$$

To estimate the average of recent values, take the sum of all capital expenditures less depreciation over the preceding five or ten years and divide this amount by the sales increase during the period. If a business continues to replace existing facilities in kind and if the prices of these facilities remain constant, then the numerator (i.e., capital expenditures less depreciation) approximates the cost of real growth in productive capacity.

However, capital expenditures usually rise each year owing to inflationary forces and regulatory requirements such as environmental control. These cost increases may be partially offset by advances in technology. Thus the numerator reflects not only the cost of real growth but price changes in facilities as well as the impact of product mix changes, regulation, and technological improvements. Whether the historical value of this variable is a reasonable basis for the forecast period depends significantly on how quickly and to what extent the company will be able to offset increased fixed capital costs with higher selling prices or more efficient use of facilities.

The *incremental working capital investment* represents the net investment in accounts receivable, inventory, accounts payable, and accruals that are required to support sales growth.[2] Since this investment is part of the firm's basic operations, it is included in the calculation of "cash flow from operations." This investment can be expressed as a percentage of incremental sales.

$$\text{Incremental working capital rate (\%)} = \frac{\text{Incremental working capital investment}}{\text{Incremental sales}}(100)$$

The *cash income tax rate* represents taxes on operating profit for a fiscal year that are either paid by installments during the year or are a liability (income taxes payable) at the end of the year. The cash income taxes are ordinarily less than the reported book income taxes which often include a deferred tax component. Deferred income taxes result from timing differences in the recognition of some revenue and expense items for book purposes and tax purposes. For example, straight-line depreciation may be used for book purposes and an accelerated depreciation method for calculating taxable operating profit.

This section has focused on the essential parameters or *value drivers* underlying cash flow from operations. To convert these cash flows to present value, we need to establish a cost of capital estimate.

Cost of Capital

The appropriate rate for discounting the company's cash flow stream is the weighted average of the costs of debt and equity capital. For example, suppose a company's after-tax cost of debt is 6 percent and its estimated cost of equity 16 percent. Further, it plans to raise capital in the following proportion—20 percent by way of debt and 80 percent by way of equity. It computes the cost of capital of 14 percent as follows:

	Weight (%)	Cost (%)	Weighted Cost (%)
Debt	20	6	1.2
Equity	80	16	12.8
Cost of capital			14.0

Estimating the cost of capital is essential for establishing the minimum acceptable rate of return or hurdle rate that management should require on new investment proposals. Investments yielding returns greater than the cost of capital will create shareholder value, while those yielding less than the cost of capital will decrease shareholder value.

The cost of capital rate incorporates the returns demanded by both debtholders and shareholders because *pre-interest* cash flows are discounted—that is, cash flows on which both debtholders and shareholders have claims. The appropriate cost of capital is therefore one that considers the claims of each group in proportion to its targeted relative capital contribution. The cash flows discounted by the cost of capital yields corporate value, and then debt is deducted to obtain shareholder value.

It is important to emphasize that the relative weights attached to debt and equity, respectively, are neither predicated on dollars the firm has raised in the past, nor do they constitute the relative proportions of dollars the firm plans to raise in the current year. Instead, the relevant weights should be based on the proportions of debt and equity that the firm targets for its capital structure over the long-term planning period. In calculating weights for target capital structure, should book (balance sheet) values or market values be used? There is widespread agreement in finance texts about the conceptual superiority of market values, despite their volatility, on the grounds that to justify its valuation the firm will have to earn competitive rates of return for debtholders and shareholders on their respective current market values.[3]

Suppose shareholders invested $5 million of initial capital in a company ten years ago. Over the ten-year period book value grew from $5 million to $7 million. Market value, however, increased to $20 million over the same period. A reasonable return in light of present market conditions is 20 percent. Would current shareholders be satisfied with a 20 percent return on the $7 million book value, or would they expect to earn 20 percent on the current market value of $20 million? Rational investors will base their decisions on current market value. Book value reflects historical costs which generally have little correspondence to economic value and therefore it is not relevant to current investment decisions.

Measuring the cost of debt is a relatively straightforward matter once it is established that what is appropriate is the cost of new debt and not the cost of previously outstanding debt. This is so because the economic desirability of a prospective investment depends upon future costs and not past or sunk costs. Since interest on debt is tax deductible, the rate of return that must be earned on debt-financed instruments is the after-tax cost of debt.

The relevant rate for the cost of debt is the long-term rate or yield to maturity which reflects the rate currently demanded by debtholders. Short-term rates do not incorporate expectations about long-term inflation. The time horizon for estimating cost of capital should be consistent with the long-term horizon of the cash flow forecast period. Even if a company routinely "rolls over" short-term debt as part of its permanent financing, the long-term rate is still a better approximation of interest costs over the forecast period because interest rates on long-term debt incorporate the expected cost of repeated short-term borrowing.

The second component of the cost of capital, the cost of equity, is more difficult to estimate. In contrast to the debt-financing case where the firm contracts to pay a specific rate for the use of capital, there is no explicit agreement to pay common shareholders any particular rate of return. Nonetheless, there is some implicit rate of return required to attract investors to purchase the firm's stock and to induce shareholders to hold their shares. This rate is the relevant cost of equity capital. Rational, risk-averse investors expect to earn a rate of return that will compensate them for accepting greater investment risk. Thus, in assessing the company's cost of equity capital, or the minimum expected return that will induce investors to buy the company's shares, it is reasonable to assume that they will demand the risk-free rate as reflected in the current yields available in government securities, plus an additional return or *equity risk premium* for investing in the company's more risky shares.[4] Specifically:

Cost of equity = Risk-free rate + Equity risk premium

Even government securities are not entirely risk-free. While they are essentially free of default risk, they are not free from increases in interest rates and the resulting capital losses. For an investor with a long-term horizon, even short-term Treasury bills carry interest rate risk because yields will fluctuate over time. In the absence of a truly riskless security, the rate on long-term Treasury bonds serves as the best estimate of the risk-free rate. Just as in the case of estimating the cost of debt earlier, the time horizon for estimating the cost of equity should be consistent with the long-term horizon of the cash flow forecast period. The use of long-term Treasury bond rates accomplishes this purpose and in addition captures the premium for expected inflation. After all, the rate of return demanded by investors includes not only the "real" interest rate (compensation for simply making the investment), but also compensation for expected inflation:

Risk-free rate = "Real" interest rate + Expected inflation rate

The second component of the cost of equity is the equity risk premium. One way of estimating the risk premium for a particular stock is by computing the product of the *market* risk premium for equity (the excess of the expected rate of return on a representative market index such as the Standard & Poor's 500 stock index over the risk-free rate) and the individual security's systematic risk, as measured by its beta coefficient[5]:

Risk premium = Beta (Expected return on Market – Risk-free rate)

The market risk premium should be based on forward-looking rates of return. This premium represents additional compensation that investors expect for holding stocks rather than "risk-free" government bonds. A number of Wall Street firms such as Goldman Sachs, Kidder Peabody, and Merrill Lynch publish their estimates for the expected rate of return on the market using discounted cash flow models. Merrill Lynch, for example, estimated the expected rate of return on the market as 14.3 percent in the March 1985 edition of its bimonthly publication, *Quantitative Analysis*. The Treasury bond rate at that time was about 11.3 percent. Thus, the implied market risk premium for equity was 3 percent.

The final factor needed for a cost of equity estimate is the beta coefficient. Individual stocks tend to be more or less risky than the overall market. The riskiness of a stock, as measured by beta, is the volatility of its return in relation to that of a market portfolio. The rate of return from dividends and capital appreciation on a market portfolio will, by definition, fluctuate identically with the market, and therefore its beta is equal to 1.0. Stocks with betas greater than 1.0 are more volatile than the market, and thus would carry a risk premium greater than the overall market risk premium. For example, if a stock moves up or down 1.5 percent when the market moves up or down 1 percent, the stock would have a beta of 1.5.

Betas for a stock are calculated by running a linear regression between past returns for that stock and past returns on a market index such as the Standard & Poor's 500. The resulting calculation is a historic beta and thereby provides a measure of how risky the stock was in the past. A number of organizations such as Value Line and Merrill Lynch calculate betas. Investors are naturally concerned with prospective rather than historic risk. In response to this need, Barr Rosenberg and a number of other researchers developed a *fundamental beta*. Recall that the historic beta measures the relative responsiveness of a company's shares to general market movements. Econometric studies indicate that fundamental characteristics such as the industry in which the company participates, along with its balance sheet characteristics (e.g., financial leverage) and earnings performance (e.g., earnings variability), provide a basis for estimating the company's exposure to general market or economy-wide developments. This multiple factor model thus provides a means of estimating *ex ante* or future betas.[6]

In summary:

Cost of equity = Risk-free rate + Beta (Expected return on market − Risk-free rate)

To illustrate, assume a risk-free rate of 11.3 percent, a company's beta equal to 0.9, and the expected return on market of 14.3 percent.

$$\text{Cost of equity} = 11.3 + 0.9\,(14.3 - 11.3) = 14\%$$

Residual Value

The last two sections on cash flow from operations and cost of capital have established the basis for calculating the discounted cash flow value attributable to the forecast period. In this section, we consider the value attributable to the period after the forecast period, that is, the residual value.

The residual value often constitutes the largest portion of the value of the firm. For most businesses only a small proportion of value can be reasonably attributed to its estimated cash flow for the next five or ten years. More than one-third of the businesses in a recent study experienced negative operating cash flow before interest expenses during the 1970–1979 period. Even large-share businesses in mature markets, the so-called cash cows, generated only an average positive cash flow of 9 cents per dollar of investment.[7]

A business attempting to increase its market share and competitive position will likely increase its new product development and marketing spending, price aggressively, and invest in expanded production capacity and working capital. While each of these activities is aimed at strengthening the organization's longer-term strategic position, cash flow may well be modest or decline over the next several years even though such actions increase market value. In sharp contrast, a harvesting strategy allows erosion in market share, and thereby increases cash flow by minimizing investment in fixed capital and freeing up working capital. Harvesting is typically appropriate for products with relatively low market share in mature or declining markets. This strategy will generate greater cash flows during the forecast period than the share-building strategy, but the residual value associated with harvesting is likely to be very small.

What emerges from the above are two important observations. First, while residual value is a significant component of corporate value, its size depends directly upon the assumptions made for the forecast period. Second, there is no unique formula for residual value. Its value depends on a careful assessment of the competitive position of the business at the end of the forecast period. There are, however, several methods for estimating residual value that can be applied in different circumstances. For example, in the case of a harvesting strategy, liquidation value would most likely be the best estimate of residual value. In contrast, for the share-building case a going concern measure rather than a liquidation measure would be relevant for estimating residual value. One such measure, the perpetuity method, is particularly useful for a wide range of situations and will be addressed in more detail now.

Value-creating strategies are those that produce excess returns over those demanded by capital markets and thereby produce positive net present values. This value creation objective is achieved by firms that can obtain funds at competitive rates from capital markets and then invest these funds to exploit imperfections in product markets. For example, a leading firm in an industry may enjoy high entry barriers due to factors such as economies of scale, product differentiation, large switching costs, substantial capital requirements, and favorable government policy.

It is, of course, much easier to talk about investing to achieve excess returns than actually to achieve such a result. Most firms operating in a highly competitive, commodity-type industry are not likely to earn excess returns. Newer industries that initially enjoy excess returns often attract additional entrants which leads to excess capacity, price competition, and finally lower returns for all participants in the industry. The video-game market of the early 1980s is an example of this phenomenon.[8]

The perpetuity method for estimating residual value is based on the foregoing competitive dynamics. It is essentially based on the assumption that a company that is able to generate returns above the cost of capital (i.e., achieve excess returns) will eventually attract competitors, whose entry into the business will drive returns down to the minimum acceptable or cost of capital rate.[9] Specifically, the perpetuity method assumes that after the forecast period, the business will earn, on average, the cost of capital on new investments. Another way of expressing this idea is to say that after the forecast period, the business will invest, on average, in strategies whose net present value is zero.

Once the rate of return has been driven down to the cost of capital rate, period-by-period differences in future cash flows do not alter the *value* of the business. Therefore, these future flows can be treated as if they were a "perpetuity" or an infinite stream of identical cash flows.

The present value of any perpetuity is simply the value of the expected annual cash flow divided by the rate of return:

$$\text{Present value of a perpetuity} = \frac{\text{Annual cash flow}}{\text{Rate of return}}$$

Using the perpetuity method, the present value (at the end of the forecast period) is therefore calculated by dividing a "perpetuity cash flow" by the cost of capital:

$$\text{Residual value} = \frac{\text{Perpetuity cash flow}}{\text{Cost of capital}}$$

Keep in mind that the perpetuity method for estimating residual value is *not* based on the assumption that all future cash flows will actually be identical. It simply reflects the fact that the cash flows resulting from future investments will not affect the value of the firm because the overall rate of return earned on those investments is equal to the cost of capital.

The following example will illustrate why using a "perpetuity cash flow" is equivalent to discounting the actual cash flows when you are calculating the value of a firm that is earning exactly the cost of capital.

A business in a mature industry generated $10 million in cash flow last year. If the company were to continue to generate $10 million annually—into "perpetuity"—and its cost of capital is 10 percent, the value of the company would simply be equal to $100 million:

$$\frac{\text{Cash flow}}{\text{Cost of capital}} = \frac{\$10\text{ million}}{.10} = \$100\text{ million}$$

Like most firms, however, this company plans to grow. Specifically, the company has decided to market a product-line extension that would cost $700,000 to develop in the first year and is expected to generate these cash flows in the following three years: $120,000, $370,000, and $379,500. These cash flows constitute a return of 10 percent which is identical to the company's cost of capital. The company's total cash flow, including both the ongoing $10 million yearly flows and the incremental flows resulting from the investment are therefore:

Year	Ongoing Cash Flows	Incremental Cash Flows	Total Cash Flow
1	$10,000,000	($700,000)	$ 9,300,000
2	10,000,000	120,000	10,120,000
3	10,000,000	370,000	10,370,000
4	10,000,000	379,500	10,379,500
5 and thereafter	10,000,000		10,000,000

The present value of these cash flows discounted at 10 percent is as follows:

Year	Total Cash Flow	Present Value
1	$ 9,300,000	$ 8,454,545
2	10,120,000	8,363,636
3	10,370,000	7,791,135
4	10,379,500	7,089,338
5 and thereafter	10,000,000	68,301,346
		$100,000,000

The value of the firm is therefore calculated to be $100 million. In other words, the value of the firm after the new investment is identical to the value of the firm assuming *no growth* in cash flows. This is because the "net present value" of the cash flows associated with the investment in the new product is zero (which is another way of saying that the firm was earning exactly its cost of capital).

There is a clear analogy between this example and the perpetuity method of calculating residual value. If, after the end of the forecast period, the firm continues to grow but earns exactly its cost of capital, then we can calculate the value of the business at that time—that is, its residual value—as if the cash flows were going to remain constant. This greatly simplifies the calculation and gives the same answer that one would obtain if the individual cash flows were discounted instead.[10]

While the standard perpetuity method is a reasonable approach to estimating residual value for a wide set of circumstances, there are situations where post-forecast period rates of return can either be expected to sustain above the cost of capital or drop below the cost of capital. These possibilities can be easily incorporated in variants of the perpetuity method.

Before concluding this discussion of residual value, two additional methods—the price/earnings (P/E) ratio method and the market-to-book (M/B) ratio method—need to be evaluated. While these methods are frequently used in valuations, each has serious limitations. Under the P/E ratio method, residual value is simply the product of earnings at the end of the forecast period times the projected P/E ratio at the end of the forecast period. An apparent advantage of this approach is that the P/E ratio is a widely used and readily available statistic. Furthermore, many executives find it to be a "comfortable concept."

There are a number of problems associated with the P/E ratio method. First, it is based on the premise that price is driven by earnings. The shortcomings of using earnings in economic valuations were outlined in Chapter 2. Second, there is an inherent inconsistency in commingling cash flows during the forecast period with accounting (earnings) numbers for the post-forecast period. Third, the P/E approach does not explicitly take into account whether the business can be expected to invest at, below, or above the cost of capital in the post-forecast period. Finally, in addition to the three previous conceptual problems, there remains a difficult practical problem. Simply stated, no reliable models exist for accurately forecasting future P/E ratios. Over the past two decades the P/E ratio for the Dow Jones Industrials has ranged from six to twenty-three.

Under the market-to-book (M/B) ratio method, residual value is the product of the book value of equity times the projected M/B ratio at the end of the forecast period. Just as for the case of the P/E ratio, the M/B ratio is an easily calculated statistic and many executives may be "comfortable" with the concept.

Except for the fact that M/B is tied to book value of equity, which is affected by earnings calculations, rather than directly to earnings, the three conceptual problems for the M/B ratio method are identical to those associated with the P/E ratio method. In addition, the practical problem of forecasting future M/B ratios remains. The M/B ratio method is a particularly troublesome application in the growing service industry sector where there are typically minimal amounts of capitalized investment.

Summary Illustration

Now that the estimation procedures for the calculational components of shareholder value—cash flow from operations, cost of capital, and residual value—have been explained, we turn to an illustration that incorporates all of the components. Consider a business with the following forecasts:

	($ IN MILLIONS)
Number of periods in forecast	5
Sales (last historical period)	100
Sales growth rate (%)	16
Operating profit margin (%)	13
Incremental fixed capital invest. (%)	21
Incremental working capital invest. (%)	15
Cash income tax rate (%)	50
Residual value income tax rate (%)	50[a]
Cost of capital (%)	20
Marketable securities & investments	3
Market value of debt & other obligations	10

[a]The residual value income tax rate is the income tax rate to be applied during the years after the forecast period. In many situations it will be reasonable to use the statutory tax rate. If the rate of investment is expected to slow, then the company will have fewer opportunities to shelter income via investment tax credits, accelerated depreciation, etc. Thus, cash income taxes can be expected to rise and eventually approach the statutory tax rate.

For purposes of simplification, forecasted value drivers are held constant over the entire five-year forecast period. The calculation of shareholder value based on the above inputs is presented as Table 3–1. The cash flow of $1.78 million in year 1 is computed as follows:

[(Sales in prior year) (1 + Sales growth rate) (Operating profit margin) (1 – Cash income tax rate)] – [(Sales in prior year) (Sales growth rate) (Incremental fixed plus working capital investment rate)]

$$= [(100)(1 + .16)(.13)(1 - .50)] - [(100)(.16)(.21 + .15)]$$

$$= 7.54 - 5.76$$

$$= \$1.78 \text{ million}$$

The residual value is calculated at the end of each year using the perpetuity method. For example, the residual value at the end of year 1 is computed as follows:[11]

$$\frac{\text{Cash flow before new investment}}{\text{Cost of capital}} = \frac{7.54}{.20} = \$37.70 \text{ million}$$

To bring the $37.70 back to present value divide by (1 + cost of capital) or 1.20 to obtain the $31.417 million residual value number displayed in the exhibit. The year 1 perpetuity residual value assumes that all subsequent investment earns exactly the cost of capital. The same assumption holds for the residual value calculations at the end of years 2, 3, 4, and 5.

The cumulative present value of cash flows for the entire five-year forecast period is $6.938 million. When the residual value at the end of the forecast period of $27.433 million is added, the total value of $34.371 million is obtained. To this sum, marketable securities of $3 million are added to arrive at corporate value of $37.371 million. Finally, the $10 million of debt is deducted to arrive at the $27.371 million shareholder value figure.

Estimating Shareholder Value Creation

In the last section the focus was on the estimation of shareholder value—the economic value of the equity of a business based on forecast data. We now shift our focus from estimating total shareholder value to estimating shareholder value *creation* that is, the amount of value created by the forecasted scenario. While shareholder value characterizes the absolute economic value resulting from the forecasted scenario, shareholder value creation addresses the *change* in value over the forecast period. Recall that value creation results from corporate investment at rates in excess of the cost of capital rate required by the capital market.

Value creation is best demonstrated by returning to the example detailed in Table 3–1. Table 3–2 is identical to Table 3–1, except for the introduction of the "increase in value" column. The value created by this five-year strategy is $1.871 million. The year-by-year increase in value is calculated by the annual change in the "cumulative PV + residual value" totals. For example, the increase in year 2 of $0.387 million is equal to $33.287 million minus $32.900 million.

Table 3–1 Present Value of Cash Flows (Cost of Capital = 20%)

Year	Cash Flow	Present Value	Cumulative Present Value	Present Value of Residual Value	Cumulative PV + Residual Value
1	$1.780	$1.483	$1.483	$31.417	$32.900
2	2.065	1.434	2.917	30.369	33.287
3	2.395	1.386	4.303	29.357	33.660
4	2.778	1.340	5.643	28.379	34.022
5	3.223	1.295	6.938	27.433	34.371
			Marketable securities & investments		3.000
			CORPORATE VALUE		$37.371
			Less: Market value of debt		10.000
			SHAREHOLDER VALUE		$27.371

Table 3–2 Base Case—Present Value of Cash Flows (Cost of Capital = 20%)

Year	Cash Flow	Present Value	Cumulative Present Value	Present Value of Residual Value	Cumulative PV + Residual Value	Increase in Value
1	$1.780	$1.483	$1.483	$31.417	$32.900	$0.400
2	2.065	1.434	2.917	30.369	33.287	0.387
3	2.395	1.386	4.303	29.357	33.660	0.374
4	2.778	1.340	5.643	28.379	34.022	0.361
5	3.223	1.295	6.938	27.433	34.371	0.349
						$1.871
		Marketable securities & investments			3.000	
		CORPORATE VALUE			$37.371	
		Less: Market value of debt			10.000	
		SHAREHOLDER VALUE			$27.371	

The value created by a strategy or the amount of shareholder value created is calculated as the difference between shareholder value and prestrategy shareholder value:

$$\text{Value created by strategy} = \text{Shareholder value} - \text{Prestrategy shareholder value}$$

Prestrategy shareholder value represents the value of the business today assuming no additional value is created. In other words, it does *not* anticipate any value creation potential associated with the firm's prospective investments. Prestrategy value is calculated by applying the appropriate residual value method to the most recent period of historical data. Returning to the example, sales for the most recent year were $100 million. With an operating profit margin of 13 percent and an income tax rate of 50 percent, cash flow before new investment amounts to $6.5 million. Assuming the perpetuity method for estimating residual value, the pre-strategy shareholder value is calculated as follows:

$$\text{Prestrategy value} = \frac{\text{Cash flow before new investment}}{\text{Cost of capital}} + \text{Marketable securities} - \text{Market value of debt}$$

$$= \frac{\$6.5}{20\%} + 3.0 - 10.0$$

$$\$25.5 \text{ million}$$

The value created by the strategy of $1.871 million is the difference between the $27.371 million shareholder value and the $25.5 million prestrategy value. Another format for presenting this information is as follows:

Cumulative PV of cash flows	$ 6.938
Present value of residual value	27.433
	34.371
Marketable securities	3.000
CORPORATE VALUE	37.371
Less: Market value of debt	10.000
SHAREHOLDER VALUE	27.371
Less: Prestrategy shareholder value	25.500
Value created by strategy	$ 1.871 million

If the liquidation or "break-up" value of a business is greater than its discounted cash flow value, then liquidation value should be used in the analysis. Under such circumstances the value created by a strategy would be assessed as:

Value created by strategy = Cumulative present value of cash flows + Present value of liquidation at end of forecast period − Current liquidation value

Threshold Margin

The case developed in Table 3–3 is identical to the base case except that the operating profit margin is assumed to be 12 percent during the forecast period rather than 13 percent assumed for the base case. As one would expect, the decrease in operating profit margin results in decreases to both annual cash flows and shareholder value. Note that the value created in each year is equal to zero. Thus, we can be certain that investment during the forecast period is projected to earn exactly the cost of capital rate of 20 percent.

The 12 percent operating profit margin is the *threshold margin* of the business. The threshold margin represents the minimum operating profit margin a business needs to attain in any period in order to maintain shareholder value in that period. Threshold margin is a new type of "break-even analysis," a *value-oriented* economic break-even analysis. Stated in yet another way, threshold margin represents the operating profit margin level at which the business will earn exactly its minimum acceptable rate of return, that is, its cost of capital.

Instructing operating managers to invest in strategies that earn more than the cost of capital is not enough. To bridge valuation concepts of modern finance theory with the needs of corporate decision makers, what is needed is an easily understood, operationally meaningful concept that enables managers to assess the value creation potential of alternative strategies. The threshold margin concept is particularly well suited to facilitate this linkage because the operating profit margin has widespread acceptance from both security analysts and corporate management as an essential ratio for assessing a firm's operating profitability and efficiency. Threshold margin can

Table 3–3 No Value Creation—Present Value of Cash Flows (Cost of Capital = 20%)

Year	Cash Flow	Present Value	Cumulative Present Value	Present Value of Residual Value	Cumulative PV + Residual Value	Increase in Value
1	$1.200	$1.000	$1.000	$29.000	$30.000	$0.000
2	1.392	0.967	1.967	28.033	30.000	0.000
3	1.615	0.934	2.901	27.099	30.000	0.000
4	1.873	0.903	3.804	26.196	30.000	0.000
5	2.173	0.873	4.678	25.322	30.000	0.000
						$0.000
		Marketable securities & investments			3.000	
		CORPORATE VALUE			$33.000	
		Less: Market value of debt			10.000	
		SHAREHOLDER VALUE			$23.000	

	($ IN MILLIONS)
Number of periods in forecast	5
Sales (last historical period)	100
Sales growth rate (%)	16
Operating profit margin (%)	**12**
Incremental fixed capital invest. (%)	21
Incremental working capital invest. (%)	15
Cash income tax rate (%)	50
Residual value income tax rate (%)	50
Cost of capital (%)	20
Marketable securities & investments	3
Market value of debt & other obligations	10

be used to evaluate the past performance of a business as well as to establish performance targets for the future.[12]

The threshold margin concept can be expressed in two ways: either as the margin required on incremental sales (i.e., incremental threshold margin) or as the margin required on total sales (i.e., threshold margin). In the case example, sales for the last historical period were \$100 million, while sales in year 1 were \$116 million. For year 1, total sales amount to \$116 million and incremental sales are \$16 million.

Because of their importance, the logic underlying incremental threshold margin and threshold margin will be reviewed briefly. The change in shareholder value for a strategy that generates incremental sales and thereby incremental cash flows as a result of fixed and working capital investment can be depicted as follows:

$$\text{Change in shareholder value} = \left(\text{Present value of incremental cash flow before new investment}\right) - \left(\text{Present value of investment in fixed and working capital}\right)$$

$$= \frac{\left(\text{Incremental sales}\right)\left(\text{Operating profit margin on incremental sales}\right)\left(1 - \text{Income tax rate}\right)}{(\text{Cost of capital})} - \frac{(\text{Incremental sales})\left(\text{Incremental fixed plus working capital investment rate}\right)}{(1 + \text{Cost of capital})}$$

The first term on the right-hand side of the equation represents the present value of the firm's incremental cash inflows, which are assumed to begin at the end of the first period and continue into perpetuity.[13] The second term represents the present value of the investment (also assumed to take place at the end of the period) necessary to generate the incremental cash inflows. The incremental threshold margin is the operating profit margin on incremental sales that equates the present value of the cash inflows to the present value of the cash outflows. The incremental threshold margin can thus be found by setting the present value of the inflows and the outflows equal to each other and then solving for the incremental threshold margin. The result is presented below:

$$\text{Incremental threshold margin} = \frac{\left(\text{Incremental fixed plus working capital investment rate}\right)\left(\text{Cost of capital}\right)}{(1 + \text{Cost of capital})(1 - \text{Income tax rate})}$$

Recall that in the case example the following values were assumed: Incremental fixed capital investment rate = 21 percent, incremental working capital investment rate = 15 percent, cost of capital = 20 percent, and income tax rate = 50 percent. Employing these numbers in the above formula, incremental threshold margin is calculated as follows:

$$\text{Incremental threshold margin} = \frac{(21\% + 15\%)20\%}{(1 + 20\%)(1 - 50\%)} = 12\%$$

While the incremental threshold margin is the "break-even" profit margin on incremental sales only, the threshold margin is equal to the "break-even" operating profit margin on total sales in any period. The threshold margin is calculated as follows:

$$\text{Threshold margin} = \frac{\begin{pmatrix}\text{Prior period}\\ \text{operating}\\ \text{profit}\end{pmatrix} + \begin{pmatrix}\text{Incremental}\\ \text{threshold}\\ \text{margin}\end{pmatrix}\begin{pmatrix}\text{Incremental}\\ \text{sales}\end{pmatrix}}{\text{Prior period sales} + \text{Incremental sales}}$$

In the case example, year-by-year forecasts were assumed to be constant. In this simplified situation, threshold margin will be identical to incremental threshold margin. Threshold margin is calculated using the above formula:

$$\text{Threshold margin} = \frac{12 + (12\%)(16)}{100 + 16} = 12\%$$

Continuing to use the case example, incremental threshold margins for a range of investment requirements per dollar of sales and cost of capital assumptions are presented below:

	Incremental Fixed and Working Capital/ Dollar of Sales (%)				
Cost of Capital (%)	*20*	*30*	*36*	*42*	*50*
15	5.2	7.8	9.4	11.0	13.0
20	6.7	10.0	12.0	14.0	16.7
25	8.0	12.0	14.4	16.8	20.0

As one would expect, threshold margins increase as cost of capital and incremental investment requirements increase. After all, more risky and capital intensive businesses will need to achieve higher operating profit margins before they can expect to be creating value.

An essential insight emerging from the analysis developed in this section is that *when a business is operating at the threshold margin sales growth does not create value*. This is illustrated clearly in Table 3–4 which maintains all of the assumptions of the "no value creation" case (Table 3–3) except that the sales growth rate is increased from 16 to 30 percent. Note that despite this substantially more rapid growth, there is still no value creation. Unlike the 16 percent growth case, the more rapid 30 percent growth case leads to negative cash flows throughout the forecast period, but the decreased values of the cash flows are offset by increased residual values.

Once the investment requirements and risk characteristics of a strategy have been established, shareholder value creation is determined by the product of three factors: (1) sales growth, (2) incremental threshold spread, that is, profit margin on incremental sales less incremental threshold margin, and (3) the duration over which the threshold spread is expected to be positive, that is, the value growth duration. More specifically, the change in shareholder value or value created by a strategy in a given period t is provided by the following equation:

$$\text{Value created by strategy} = \frac{\begin{pmatrix}\text{Incremental}\\ \text{sales in}\\ \text{period } t\end{pmatrix}\begin{pmatrix}1-\text{Income}\\ \text{tax rate}\end{pmatrix}\begin{pmatrix}\text{Incremental}\\ \text{threshold spread}\\ \text{in period } t\end{pmatrix}}{(\text{Cost of capital})(1+\text{Cost of capital})^{t_{\text{periods}}-1}}$$

To illustrate, we return to the base case (see Table 3–3) to calculate the $1.871 million value creation using the above equation.

	YEARS					
	1	*2*	*3*	*4*	*5*	*Total*
Sales	$116.00	$134.56	$156.09	$181.06	$210.03	
Incremental sales	16.00	18.56	21.53	24.97	28.97	
Income tax rate	50%	50%	50%	50%	50%	
Incremental threshold spread (13% – 12%)	1%	1%	1%	1%	1%	
Value created by strategy	.400	.387	.374	.361	.349	1.871

Table 3–4 Rapid Growth, No Value Creation—Present Value of Cash Flows (Cost of Capital = 20%)

Year	Cash Flow	Present Value	Cumulative Present Value	Present Value of Residual Value	Cumulative PV + Residual Value	Increase in Value
1	$(3.000)	$(2.500)	$(2.500)	$32.500	$30.000	$0.000
2	(3.900)	(2.708)	(5.208)	35.208	30.000	0.000
3	(5.070)	(2.934)	(8.142)	38.142	30.000	0.000
4	(6.591)	(3.179)	(11.321)	41.321	30.000	0.000
5	(8.568)	(3.443)	(14.764)	44.764	30.000	0.000
						$0.000
		Marketable securities & investments			3.000	
		CORPORATE VALUE			$33.000	
		Less: Market value of debt			10.000	
		SHAREHOLDER VALUE			$23.000	

	($ in millions)
Number of periods in forecast	5
Sales (last historical period)	100
Sales growth rate (%)	**30**
Operating profit margin (%)	12
Incremental fixed capital invest. (%)	21
Incremental working capital invest. (%)	15
Cash income tax rate (%)	50
Residual value income tax rate (%)	50
Cost of capital (%)	20
Marketable securities & investments	3
Market value of debt & other obligations	10

The Shareholder Value Network

The approach developed in this chapter is best summarized by the shareholder value network (see Figure 3–1). The network depicts the essential link between the corporate objective of creating shareholder value and the basic valuation parameters or *value drivers*—sales growth rate, operating profit margin, income tax rate, working capital investment, fixed capital investment, cost of capital, and value growth duration.

Operating decisions such as product mix, pricing, promotion, advertising, distribution, and customer service level are impounded primarily in three value drivers—sales growth rate, operating profit margin, and income tax rate. *Investment* decisions such as, for example, increasing inventory levels and capacity expansion are reflected in the two investment value drivers—working capital and fixed capital investment. The cost of capital value driver is governed not only by business risk but also by management's *financing* deci-

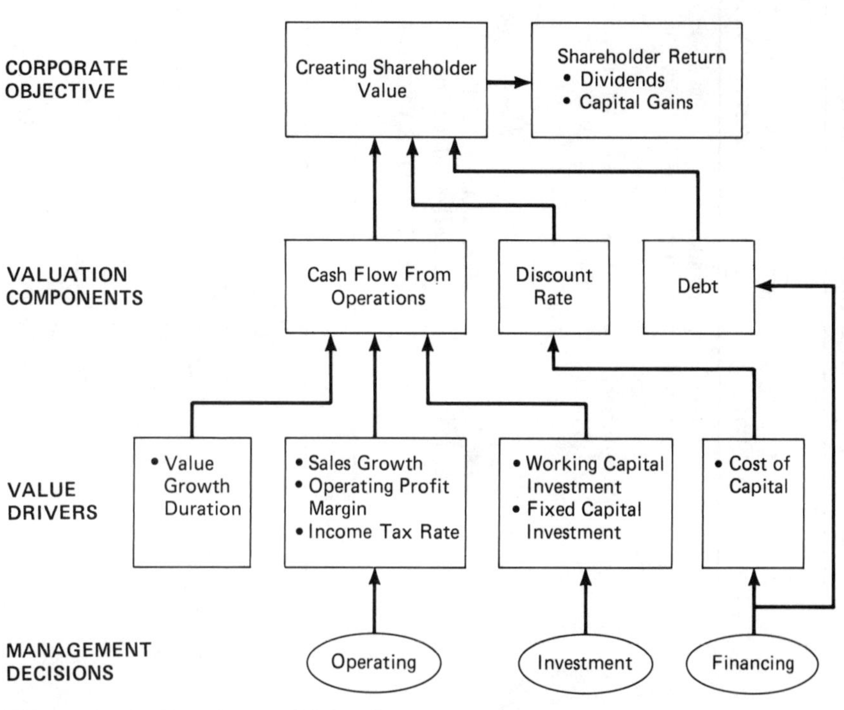

Figure 3–1 The Shareholder Value Network

sions, that is, the question of the proper proportions of debt and equity to use in funding the business as well as appropriate financing instruments. The final value driver, value growth duration, is management's best estimate of the number of years that investments can be expected to yield rates of return greater than the cost of capital.

As shown in Figure 3–1, the first valuation component, cash flow from operations, is determined by operating and investment value drivers along with the value growth duration. The second component, the discount rate, is based on an estimate of cost of capital. Recall that discounting cash flow from operations yields corporate value. To obtain shareholder value, the final valuation component, debt, is deducted from corporate value. Shareholder value creation, in turn, serves as the foundation for providing shareholder returns from dividends and capital gains.

PART *II*

Linking Competitive and Shareholder Value Analysis

Chapter 4

Competitive Strategy Framework

It is essential to distinguish between two activities in the strategic analysis of any business—*formulating* business strategies and *valuing* business strategies. Strategy formulation typically entails analyzing the attractiveness of the industry and the position of the business vis-à-vis its competitors. The analysis then seeks to understand how alternative strategies might affect industry attractiveness and the competitive position of the business. In contrast, strategy valuation involves an estimation of the economic value created by alternative strategies. Successful planning requires sound analysis for *both* formulating business strategies as well as for valuing strategies. This chapter describes some important new advances in strategy formulation and then links this analysis with the shareholder value approach to valuing business strategies.

An Overview

While there is no shortage of "systematic frameworks" for strategy formulation, none has had a greater impact during the past few years than the competitive strategy framework developed by Michael E. Porter. In his seminal work, *Competitive Strategy*,[1] Porter presents a framework for assessing industries and competitors, and then formulating an overall competitive strategy. The core of Porter's framework is the analysis of the five competitive forces that drive industry structure and thereby the long-run rates of return that firms in an industry can expect to earn. The five competitive forces and their structural determinants are presented in Figure 4–1.

The five competitive forces—threat of new entrants, threat of substitute products, bargaining power of buyers, bargaining power of suppliers, and rivalry among current competitors—reflect the fact that current competitors determine only a part of the competitive setting. Customers, suppliers, potential entrants, and substitute products also affect competitive structure and thereby industry and individual company rates of return. The relative importance of the five forces differs by industry and may well change over time. For example, the impressive returns achieved during the 1970s by leading computer time-sharing companies were recently disrupted by a substitute technology. The advent of microcomputers coupled with the steadily declining cost of mainframe computers has led to a significantly decreased demand for time-sharing services.

For those not familiar with the framework presented in Figure 4–1, a detailed discussion of the five competitive forces and their structural determinants can be found in Porter's *Competitive Strategy*, Chapter 1. For our purposes it is important to establish that the five competitive forces govern shareholder returns because they influence prices, quantities sold, costs, investment, and the riskiness of firms in an industry. These variables, in turn, are the building blocks for the value driver determinants of shareholder value. Specifically, price and quantity determine sales growth. The operating profit margin is affected by costs relative to prices and quantities sold. Investment is divided into two essential value drivers—working capital and fixed capital investment.[2] Finally, risk is conditioned by management's investment choices and its capital structure or financing policy.

Consider some relationships between Porter's five competitive forces and the value drivers. The *threat of new entrants* into an industry depends on the barriers to entry. The higher the barriers, the lower the threat of new entrants. The height of entry barriers depends on factors such as economies of scale, product differentiation, switching costs, capital requirements, and government policy.

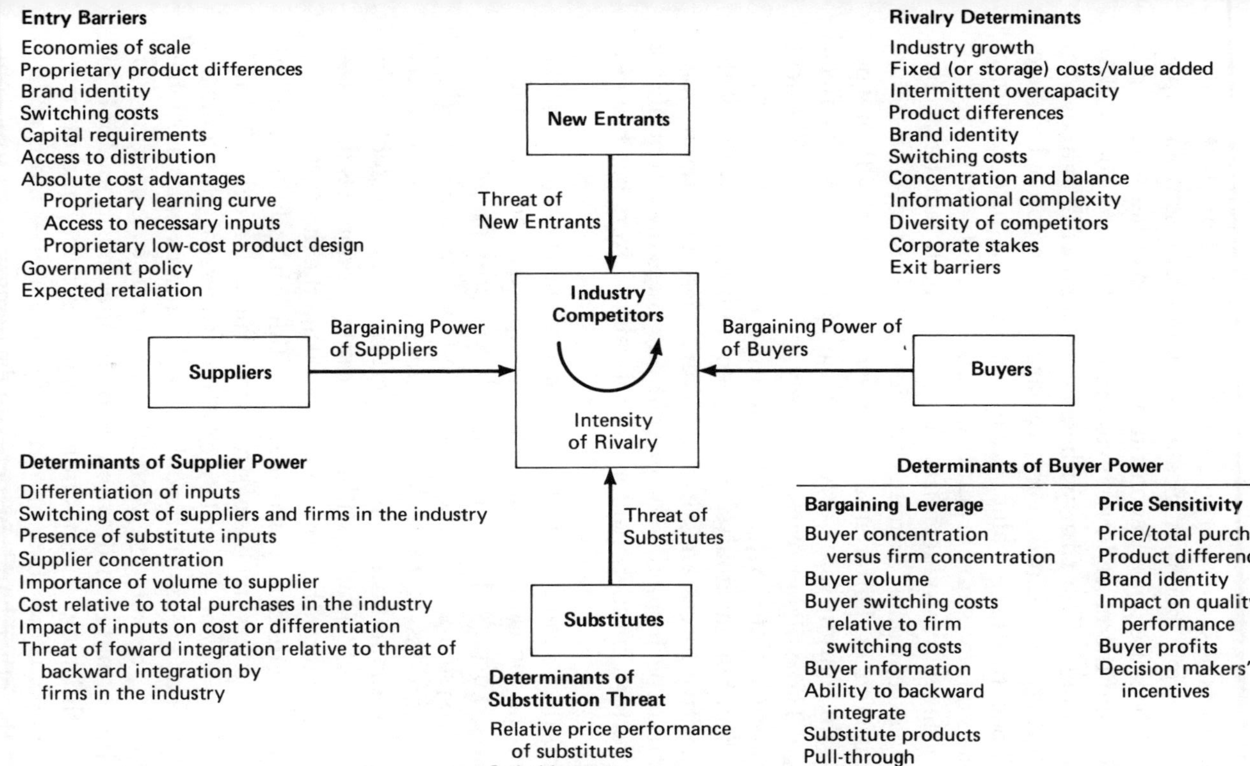
Entry Barriers
Economies of scale
Proprietary product differences
Brand identity
Switching costs
Capital requirements
Access to distribution
Absolute cost advantages
Proprietary learning curve
Access to necessary inputs
Proprietary low-cost product design
Government policy
Expected retaliation
New Entrants
Threat of New Entrants
Rivalry Determinants
Industry growth
Fixed (or storage) costs/value added
Intermittent overcapacity
Product differences
Brand identity
Switching costs
Concentration and balance
Informational complexity
Diversity of competitors
Corporate stakes
Exit barriers
Suppliers
Bargaining Power of Suppliers
Industry Competitors
Intensity of Rivalry
Bargaining Power of of Buyers
Buyers
Determinants of Supplier Power
Differentiation of inputs
Switching cost of suppliers and firms in the industry
Presence of substitute inputs
Supplier concentration
Importance of volume to supplier
Cost relative to total purchases in the industry
Impact of inputs on cost or differentiation
Threat of foward integration relative to threat of backward integration by firms in the industry
Threat of Substitutes
Substitutes
Determinants of Substitution Threat
Relative price performance of substitutes
Switching costs
Buyer propensity to substitute
Determinants of Buyer Power
Bargaining Leverage
Buyer concentration versus firm concentration
Buyer volume
Buyer switching costs relative to firm switching costs
Buyer information
Ability to backward integrate
Substitute products
Pull-through
Price Sensitivity
Price/total purchases
Product differences
Brand identity
Impact on quality/ performance
Buyer profits
Decision makers' incentives

Figure 4–1 Elements of Industry Structure

SOURCE: Michael E. Porter, *Competitive Advantage* (New York: Free Press, 1985), p. 6.

Economies of scale refer to the decrease in unit product costs as volume per period increases. Scale economies represent an important barrier because potential entrants are forced either to enter at a large scale, and therefore large investment, or to face a competitive cost disadvantage. The firm with scale economies in purchasing, manufacturing, distribution, and research enjoys cost advantages that can benefit three value drivers—operating profit margin, working capital investment, and fixed capital investment. A second barrier to entry is product differentiation which can be accomplished by exceptional customer service, advertising, and actual product differences. Differentiation affects the sales growth and operating profit margin value drivers by the higher prices that firms can charge. These higher prices are likely to be offset to some extent by the costs associated with differentiation activities such as customer service. Similar analysis for conceptually linking each of the five competitive forces and their structural determinants to value drivers can be performed.[3] For present purposes, the essential link between Porter's competitive forces and value drivers has been established.

Recall that strategy formulation involves assessing the attractiveness of the industry and the firm's competitive position within the industry. Porter's five competitive forces provide an economically sound, systematic framework for analyzing industry attractiveness. Regardless of the relative attractiveness of an industry, firms in the same industry will often perform very differently. The wide range of performance within an industry underlines the necessity of understanding the firm's position within the industry.

Differences in firm performance within an industry may be driven by differences in chosen strategies. These strategies, in turn, can materially affect the relative attractiveness of the industry. Competitors may exercise different strategic options in areas such as product quality, technology, vertical integration, cost position, service, pricing, brand identification, and channel selection. IBM, for example, with its low cost position, excellent service, and distribution network continues its dominance of the computer industry. Auditing, on the other hand, is increasingly being viewed as a commodity by price-sensitive corporate buyers. The "Big Eight" public accounting firms have largely responded with price cutting and cost containment in their audit practice and increased investment in their management consulting practice. The economic attractiveness of the public accounting industry has been affected adversely by these structural changes.

Once a company's planners assess industry structure and its competitive position in the industry, the focus shifts to translating this knowledge into a *competitive advantage*. Porter describes competitive advantage as follows:

> Competitive advantage grows out of value a firm is able to create for its buyers that exceeds the firm's cost of creating it. Value is what buyers are willing to pay, and superior value stems from offering lower prices than competitors for equivalent benefits or providing unique benefits that more than offset a higher price. There are two basic types of competitive advantage: cost leadership and differentiation.[4]

Value Chains

Porter goes on to develop the value chain as a tool to identify the two types of competitive advantage mentioned above—cost leadership and differentiation. In contrast to five-forces analysis which focuses on an entire industry, value chain analysis is oriented to a specific business within the industry. Porter views a business as a "collection of activities that are performed to design, produce, market, deliver, and support its product." Disaggregating a firm into its strategically relevant activities enables the manager to understand both the behavior of costs and possible bases for differentiation. Competitive advantage potential can then be assessed by examining essential differences among competitor value chains.

The Porter value chain with its component parts is shown in Figure 4–2. The recommended level for developing a value chain is the company's activities in a specific industry, that is, the business unit level. Note that total value in the value chain is the sum of value activities and margin. Margin, in Porter's terminology, is the difference between total value or revenue and the total cost of performing the various value activities. As shown in Figure 4–2, value activities are divided into primary and support activities. Primary activities are those involved in creation of the product, its sale and transfer to the buyer, and service after the sale. Support activities include:

- *Procurement*. The function of purchasing inputs used in the firm's value chain.

- *Technology development.* Activities aimed at improving the product or any of the primary activities, e.g., computerized order entry system.
- *Human resource management.* Activities involved in the recruiting, hiring, training, development, and compensation of personnel involved in the primary activities.
- *Firm infrastructure.* Activities including general management, planning, finance, accounting, legal, and government affairs.[5]

The link between competitive strategy analysis using value chains and the cash flows fundamental to the shareholder value approach to valuing business strategies is shown in Figure 4–3. To derive cash flow from operations, we begin with sales. Operating expenses are then deducted. Major classes of operating expenses for a typical manufacturing business are shown for each of the five primary activities. This activity-oriented classification scheme has important advantages over conventional accounting classifications which often merge costs involving several activities or, in other cases, may separate costs that properly belong to a single activity. Strategic alternatives are essentially based on scenarios involving tradeoffs within an activity or between activities and therefore are more easily assessed by an activity-based financial information system than by conventional accounting systems.

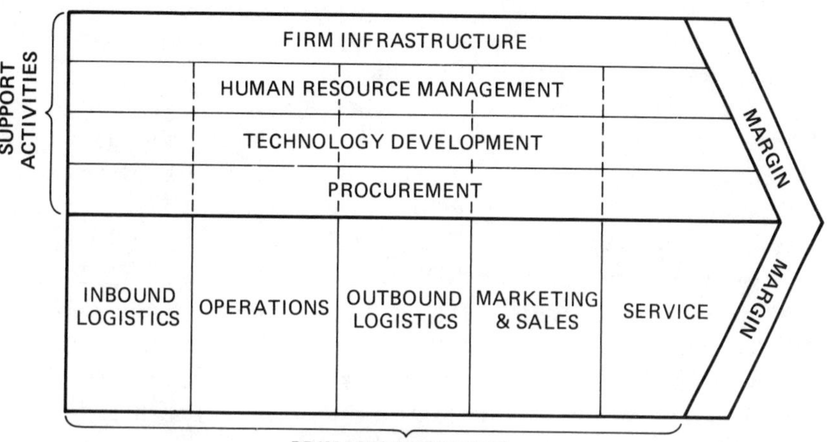

Figure 4–2 The Generic Value Chain

SOURCE: Michael E. Porter, *Competitive Advantage* (New York: Free Press, 1985), p. 37.

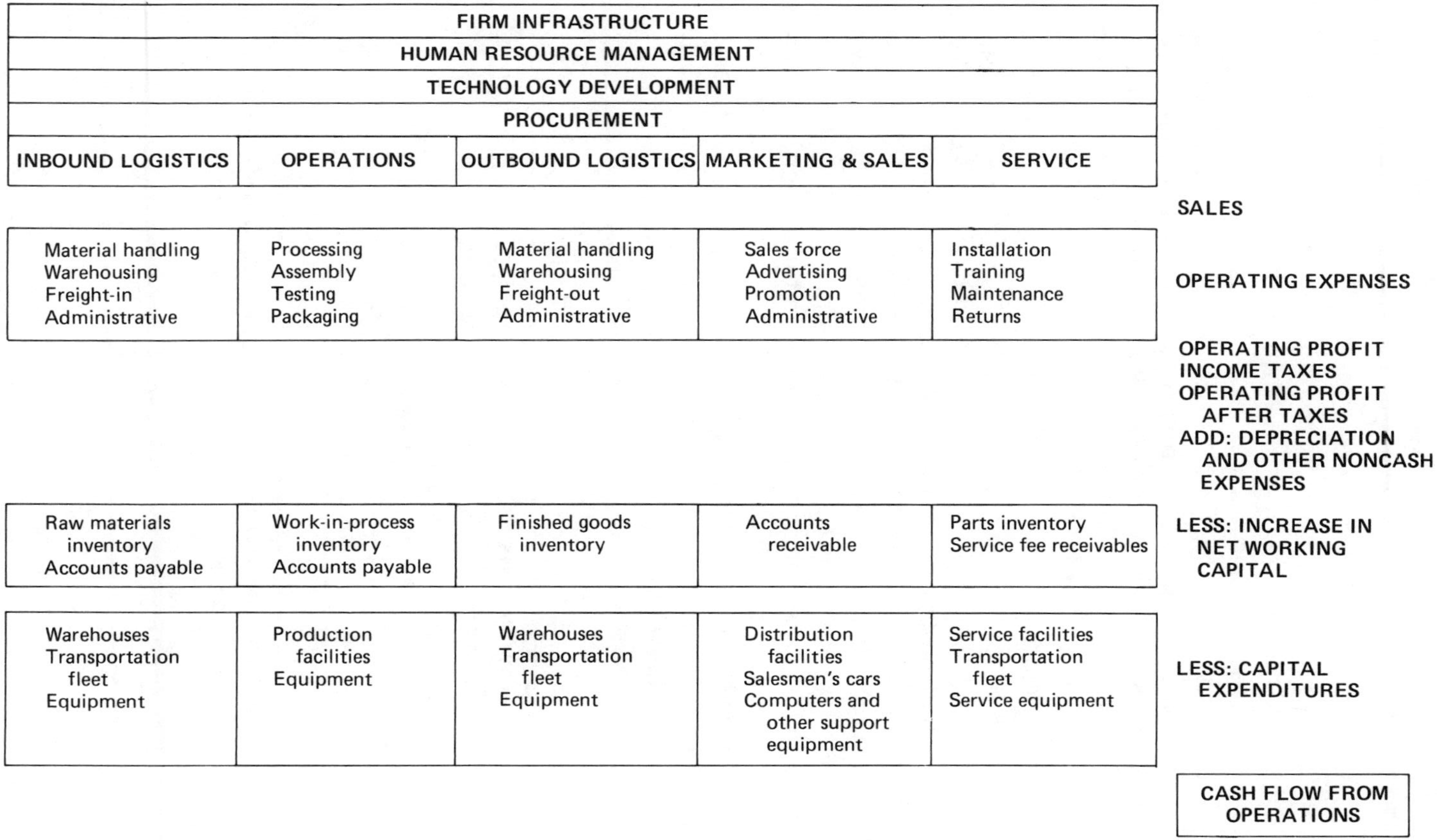

FIRM INFRASTRUCTURE					
HUMAN RESOURCE MANAGEMENT					
TECHNOLOGY DEVELOPMENT					
PROCUREMENT					
INBOUND LOGISTICS	OPERATIONS	OUTBOUND LOGISTICS	MARKETING & SALES	SERVICE	
					SALES
Material handling Warehousing Freight-in Administrative	Processing Assembly Testing Packaging	Material handling Warehousing Freight-out Administrative	Sales force Advertising Promotion Administrative	Installation Training Maintenance Returns	OPERATING EXPENSES
					OPERATING PROFIT INCOME TAXES OPERATING PROFIT AFTER TAXES ADD: DEPRECIATION AND OTHER NONCASH EXPENSES
Raw materials inventory Accounts payable	Work-in-process inventory Accounts payable	Finished goods inventory	Accounts receivable	Parts inventory Service fee receivables	LESS: INCREASE IN NET WORKING CAPITAL
Warehouses Transportation fleet Equipment	Production facilities Equipment	Warehouses Transportation fleet Equipment	Distribution facilities Salesmen's cars Computers and other support equipment	Service facilities Transportation fleet Service equipment	LESS: CAPITAL EXPENDITURES
					CASH FLOW FROM OPERATIONS

Figure 4–3 Link Between Value Chain and Cash Flows

After subtracting income taxes from operating profit we arrive at operating profit after taxes. To convert this amount to a cash basis, depreciation and other noncash expenses deducted as part of operating expenses are added back. Investments in working capital and fixed capital, which are classified by activities, are then deducted to arrive at cash flow from operations. These cash flows when discounted by the appropriate cost of capital serve as the essential basis for valuing businesses and the value created by their strategies. Figure 4–3 thus establishes the link between value chains and the value drivers—sales growth rate, operating profit margin, income tax rate, working capital investment, fixed capital investment, and cost of capital—which are the essential building blocks of the shareholder value approach to valuing business strategies. The Porter value chain framework enables management to project value driver estimates more systematically and thereby more confidently.

Figure 4–4 summarizes the relationship between competitive analysis and strategy valuation as outlined in this section. The Porter competitive analysis framework provides a powerful aid to strategic thinking. The shareholder value approach, on the other hand, evaluates the chosen strategies to see whether they are in fact likely to create a sustainable competitive advantage.

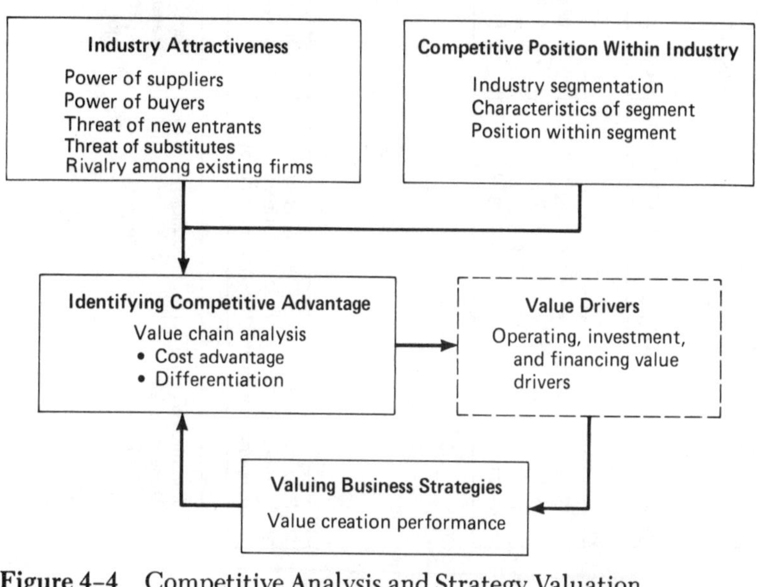

Figure 4–4 Competitive Analysis and Strategy Valuation

Competitive Analysis Process

As shown in Figure 4–4, the competitive analysis process involves three basic steps: to assess industry attractiveness, to evaluate a business's competitive position within an industry, and to identify sources of competitive advantage. In this section, the steps involved in the process are discussed. In addition, the integral relationship between competitive strategy variables and the financially-oriented value drivers underlying strategy valuation is demonstrated.

Industry Attractiveness

The fundamental purpose of industry attractiveness analysis is to gauge the value creation potential of each of the industries in which the company competes. Identifying competitive risk is a key consideration in industry attractiveness analysis. Industry attractiveness analysis using Porter's five-forces framework is particularly useful for assessing risk.

In Chapter 3, risk was viewed from the investor's perspective. Recall that total risk is the sum of unsystematic or firm-specific risk (which can be largely eliminated by investing in a diversified portfolio) and systematic or market risk (which cannot be avoided). Since firm-specific risk can be eliminated, investors can expect to be rewarded only for bearing market risk. When viewed from the manager's perspective, total risk is often characterized as *business risk* plus *financial risk*. Business risk is the uncertainty inherent in business operations and may be measured by the variability of cash flows. Financial risk represents the additional risk borne by common stockholders as a result of the introduction of fixed obligations such as debt and preferred stock in the capital structure. As financial leverage increases so does the variability of cash flows available for shareholders because these flows are subordinate to the contractually fixed interest payments. In effect, the risk inherent in operations, business risk, is now spread over a smaller equity base, thus increasing the risk for each share.[6]

While strategies that increase business risk will more than likely increase a firm's systematic risk as measured by its beta coefficient, a part of the increased business risk will generally be unsystematic or firm-specific and therefore can be eliminated by diversification. Thus, methods that establish cost of capital or hurdle rates based on business unit or corporate cash flow variability are essentially including diversifiable risk as well as the systematic component of risk. This, in turn, leads to higher hurdle rates than those demanded by investors who require compensation based on systematic market risk only.

Two observations are pertinent here. First, under some circumstances determining a business's cost of equity by its systematic risk may understate the risk assumed by shareholders because bankruptcy costs are not taken into account. Assuming that the bankruptcy losses associated with one stock are only partially offset by gains in other stocks held in a diversified portfolio, then the higher the probability of a business going bankrupt, the greater will be investors' concern with *total risk* rather than just systematic risk. As a consequence, investors will demand a higher rate of return for the business than that dictated solely by its systematic risk. Second, the manager's focus on cash flow variability of the business (total risk approach) rather than cash flow variability relative to the overall market or economy (systematic risk approach) is perhaps explained by the fact that unlike well-diversified shareholders, managers, who typically have most of their wealth (stock, stock options, future compensation) linked to the firm, cannot easily balance the risk of business unit or company failure against other risks in their portfolio. Thus, managers view bankruptcy or failure with substantially greater concern than well diversified shareholders and this aversion to risk may well manifest itself in overly high hurdle rates for risky projects and strategies.[7]

Keeping the foregoing discussion in mind, we are now ready to examine how the five-forces approach to industry attractiveness analysis facilitates the assessment of business risk. Business risk depends on a variety of factors, some of the more important of which include:

- *Demand variability.* The more stable the demand for a firm's products, other things held constant, the lower its business risk.
- *Sales price variability.* Firms whose products are sold in highly volatile markets are exposed to more business risk than similar firms whose output prices are more stable.
- *Ability to adjust output prices for changes in input prices.* Some firms are better able to raise their own output prices when input costs rise. The greater the ability to adjust output prices, the lower the degree of business risk, other things held constant. This factor

becomes increasingly important during the 1970s and 1980s because of inflation.

- *Input price variability.* Firms whose input prices are highly uncertain are exposed to a high degree of business risk.
- *The extent to which costs are fixed: operating leverage.* If a high percentage of a firm's cost are fixed, and hence do not decline when demand falls off, then it is exposed to a relatively high degree of business risk.[8]

Table 4–1 shows which of Porter's five competitive forces principally impact each of the above business risk factors. The first three business risk factors jointly determine the variability of the sales growth value driver. When the other two business factors, input price variability and operating leverage, are added we have the factors that affect the variability of the operating profit margin value driver. Operating leverage establishes the tradeoff between two value drivers—fixed capital investment and operating profit margin. Each of the business risk factors, of course, affects the cost of capital value driver.

The principal competitive forces that affect the first four business risk factors are apparent. The fifth business risk factor, operating leverage, deserves a comment. The economic tradeoff between variable and fixed costs is influenced by the bargaining power of suppliers. For example, a business wishing to become the low-cost producer in the industry will examine carefully the labor versus fixed capital investment tradeoff. Rivalry also impacts operating leverage. More precisely, the current level of operating leverage within the industry may affect rivalry. For example, high levels of operating leverage create substantial pressure for firms to operate at

Table 4–1 Impact of Competitive Forces on Business Risk Factors

Business Risk Factor	Principally Impacted by
Demand variability	Threat of substitute products
	Threat of new entrants
Sales price variability	Bargaining power of buyers
	Rivalry among existing firms
Ability to adjust prices	Bargaining power of buyers
Input price variability	Bargaining power of suppliers
Operating leverage	Bargaining power of suppliers
	Rivalry among existing firms

high levels of capacity which is often achieved by price cutting. Operating leverage thus can have an important effect on business risk not only in its own right but also because of its impact on sales price variability.

At the conclusion of the industry attractiveness analysis, insights into the following questions should have been developed:

- How attractive is the industry as a whole?
- Which factors are generally most critical for creating value in this industry?
- How sensitive is the value of various companies in this industry to changes in key factors?
- How might individual entities and the industry as a whole be affected by changes in industry structure, by the competitive and general economic environment, and by other pressures?

Competitive Position

The second basic step in competitive analysis is to evaluate the business unit's competitive position within the industry. The business unit may find itself in a very attractive industry, but a poor competitive position may nonetheless seriously limit its value creation potential. The reverse is also true. A strong competitive position in a lackluster industry can lead to excellent shareholder value prospects.

As Porter points out, while industry attractiveness reflects factors over which the firm has minimal control, differences in firm performance and competitive position can be driven by differences in chosen strategies. By its choice of strategy, a firm can change its relative position within its industry thereby making the industry more or less attractive *for the firm*. Industries are not, however, homogeneous. Segments of a single industry may have very different structures as reflected in differences in the behavior of the five competitive forces. Competitive position must be analyzed in the context of the industry segment in which the business chooses to compete. Industry segmentation thus becomes an essential part of the competitive analysis process. It is a prerequisite for determining what part of an industry a business should serve as well as how to compete within the chosen segment. Porter makes the case for segmentation as follows:

> The reason that industries must be segmented for competitive strategy formulation is that the products, buyers, or both within an indus-

try are dissimilar in ways that affect their *intrinsic attractiveness* or the way in which a firm gains *competitive advantage* in supplying them. Differences in structural attractiveness and in requirements for competitive advantage among an industry's products and buyers create industry segments.[9]

Porter suggests that segmentation be based on one or more of the following strategically relevant dimensions that carry potentially important value chain implications:

- *Product variety.* The discrete product varieties that are, or could be, produced.
- *Buyer type.* The types of end buyers that purchase, or could purchase, the industry's products.
- *Channel (intermediate buyer).* The alternative distribution channels employed or potentially employed to reach end buyers.
- *Geographic buyer location.* The geographic location of buyers, defined by locality, region, country, or group of countries.[10]

Product differences that could lead to structural and value chain differences that help define segments include physical size, price level, features, input employed, packaging, performance, new versus replacement, and bundled versus unbundled. Price level, for example, may affect both buyer price sensitivity and manufacturing activities associated with the product. Porter broadly classifies buyer segments into industrial and commercial buyers and consumer-goods buyers. Segmentation within the industrial and commercial category can be based on buyer's industry, buyer's strategy (e.g., cost leadership, differentiation), technological sophistication, degree of vertical integration, size, ownership, financial strength, and order pattern. Segments among consumer-goods buyers may be defined by demographics, lifestyle, language, and purchasing process. Porter provides similar segmentation bases for channel and geography segments.[11]

Once a business unit has properly identified its industry segment and the firms competing in that segment, it can continue its data gathering and analysis of competitive position with substantially greater confidence.[12] The analysis should yield insights into questions such as:

- What appear to be the relative strengths and weaknesses of the competitors in the relevant industry segment?
- How might a company respond to a competitor's strategy, and how would a retaliatory strategy affect the company?

- How well will a competitor be able to pursue its apparent strategy given its current competitive position, cost structures, and available funding?
- How might individual competitors and the industry as a whole be affected by changes in industry structure, the competitive and general economic environment, and other pressures?

Competitive Advantage

Industry attractiveness analysis, along with an assessment of the business unit's position within its industry segment, provides the background for the third step in competitive analysis—the identification of competitive advantage. Estimating the shareholder value creation potential of strategies is a theoretically sound and practical means of evaluating the absence or presence of competitive advantage. More precisely, *sustainable value creation*, that is, developing long-run opportunities to invest above the cost of capital, is the ultimate test of competitive advantage. The value chain is a robust tool for identifying competitive advantage. Moreover, as shown previously, there is a direct link between value chain analysis and the cash flow forecasts required for estimating the value created by business unit strategies.

Because the most rewarding value-creating strategies emerge from exploiting a *sustainable* competitive advantage, it becomes important not only to identify how competitive forces can yield competitive advantage for the business, but also to predict the relative stability of these forces. Without consideration of the dynamics of the five competitive forces over time and their impact on the value chains, the business may find that it has developed a strategy with short-term rather than sustainable competitive advantage. In some industries the relationships among skills embodied in its value chain, strategies, and competitive forces shaping industry structure change very little over time. In other, more dynamic, industries these relationships are undergoing rapid change. Williams, in an important contribution to the competitive strategy literature, extends the Porter framework by incorporating this time dimension into value chain analysis. He classifies industry environments into three types:

- *Class I Industries*—characterized by *competitively stable* value chains which over time are relatively unchanged

- *Class II Industries*—characterized by *smoothly evolving* value chains which are reinforced through scale-based learning
- *Class III Industries*—characterized by *dynamic and unstable* value chains which accelerate rapidly to maturity.[13]

A brief summary of each of these three industry classes follows. Competitive advantage in Class I industries is generally unrelated to economies of scale. What dominate are nonscale factors such as patents, government regulation, reputation of key individuals, specialized service, creative talent, and location. For example, before they were deregulated, banking, telecommunications, trucking, airlines, and the health care industry were Class I by virtue of government regulation that limited competition. In summary, Class I industries, because they are not scale-driven, do not necessarily view cost or market share leadership as the basis for competitive advantage, but instead flourish on nonscale factors which promote high switching costs for the buyer. In addition to regulated industries, Williams provides Class I industry examples such as defense contractors, embryonic technologies, universities, professional services (law, accounting, management consulting), investment banking, custom engineering, and job-shop manufacturing.

Class II industries, which are characterized by smoothly evolving value chains, compete in terms of productivity. Productivity is achieved from four basic sources—economies of scale, organizational learning, product standardization, and process engineering (replacement of costly labor with state-of-the-art production equipment and less costly labor). Class II industries would include many of the so-called "basic industries" such as steel, tire, automobile, appliance, and chemical. General Motors' huge investment in productivity including the acquisitions of EDS and Hughes Aircraft provides an excellent example of a productivity-based strategy in the manufacturing sector. As Williams observes, productivity or scale-based strategy can be developed in companies dominated by marketing and distribution as well. He cites Anheuser-Busch in beer, Procter and Gamble in consumer products, IBM in office equipment, and McDonald's in the fast-food industry as leading examples. Because productivity is achieved from economies of scale and organizational learning, there is active competition to gain and hold market share oftentimes by pricing tied closely to the cost of production. As a result, typically only a few firms survive and dominate the industry. While new products and processes are continually introduced in Class II industries, both the rate and magnitude of innovation are relatively predictable and manageable. Thus, these industries are characterized by smoothly evolving value chains.

Class III industries are characterized by a relatively high degree of instability in value chains. Part of this instability is due to the "surprise" entry of nontraditional competitors in this innovation-based environment. At the early stages there is great uncertainty about which innovations will succeed. After a shakeout period, successful Class III products gain quick and pervasive (oftentimes global) appeal which leads to rapid volume growth. Examples cited by Williams include semiconductors, consumer electronics, small telecommunications equipment, personal computers, and high fashion consumer goods.

Productivity gains can be very substantial in the early stages of innovation. However, technology and the benefits of organizational learning are quickly diffused to competitors. Previously unique products that were value-priced quickly become commodities characterized by rapidly falling prices. A good example of this in a non-technology environment is the Cabbage Patch doll which initially sold for several hundred dollars, but was quickly copied, produced at high volumes, and now sells for a small fraction of the original price.

Classifying industries by the relative stability of their value chains and then examining a plausible set of alternative scenarios is essential for establishing a basis for sustainable competitive advantage. This industry classification also underscores the positive correlation between value chain stability and the relative confidence with which planning assumptions (i.e., forecasts) are made. Competing, for example, in a Class III environment is most precarious and managers' forecasts of the value drivers would undoubtedly have the least degree of accuracy. Indeed, the three classes provide yet another way of viewing business risk, that is, business risk increases as the stability of value chains decrease.

Any strategy designed to promote competitive advantage must, in the final analysis, meet the test of sustainable value creation. The value creation process in turn depends on the translation of competitive dynamics into forecasts of value drivers. Thus, competitive advantage, whether driven by cost leadership or differentiation, involves a number of supporting strategies which affect each of the value drivers and collectively yield the best value creation prospects. To illustrate, Tables 4–2 and 4–3 present some relevant tactics, classified by their impact on value drivers, for cost leadership and differentiation approaches to competitive advantage.

Table 4–2 Cost Leadership Strategy and Supporting Tactics Classified by Value Drivers

Value Drivers	Tactics Supporting Cost Leadership Strategy
Sales growth rate	• Maintain competitive prices • Pursue market share opportunities to gain scale economies in production, distribution, etc.
Operating profit margin	• Achieve relevant economies of scale for each of the value activities • Introduce mechanisms to improve the rate of learning, e.g., standardization, product design modifications, improved scheduling, etc. • Search for cost-reducing linkages with suppliers based on supplier's product design, quality, packaging, order processing, etc. • Search for cost-reducing linkages with channels • Eliminate overhead that does not add value to the product
Working capital investment	• Minimize cash balance • Manage accounts receivable to reduce average number of days outstanding • Minimize inventory without impairing required level of customer service
Fixed capital investment	• Promote policies to increase utilization of fixed assets • Obtain productivity-increasing assets • Sell unused fixed assets • Obtain assets at least cost, e.g., lease versus purchase
Cost of capital	• Target an optimal capital structure • Select least-cost debt and equity instruments • Reduce business risk factors in manner consistent with strategy

Cost leadership (Table 4–2) is attained by controlling costs (by controlling scale, learning, capacity utilization) and reconfiguring the value chain, that is, developing more efficient ways to design, produce, distribute, or market the product.[14] The reduction of services at ticket counters, gates, during the flight, and for baggage handling by the no-frills airlines such as People Express is an excellent example of reconfiguring value chains. Differentiation (Table 4–3), which seeks to provide something both different from competitors and valuable to the buyer, calls for a set of supporting tactics that are clearly distinct from those appropriate for a cost leadership strategy. These differences in supporting tactics will be reflected in forecasts for each of the value drivers. For example, value creation is ordinarily very sensitive to even small changes in operating profit margin. In the cost leadership case the key to achieving target mar-

Table 4–3 Differentiation Strategy and Supporting Tactics Classified by Value Drivers

VALUE DRIVERS	TACTICS SUPPORTING DIFFERENTIATION STRATEGY
Sales growth rate	• Command a premium price • Pursue growth in market segments in which buyer is willing to pay premium for differentiation
Operating profit margin	• Choose combination of value activities that create the most cost-effective means of differentiating, e.g., by lowering buyer's cost and risk and by raising performance • Eliminate costs that do not contribute to buyer needs
Working capital investment	• Minimize cash balance • Link accounts receivable policy to differentiation strategy • Maintain inventory level consistent with differentiating level of service • Obtain best terms with suppliers for accounts payable
Fixed capital investment	• Invest in specialized assets that create differentiation • Purchase assets for optimal utilization • Sell unused fixed assets • Obtain assets at least cost, e.g., lease versus purchase
Cost of capital	• Target an optimal capital structure • Select least-cost debt and equity instruments • Increase differentiation and thereby make demand less dependent on general economy

gins is likely to be effective cost control, while for the differentiation strategy the critical focus is more likely to be on the firm's ability to command a premium price.

Regardless of how a firm plans to achieve a competitive advantage, it is essential that management become familiar with the tradeoffs between various value drivers. Below are some illustrative questions germane to cost leadership and then to differentiation strategies:

Cost Leadership

- Do the labor savings justify the productivity-motivated capital expenditures?
- Are the tight controls on inventory levels offset by reduced customer service and consequent loss of revenue?
- Can a less restrictive accounts receivable policy lead to increased market penetration and greater scale economics?
- Would increasing the sales growth rate also lead to an increase

in financial risk which would result from debt-financing the growth?

- If increased growth is due principally to lower selling prices, will cost savings improve operating profit margin sufficiently to justify the growth strategy?

Differentiation

- Does the premium price justify the costs of product features and other costs required to differentiate the product or service?
- Is the cost of maintaining inventory levels to ensure the highest service level necessary to attract and maintain buyers willing to pay the premium price?
- Is the cost of granting liberal credit terms necessary to attract and maintain buyers willing to pay the premium price?
- What would be the impact on sales growth and operating profit margin of a selling price reduction aimed at capturing a larger market share?

This concludes the discussion of the competitive analysis process consisting of industry attractiveness, competitive position, and competitive advantage. We are now ready to move from strategic analysis and diagnosis to the testing of alternative strategies. The ultimate purpose is to ensure that the best value-creating strategy is selected and implemented.

Chapter 5

Value-Creating Business Strategies

In today's fast-changing, often bewildering business environment, formal systems for strategic planning have become one of top management's principal tools for evaluating and coping with uncertainty. Corporate board members are also showing increasing interest in ensuring that the company has adequate strategies and that these are tested against actual results. While the organizational dynamics and the sophistication of the strategic planning process vary widely among companies, the process almost invariably culminates in projected (commonly five-year) financial statements.

This accounting format enables top managers and the board of directors to review and approve strategic plans in the same terms that the company uses to report its performance to shareholders and the financial community. Under current practice the projected financial statements, particularly projected earnings-per-share performance, commonly serve as the basis for judging the attractiveness of the strategic or long-term corporate plan.

The conventional accounting-oriented approach for evaluating the strategic plan does not, however, provide reliable answers to such basic questions as:

- Will the corporate plan create value for shareholders? If so, how much?

- Which business units are creating value and which are not?
- How would alternative strategic plans affect shareholder value?

The material in this chapter will provide top management and board members with a theoretically sound, practical approach for assessing the contributions of business unit plans and overall corporate strategic plans toward creating shareholder value.

Over the past few years, there has been a virtual revolt against corporate strategic planning staffs that mushroomed during the 1970s. In company after company planning staffs have been cut, often by more than 50 percent. Critics point to companies with presumably sophisticated planning systems who were blindsided by unanticipated phenomena such as changes in oil prices, inflation, technology changes, and strategic moves by competitors. Fueled by the growth-share matrix and other "formula" techniques, rather than fundamental strategic analysis, many companies placed too much reliance on market-share growth. Often this led to acquisition of growth businesses that the buying company did not know how to manage.

The most telling criticism comes from operating managers, who claim that some corporate staffs responsible for designing the planning systems are simply out of touch with the markets in which the business operates. In brief, the planning process was not linked to the operational realities and difficult requirements of the implementation process. Roger Smith, chairman of General Motors, described the problem as follows: "We got these great plans together, put them on the shelf, and marched off to do what we would be doing anyway. It took us a little while to realize that wasn't getting us anywhere."[1]

The result of this recent turmoil has been a redirection of strategic planning from corporate staff to line managers who bear the responsibility of implementing the plans. The decentralization of the planning process is a promising development, but does not alter the essential purpose of the planning *process*: to provide managers with a systematic framework to think strategically and thereby shape the future of their businesses. It is important to emphasize that qualitative strategic thinking, based on judgments and even intuition, and the discipline of analytic and quantitative analysis are neither mutually exclusive nor contradictory. To the contrary, they are complementary. Ultimately, it is necessary to translate qualitative, and hopefully creative, strategic analysis into plans that specify resources required and expected rates of return. All of this is perhaps best summarized by a comment attributed to President Eisenhower: "Plans are nothing, planning is everything."

I proceed with two basic beliefs: first, that businesses can create shareholder value by superior planning; second, that managers are particularly motivated in the current climate of corporate takeovers by the knowledge that "capitalism offers no refuge for companies that don't maximize their value."[2]

Business Unit and Corporate Level Strategies

Diversified and decentralized companies typically have an organizational structure consisting of corporate, group, and business unit levels. Strategic planning should take place at both the corporate and business unit levels. Although each level is faced with different strategic tasks, they should be linked by one common objective—to create shareholder value. In those cases in which potential synergies between business units can be exploited, planning at the group level is appropriate as well.

A central task of strategic management is to identify individual businesses as strategic business units (SBUs). Collier[3] suggests that a properly defined SBU meets the following criteria:

- It has a clearly defined served market(s).
- It is a full-fledged competitor in an external market as opposed to being an internal supplier.
- It is a discrete unit—separable, distinct, and identifiable. It is possible to conduct integrated strategic planning related to markets, products, organizations, and facilities for this business, and its assets do not depend upon the existence of another SBU.
- Its manager has full control (within the scope of an approved plan) over most areas critical to the success of the business, including marketing, manufacturing, R&D, and asset management.

Another test of the degree of independence of the business is whether it could divest itself of a product line without affecting another of the company's businesses.

At the business unit level, strategy is product-market driven. It is governed by questions such as: What does the customer want to buy? How can the customer's product needs be filled best? How is the business positioned in relationship to competitors? And in the final analysis, the issue is how a sustainable competitive advantage can be established. The optimal strategy for a business unit will naturally be influenced by industry structure and the competitive position of the business in that industry.

Strategic planning at the corporate level has a portfolio orientation. Here the concern is with allocating resources among the various businesses so that the overall value of the portfolio is improved. If the current portfolio cannot generate the target level of shareholder value creation, corporate strategy may be directed toward restructuring the company's business mix via acquisitions, divestitures, internally developed new business ventures, or changing the mix of capital allocated to the company's existing businesses. In addition to the above operational restructurings, companies are frequently involved in financial restructurings such as stock repurchases, swapping debt for equity, debt swaps, revising terms of debt, and liquidation of overfunded pension funds. Some corporate restructurings involve both operational and financial restructuring. A recent example is Atlantic Richfield's plan which involves the sale of its oil-refining and gasoline-retailing businesses east of the Mississippi River, a two-year stock repurchase plan, a 33 percent dividend increase, and a 20 percent reduction in its work force.

One of the forerunners of corporate restructuring and one of the most successful was Esmark's substantial shrinking of its size, which led to significant shareholder value creation. The transaction is best described by Donald P. Kelly, CEO of Esmark, in the company's 1980 annual report:

> Esmark's Board and management's underlying philosophy of striving to increase the value of your investment in Esmark was tested in a rather dramatic fashion in the 1980 fiscal year. The basic question addressed involved determining whether current appreciation in realizable value from a shareholder point of view was more important than growth in the size of the corporation.
>
> The Board and management, looking at potential appreciation in excess of 100 percent in share values versus continuing business as usual, elected the route of improving the market value of Esmark shares. To enable this to be accomplished, a series of activities was undertaken to significantly restructure the company.
>
> Esmark: 1) disposed of Vickers Energy Corporation, including Vickers Petroleum Corporation, Doric Petroleum, Inc. and Trans-Ocean Oil, Inc.; 2) structured part of this disposition in such a way

> that one of the purchasers implemented a tender offer for some 12 million Esmark shares; 3) announced that certain units of Swift's Fresh Meats Division were to be closed and the remaining units were to be placed in a separate company which would continue the fresh meat production and distribution activities conducted by Swift's Fresh Meats Division; 4) arranged for substantial charges to income to provide for the ultimate funding of certain pension and pensioners' health care program liabilities related to Swift; 5) restructured Swift & Company with major activities in the processed foods area; and 6) provided for the disposition or closing of a number of non-food related activities.
>
> The contrast between Esmark in 1980 and Esmark in 1979 is certainly significant. At the end of the 1979 fiscal year, Esmark reported revenues of $6.8 billion, employed about 44,000 people, and stated the company had some 48,000 shareholders owning 20,311,000 shares of stock with a book value of $39.88 per share. Total market value of the company approximated $550 million.
>
> One year later, as Esmark completed its fiscal 1980 year, the company finds itself starting the 1981 fiscal year employing fewer than 31,000 people and having some 33,900 shareholders who own 10,083,000 shares of common stock with a book value of $57.06 per share and a year-end market value of approximately $500 million. Anticipated revenues for the coming year will approximate $3.5 billion.
>
> Management believes the restructuring provided three great basic strengths: 1) an increase in market value of our shareholders' investment; 2) improvement in the financial capacity of the company; and 3) a general strengthening of those companies that make up Esmark in 1981.

Before concluding this discussion of business unit and corporate level strategy, the organizational issue of how to allocate capital most efficiently needs to be addressed. Typically, total capital requested by various parts of the company exceeds the amount corporate headquarters has available. While there is broad agreement that resources should be allocated on the basis of credible value-creating plans, there is the question of whether capital should be allocated directly to business units or to groups that in turn allocate capital to their constituent business units.

If resources were allocated to groups, corporate management's burden would be substantially reduced because there are usually five to ten times as many business units as groups. But allocation to groups is not likely to optimize shareholder value creation. Collier[4] offers a simplified illustration. Assume a company has two groups and each group consists of three business units. Each of the six business units requests $100 million of new capital. The plans generate varying amounts of shareholder value as shown below:

Business Unit	Group A ($ in millions) Capital Requested	Group A Value Created	Group B ($ in millions) Capital Requested	Group B Value Created
1	$100	$130	$100	$ 50
2	100	15	100	50
3	100	5	100	50
	$300	$150	$300	$150

Assume that the company has only $400 million available rather than the $600 million total requested. If the capital allocation were made to groups, each group would receive $200 million since each is forecasting $150 million of value creation. The groups, in turn, would allocate $100 million to each of their respective two top value-creating units. Shareholder value created would total $245 million computed as follows:

Group A	
Business Unit 1	$130 million
Business Unit 2	15
Group B	
Business Unit 1	50
Business Unit 2	50
	$245 million

If capital were allocated directly to business units, shareholder value created would total $280 million computed as follows:

Group A	
Business Unit 1	$130 million
Group B	
Business Unit 1	50
Business Unit 2	50
Business Unit 3	50
	$280 million

The total value created by direct allocation to business units exceeds the group allocation approach by $35 million. In the more complex real world these differences can be even greater. While it is desirable from a shareholder value perspective for the corporate level to allocate resources directly to business units, once plans have been agreed to, group heads are responsible for the performance of the business units assigned to them.

Strategy Valuation Process

The basic inputs into the strategy valuation process, alternative strategies for gaining competitive advantage, are a direct outgrowth of the competitive analysis process. For each strategy the valuation process involves establishing reasonable input assumptions or forecasts and then evaluating the outputs including the impact on value of variations from the "most likely" scenario.

At the conclusion of the valuation process business unit managers should be able to answer questions such as:

- How would alternative strategies affect shareholder value creation?
- Which strategy is likely to create the most value?
- For the selected strategy, how sensitive is value to internal and external business factors not contemplated in the "most likely" scenario?

At the corporate level these additional questions must be satisfactorily answered:

- Which business units in the corporate portfolio are creating the most value for shareholders?
- Which business units have limited value creation potential and thereby should be candidates for divestiture?
- Which combination of strategies will generate the most total value?
- Which business units are cash generators and which are cash drains?
- To what extent can the corporation fund its proposed strategies from internal sources, and how much additional debt or equity might have to be raised?

The first step of the valuation process, establishing the reasonableness of forecasts, will be discussed briefly now. The second step, evaluating the resulting valuations, is better demonstrated in the context of case illustrations presented in the next section.

In all but the most dynamic settings historical performance represents a useful point of departure in developing forecasts. After establishing forecasts for each of the value drivers, these projections should be compared with recent performance. Beware of unrealistically optimistic projections such as a sharp upturn in the sales growth rate or operating profit margin. This phenomenon, sometimes referred to as the "hockey-stick effect," may be motivated by a wish to gain funding for the strategy. On the other hand, if projections are used subsequently to evaluate management performance, they are more likely to be too conservative rather than too optimistic because then actual performance is more likely to be better than budgeted performance.

If projections are, in part, based on historical averages, do these averages represent the probable future performance of the business? The projections may rely too heavily on historical performance without taking into full consideration management's plans for the business and some anticipated changes in the competitive environment. For example, an energy-intensive chemical company's plan to vertically integrate backwards to gain control of and reduce the cost of its energy supply is likely to alter several value drivers. The cost savings would presumably be translated into higher operating profit margins. The new commitment to capital expenditures would lead to an increase in the fixed capital investment value driver. Gaining greater stability and control over a critical input to its production process may also reduce the total risk of the business and thereby lower the cost of capital.

The historical averages of value drivers may also be affected by a number of environmental factors anticipated in the plan. Below are several examples.

Environmental Factor	Value Drivers Most Likely to Be Affected
Entry of new competitors	Sales growth rate Operating profit margin
Introduction of new products and technologies	Sales growth rate Operating profit margin Fixed capital investment
Competitors' strategic action (price-cutting tactics, major advertising campaigns, etc.)	Operating profit margin
Regulatory actions (changes in income tax laws, pollution control laws, or safety procedures)	Operating profit margin Fixed capital investment Cash income tax

In testing the reasonableness of projections, it is always useful to try to obtain an external benchmark. When available, projections for the industry developed by security analysts, industry experts, and government agencies are useful sources of information. In comparing the firm's projections with industry forecasts, several questions are relevant:

- Are your projections consistent with industry averages forecast by investment firms and industry experts?
- If yes, is it realistic to assume that the firm will perform at the "average" level?
- If no, where do your projections deviate from those of the industry as a whole? (sales growth rate, operating profit margin, fixed capital investment?) Are those divergences realistic?

Another useful technique for generating forecasts with greater confidence is to learn from poor forecasts made in previous years. Reviewing where previous forecasts deviated from actual performance may enable one to avoid repeating the same errors. After following each of these forecasting guidelines, one should step back from the detail and continually ask, "Do the numbers make sense?"

Three Case Illustrations

To provide a more meaningful context for discussing the strategy valuation process, three case illustrations are presented in this section. The first covers valuation issues both at the business unit and corporate levels. The second case illustrates how value can be created by exploiting intracompany synergies. The last case contrasts the shareholder value approach to product mix analysis with the more conventional approach.

Business Unit/Corporate Strategy Valuation[5]

Econoval, a diversified manufacturing company, divides its operations into three business—telecommunications, industrial systems, and automotive parts (see Table 5–1).

Before beginning their detailed analysis, Econoval managers must choose appropriate time horizons for calculating the value

Table 5–1 Strategic Overview of Econoval's Business Units

Business Unit	Product Life Cycle Stage	Strategy	Risk	Current Year's Sales ($ in millions)
Telecommunications	Embryonic	Invest aggressively to achieve dominant market position	High	50
Industrial systems	Expanding	Invest to improve market position	Medium	75
Automotive parts	Mature	Maintain market position	Low	125

contributed by each business unit's strategy. The product life cycle stages of the various units should determine the length of the forecast period. If we were to measure value creation for all businesses arbitrarily in a common time horizon, say five years, then embryonic businesses with large capital requirements in early years and large payoffs in later years would be viewed as poor prospects even if they were expected to yield exceptional value over the life cycle. Therefore, in this case, the projections for the telecommunications unit were extended to ten years and projections for the industrial systems and auto parts units were limited to five years.

The telecommunications unit designs, manufactures, and sells sophisticated computerized PBX systems. Its customers (end users, distributors, and independent telephone companies) are particularly attracted to its least-cost routing software features which can lead to significant savings in usage-sensitive communication costs. The recent development of the ability to handle voice and data transmission simultaneously gives the telecommunications unit an early technological lead. Despite this lead, the telecommunications unit can expect serious competition as the PBX technology moves from its current third generation stage to fourth generation switches. In addition, the threat of substitute technology is ever present in the competition for office-of-the-future dollars.

Once business unit managers have developed and analyzed their initial planning projections, they can prepare more detailed analyses for evaluating alternative planning scenarios. Table 5–2 shows the telecommunications unit's planning parameters for conservative, most likely, and optimistic scenarios.

The worst case, or conservative scenario, assumes significant market penetration by other producers via major technological ad-

Table 5–2 Telecommunications Unit's Forecasts for Three Scenarios (in percent)

	Year									
	1	*2*	*3*	*4*	*5*	*6*	*7*	*8*	*9*	*10*
Sales Growth Rate										
Conservative	25	25	20	20	18	18	18	18	18	18
Most likely	30	28	25	22	20	20	20	20	20	20
Optimistic	32	30	30	25	25	25	25	25	25	25
Operating Profit Margin										
Conservative	11.5	12	12.5	13	13.5	13.5	13.5	13.5	13.5	13.5
Most likely	12	12.5	13	13.5	14	14.5	15	15	15	14.5
Optimistic	12.5	13	14	14.5	15	15	15	15	15	15
Incremental Working Capital Investment										
Conservative	20	20	20	20	20	20	20	20	20	20
Most likely	20	20	20	20	20	20	20	20	20	20
Optimistic	18	18	18	18	18	18	18	18	18	18
Incremental Fixed Capital Investment										
Conservative	42	42	42	40	40	35	35	35	35	35
Most likely	45	45	44	42	42	40	38	38	35	35
Optimistic	40	38	38	36	36	35	35	35	35	35
Cash Income Tax Rate										
Conservative	41	41	41	41	41	41	41	41	41	41
Most likely	40	40	40	40	40	40	40	40	40	40
Optimistic	39	39	39	39	39	39	39	39	39	39

vances coupled with aggressive price competition. The most likely scenario assumes the telecommunications unit's continued dominance in the PBX market, substantial R&D expenditures to enable it to maintain its competitiveness in the learning curve race, and gradual technological parity, which will place pressure on operating profit margins. The optimistic scenario projects more rapid industry growth and greater success in the unit's effort to carve out high-margin proprietary niches.

Table 5–3 presents the shareholder value contribution for each of these three scenarios and for a range of discount rates.

Econoval expects the telecommunications unit's ten-year plan for the most likely scenario to contribute $10.6 million to shareholder value. The range of value creation from conservative to optimistic scenarios is from $4.87 million to $29.93 million for the estimated cost of capital or discount rate of 15 percent. An assessment of the likelihood of each scenario will provide further insight into the relative riskiness of business unit investment strategies. For example, if all three scenarios are equally likely, the situation would be riskier than if the most likely scenario is 60 percent probable and the other two are each 20 percent probable.

Table 5–4 presents the cash flows and shareholder value calculations for the "most likely" scenario. The combination of fast growth and relatively large working capital and fixed capital investment requirements results in negative cash flows throughout the forecast period. Despite this, as can be seen from the "increase in value" column the business is operating above its cost of capital in all years except years 2 and 10. Over the entire ten-year period the value created by the strategy amounts to $10.6 million. Table 5–5 provides further insight into the unit's value creation process. The "operating profit margin" column reproduces the projections for the forecast period. The "threshold margin" entries provide manage-

Table 5–3 Shareholder Value Created by the Telecommunications Unit Under Different Scenarios and Discount Rates ($ in millions)

	Cost of Capital (Discount Rate)				
Scenario	*14%*	*14.5%*	*15%*	*15.5%*	*16%*
Conservative	$ 9.30	$ 6.96	$ 4.87	$ 2.99	$ 1.30
Most likely	16.92	13.59	10.60	7.91	5.48
Optimistic	39.64	34.53	29.93	25.79	22.05

Table 5–4 Cash Flows and Shareholder Value for Telecommunications—Most Likely Scenario (Cost of Capital = 15.0%) ($ in millions)

Year	Cash Flow	Present Value	Cumulative Present Value	Present Value of Residual Value	Cumulative PV + Residual Value *	Increase in Value
1	$(5.1)	$(4.4)	$ (4.4)	$24.4	$20.0	$0.2 †
2	(5.6)	(4.2)	(8.6)	28.3	19.7	(0.3)
3	(5.2)	(3.4)	(12.0)	32.0	20.0	0.3
4	(3.9)	(2.2)	(14.2)	35.2	21.0	1.0
5	(2.9)	(1.5)	(15.7)	38.1	22.4	1.4
6	(2.4)	(1.0)	(16.7)	41.2	24.5	2.1
7	(1.5)	(0.5)	(17.3)	44.5	27.2	2.7
8	(1.8)	(0.6)	(17.9)	46.4	28.5	1.3
9	(0.5)	(0.2)	(18.1)	48.5	30.4	1.9
10	(1.8)	(0.4)	(18.5)	48.9	30.4	0.0
						$10.6
			CORPORATE VALUE		$30.4	
			Less: Market value of debt		5.0	
			SHAREHOLDER VALUE		$25.4	

*Assumes a 46 percent residual value income tax rate.
†Operating profit margin in year 0 = 11 percent.

Table 5–5 Profit Margins for Telecommunications—Most Likely Scenario (in percent)

Year	Operating Profit Margin	Threshold Margin	Threshold Spread
1	12.0	11.9	0.1
2	12.5	12.6	(0.1)
3	13.0	12.9	0.1
4	13.5	13.2	0.3
5	14.0	13.6	0.4
6	14.5	13.9	0.6
7	15.0	14.2	0.8
8	15.0	14.6	0.4
9	15.0	14.5	0.5
10	14.5	14.5	0.0

ment with minimum acceptable margins the business must attain in each period for value to be created in that period. The difference between the projected and threshold margins is the "threshold spread." Consistent with Table 5–4, the threshold spread is positive, thus indicating value creation, in all years except years 2 and 10.

Once the initial value creation calculations have been completed and reviewed, it becomes important to identify which of the value drivers have the greatest impact on shareholder value. Table 5–6 presents the changes in shareholder value resulting from a 1 percent increase in each of the value drivers. Note that the 1 percent increase represents a change in a variable from, say, 10 percent to 10.1 percent, not to 11 percent; that is, it represents a point elasticity for each item, assuming other items are held constant.

Table 5–6 Relative Impact of Key Variables on Shareholder Value for Telecommunications—Most Likely Scenario

A 1% Increase in:	Increases Shareholder Value Created by
Sales growth rate	$ 94,000
Operating profit margin	1,135,000
Incremental fixed capital investment	(555,000)
Incremental working capital investment	(276,000)
Cash income tax rate	(431,000)
Residual value income tax rate	(416,000)
Cost of capital	(1,033,000)

Understanding the aspects of the business that are most critical to value creation enables management to focus its analysis more efficiently on key elements of a strategy. Telecommunications' strategy value is most sensitive to changes in operating profit margin and cost of capital. In addition, because most business decisions involve tradeoffs between two or more value drivers, establishing the relative impact of value drivers can provide useful direction for decision making. To illustrate, suppose the telecommunications unit wishes to evaluate the attractiveness of a proposed promotional campaign. The campaign is expected to stimulate product demand and thereby increase sales growth, but the campaign costs would result in a decrease in operating profit margin. Table 5–6 shows that a 1 percent increase in the sales growth rate would increase shareholder value created by $94,000 and a 1 percent increase in operating profit margin would increase value by $1,135,000, respectively. The analysis proceeds as follows:

Step 1: Compare the relative impacts of changes in sales growth rate and operating profit margin.

$$\frac{\text{Impact of 1\% change in operating profit margin}}{\text{Impact of 1\% change in sales growth rate}} = \frac{\$1{,}135{,}000}{94{,}000} = 12$$

Shareholder value creation is about twelve times more sensitive to a change in operating profit margin than to a change in the sales growth rate. The relative insensitivity of value creation to sales growth is not surprising since the business is operating relatively close to the threshold margin throughout the forecast period (as shown by the small threshold spreads in Table 5–5).

Step 2: Estimate the anticipated change in the more critical variable. In this case, the promotional campaign is projected to reduce operating profit margin by 0.5 percent.

Step 3: Evaluate whether the decision is advisable. To justify the promotional campaign, the sales growth rate would need to increase by more than 6 percent, that is, twelve times 0.5 percent.

The relative impact analysis tests only a 1 percent change in each of the value drivers and is very useful for an initial understanding of the financial dynamics of the business. Invariably managers want to test the sensitivity of shareholder value to changes in the value drivers for ranges other than 1 percent as well as using pairs of value drivers to conduct "what if" analysis. Table 5–7 illustrates this type of analysis. (In these sensitivity exhibits percentage changes are additive, i.e., a 1 percent increase represents an increase in a variable from, say, 10 to 11 percent not to 10.1 percent.)

The telecommunications unit is actively considering the possibility of increasing its capital investment outlays to gain labor-saving production efficiencies that should improve operating profit margin. It estimates that to gain a 1 percent improvement in margin it will have to increase its capital expenditures by 5 percent for each dollar of sales increase. Table 5–7a presents the results of the analysis. The center cell reflects the most likely scenario value contribution of $10.6 million. The combination of a 5 percent increase in incremental capital expenditures and a 1 percent margin improvement results in a strategy value of $11.7 million—an improvement of just over $1 million. If the unit makes the outlays and no margin improvement is forthcoming, then the value of the strategy decreases significantly to only $3.7 million.

The identical analysis is performed in Table 5–7b except that now the results are expressed in terms of discounted cash flow rates of return, that is, internal rates of return. Because the most likely strategy does create value ($10.6 million), we can be certain that it yields a rate greater than its 15 percent cost of capital. As shown in

Table 5–7

a. Sensitivity of Shareholder Value Created by Strategy for Telecommunications

		Operating Profit Margin		
		– 1.00%	0.00%	1.00%
Increm. Fixed Capital Invest.	– 5.00%	9.5	17.5	25.5
	0.00%	2.6	10.6	18.6
	5.00%	(4.3)	3.7	11.7

b. Sensitivity of Internal Rate of Return for Telecommunications

		Operating Profit Margin		
		– 1.00%	0.00%	1.00%
Increm. Fixed Capital Invest.	– 5.00%	18.13	20.58	22.90
	0.00%	15.85	18.34	20.70
	5.00%	13.61	16.15	18.34

Internal rate of return uses prestrategy residual value as investment ($19.8 million).

the center cell, the rate of return is 18.34 percent. If the capital outlays are made without margin improvement, the rate of return falls to 16.15 percent.

Econoval performed similar analyses for the industrial systems and automotive parts units.[6] Table 5–8 summarizes the results for most likely scenarios. To ensure consistency in comparing or consolidating scenarios of various business units, it is important for the corporate planning group to establish that such scenarios share common assumptions about critical environmental factors such as inflation and energy prices.

The analysis in Table 5–8 provides support for corporate level management's concern about the automotive unit's performance. While the unit now accounts for 50 percent of Econoval's sales, the company expects it to create only $3.57 million, or about 15 percent of the total increase in shareholder value.

On the basis of traditional criteria such as sales and earnings growth rates, the telecommunications unit clearly emerges as the star performer. However, its high investment requirements and risk vis-à-vis its sales margins combine to limit its value-creating potential. Despite the fact that the telecommunications unit's sales and earnings growth rates are substantially greater than those of the industrial systems unit, the telecommunications unit is expected to contribute only modestly more shareholder value in ten years than the industrial systems unit in five years.

The shareholder value increase per discounted dollar of investment provides management with important information about where it is realizing the greatest benefits per dollar of investment.

Table 5–8 Shareholder Value, Sales Growth, and Earnings Growth Rates by Business Unit for Most Likely Scenarios

		Shareholder Value Increase			Growth Rates	
Business Unit	*Years in Plan*	*$ in millions*	*Per Discounted $ Of Sales (Value ROS)*	*Per Discounted $ of Investment (Value ROI)*	*Sales*	*Earnings*
Telecommunications	10	10.60	7.7%	12.8%	22.4%	26.1%
Industrial Systems	5	8.79	17.5	43.8	15.0	17.7
Automotive Parts	5	3.57	6.8	19.4	10.0	11.9
Consolidated		22.96				

Indeed, this value ROI, rather than the traditional accounting ROI, enables management to rank various business units on the basis of a substantive economic criterion.

Value ROI is simply the amount of shareholder value created per dollar of investment.

$$\text{Value ROI} = \frac{\text{Value created by strategy}}{\text{Present value of investment}}$$

When value ROI is equal to zero, the strategy yields exactly the cost of capital, and when value ROI is positive, the strategy yields a rate greater than its cost of capital. Telecommunications, for example, creates 12.8 cents of value per dollar of investment. Recall that the telecommunications strategy is forecasted to yield a rate of return of 18.34 percent while its cost of capital is 15 percent. Note, however, that the telecommunications unit ranks last, even behind the auto parts unit, in this all-important performance measure.

Ranking units on the basis of value ROI can be particularly helpful to corporate headquarters in capital-rationing situations where the various parts of the company are competing for scarce funds. In the final analysis, however, corporate resources should be allocated to units so as to maximize the shareholder value creation of the company's total product-market portfolio.

Once the company has established a preliminary plan, it should test its financial feasibility, that is, whether it is fundable. This involves integrating the company's planned investment growth strategies with its dividend and financing policies. A more detailed discussion of how to assess the fundability of strategic plans will be presented in Chapter 6. In this case, Econoval management concluded that the strategic plan was financially feasible. The analysis did, however, raise two concerns. First, the current dividend payout rate could not be sustained without issuing additional equity or issuing debt in excess of its target capital structure unless the plans fully materialized. The company would be particularly vulnerable if actual operating margins were lower than those projected. Second, management was concerned about the riskiness of the telecommunication unit's aggressive competitive positioning and the related high level of investment requirements. This unit's large cash requirements, coupled with its relatively modest value ROI, prompted Econoval management to launch a study of alternative product portfolio strategies and related restructuring activities.

Increasingly, companies are adding financial self-evaluation to their strategic planning process. A financial evaluation poses two fundamental questions: How much is the company and each of its major lines of business worth? How much would each of several plausible scenarios involving various combinations of future environments and management strategies affect the value of the company and its business units?

The following types of companies would especially benefit from conducting a financial evaluation:

- Companies that wish to sell and need to establish a minimum acceptable selling price for their shares
- Companies that are potential takeover targets
- Companies considering selective divestments
- Companies evaluating the attractiveness of repurchasing their own shares
- Private companies wanting to establish the proper price at which to go public
- Acquisition-minded companies wanting to assess the advantages of a debt-financed versus a equity-financed offer

The shareholder value of any business unit, or the entire company, is the sum of the estimated shareholder value contributed by its strategic plan and the current cash flow level discounted at the risk-adjusted cost of capital (i.e., prestrategy value) less the market value of outstanding debt. Table 5–9 summarizes these values for Econoval and its three major business units. For example, the tele-

Table 5–9 Business Unit and Corporate Financial Evaluation Summary for Most Likely Scenarios ($ in millions)

	TELECOMMUNICATIONS	INDUSTRIAL SYSTEMS	AUTOMOTIVE PARTS	CONSOLIDATED
Prestrategy shareholder value	$14.80	$20.93	$25.10	$60.83
Shareholder value created by strategy (see Table 5–8)	10.60	8.79	3.57	22.96
Shareholder value	$25.40	$29.72	$28.67	$83.79
Percent of total shareholder value	30.3%	35.5%	34.2%	
Econoval shareholder value at corporate cost of capital of 14%				87.57

communications unit's current cash flow perpetuity level is $2.97 million, which, when discounted at its risk-adjusted cost of capital of 15 percent produces a value of $19.8 million. Subtracting the $5 million of debt outstanding provides the $14.8 million prestrategy shareholder value. To obtain the total shareholder value of $25.4 million for the telecommunications unit, simply add the $10.6 million value created by the strategic plan.

The sum of the three business unit values is $83.79 million. Combining the cash flows of the individual businesses and discounting them at the 14 percent corporate cost of capital yields a value of $87.57 million. In this case, the differences between the value of the whole and the sum of the parts is relatively small. However, this may not always be the case.

Aggregating the values of the company's business units is consistent with the assumption that the riskiness of each unit must be considered separately. If, however, the company's entry into unrelated businesses reduces the overall variability of its cash flows, then the lower expected probability of bankruptcy can decrease its cost of debt and increase its unused debt capacity.

What happens to the company's overall cost of capital naturally depends on any changes in the cost of equity as well as on the cost of debt. Analysis of the impact of business units on the overall risk of the company is generally a difficult and subjective exercise.

A more attractive alternative is to (1) assume risk independence in establishing the cost of capital for business units and (2) interpret the difference between the value of the company and the aggregate value of its individual businesses as a broad approximation of the benefits or costs associated with the company's product portfolio balancing activities.

Value Creation by Exploiting Synergies[7]

The purpose of this case is to illustrate the shareholder value approach for choosing between two strategies involving organizationally independent operating units which have potentially synergistic relationships.

This case deals with a manufacturer of telephones. The company has two operating divisions: (1) Home Phones, which makes state-of-the-art telephones for home use; and (2) Biz Phones, which makes sophisticated equipment for businesses. Some common core components are used in both products lines, although each division currently manufactures the components separately for its own use. The buyers of Home Phones' products are extremely price sensitive, while Biz Phones' buyers are much less price sensitive.

Each of the two divisions has prepared a plan to submit to the corporate office. First, I will examine how the Home Phones division would assess its own value creation opportunities. This will be followed by a discussion of how the corporate office would make its funding allocation decision in light of both divisions' plans.

The manager of the Home Phones division begins the analysis by preparing forecast data for a "base scenario" (i.e., strategy 1) that would assess Home Phones' value contribution if the division continues "business as usual"—that is, without making any significant changes to its current strategy. A summary of value driver forecasts appears below:

	YEAR				
	1	*2*	*3*	*4*	*5*
Sales growth rate	15%	15%	15%	15%	15%
Operating profit margin	20	20	20	20	20
Incremental fixed capital investment (as a percentage of each dollar of sales increase)	40	40	40	40	40
Incremental working capital investment (as a percentage of each dollar of sales increase)	18%	18%	18%	18%	18%
Cash income tax rate	38	38.4	38.7	38.9	39.2
Residual value income tax rate	45	45	45	45	45
Cost of capital	14	14	14	14	14

Table 5–10 presents the cash flows and Table 5–11 shows that if Home Phones pursues basically a "business as usual" strategy, it can expect to increase its shareholder value by $35.5 million, resulting in a total shareholder value of $106.2 million. An analysis of the relative impact of the value drivers reveals that shareholder value is most sensitive to changes in the operating profit margin.

Because Home Phones' market is so price sensitive, it is considering a price-cutting strategy to gain market share. To get a preliminary estimate of how much sales would need to increase to offset a 1

Table 5–10 Cash Flow Statement for Home Phones Division

	YEAR				
	1	2	3	*4*	5
Sales	$115.000	$132.250	$152.087	$174.901	$201.136
Cost of goods sold	48.875	56.206	64.637	74.333	85.483
Gross profit	66.125	76.044	87.450	100.568	115.653
Selling, general & adminstrative expense	43.125	49.594	57.033	65.588	75.426
Taxable operating profit	23.000	26.450	30.417	34.980	40.227
Depreciation expense	10.000	10.600	11.290	12.083	12.996
Funds from operations before tax	33.000	37.050	41.708	47.064	53.223
Cash income taxes	8.750	10.152	11.765	13.620	15.753
Funds from operations after tax	$ 24.250	$ 26.897	$ 29.942	$ 33.443	$ 37.470
Incremental working capital investment	2.700	3.105	3.571	4.106	4.722
Fixed capital investment	16.000	17.500	19.225	21.209	23.490
Cash flow from operations	$ 5.550	$ 6.292	$ 7.146	$ 8.128	$ 9.258

Table 5–11 Cash Flows and Shareholder Value for Home Phones Division—Strategy 1 (Cost of Capital = 14%) ($ in millions)

Year	Cash Flow	Present Value	Cumulative Present Value	Residual Value	Cumulative PV + Residual Value	Increase in Value
1	$5.550	$4.868	$ 4.868	$79.261	$ 84.129	$13.415
2	6.292	4.842	9.710	79.956	89.666	5.537
3	7.146	4.824	14.534	80.657	95.191	5.525
4	8.128	4.813	19.347	81.365	100.711	5.520
5	9.258	4.808	24.155	82.079	106.233	5.522
						$35.519
		Marketable securities			0.000	
		DIVISION VALUE			$106.233	
		Less: Market value of debt			0.000	
		SHAREHOLDER VALUE			$106.233	

Note: Neither division carries any marketable securities or debt on its balance sheet.

percent decline in profit margin, a sensitivity analysis is performed (Table 5–12).

This exhibit shows that if prices were cut (and the operating profit margin declined by 1 percent, from 20 to 19 percent), even a 4 percent increase in sales (from 20 to 24 percent) would not offset the reduction in profit margin: as the upper right-hand corner of the matrix indicates, shareholder value would decline by $85,000. Sales would need to increase by almost 5 percent before there begins to be any significant increase in shareholder value, offsetting the 1 percent decline in the profit margin.

Home Phones is also considering a strategy that would entail investing $25 million in a new, more efficient production process that would reduce the cost of making the core components. The cost savings would enable the division to lower its prices and thereby obtain a much larger share of its price-sensitive market—while still maintaining its profit margins.

However, these savings can be realized only if the division sells enough units to take advantage of economies of scale. A Home Phones study showed that the new production line would be too large for Home Phones to use efficiently on its own. But the combined volume of production by both Home Phones and Biz Phones would be sufficient to make full use of the new production line.

The strategy would involve a $25 million investment, shared equally by the divisions in year 1 (each would pay $7.5 million) and in year 2 (each would pay $5 million). The resulting cost savings would enable Home Phones to cut its prices without reducing its operating profit margin and also achieve a sharp increase in sales. (The impact on Biz Phones will be explored later.)

Home Phones developed a forecast for the new strategy involving a shared investment in the new production facilities. The projections shown below reflect Home Phones' portion of the fixed capital investment as well as the increased sales growth that could result

Table 5–12 Sensitivity of Changes in Shareholder Value Creation for Home Phones Division—Strategy 1

		Sales Growth Rate		
		– 4.00%	0.00%	4.00%
Operating Profit Margin	– 1.00%	(13.596)	(7.253)	(0.085)
	0.00%	(7.323)	0.000	8.278
	1.00%	(1.050)	7.253	16.642

when Home Phones cuts its prices. All other forecasts from Strategy 1 are unchanged except for the cash tax rates which are less because of the increase in depreciation. The new forecast is shown following the earlier Strategy 1 projections.

	YEAR				
	1	*2*	*3*	*4*	*5*
Sales Growth Rate					
Strategy 1	15%	15%	15%	15%	15%
Strategy 2	15	25	30	30	30
Incremental Fixed Capital Investment					
Strategy 1	40	40	40	40	40
Strategy 2	90	57.4	40	40	40
Cash Income Tax Rate					
Strategy 1	38	38.4	38.7	38.9	39.2
Strategy 2	34.8	34.3	34.9	35.4	35.7

The valuation summary for Strategy 2 (Table 5–13) shows that the shareholder value contributed by the new strategy is almost $53 million or $17.5 million more than the $35.5 million that would be generated under Strategy 1. Based on this analysis, Home Phone has decided it would like to pursue the new strategy. The division therefore proposed that the two divisions invest jointly in the new production process to manufacture the common component.

The corporate staff recognizes that the Biz Phones Division, whose buyers are not nearly as price-sensitive, has no interest in sharing the investment because the cost savings would not improve their profit margins enough to offset the negative effect of the increased investment. When the managers at Biz Phones had conducted a similar analysis of the shared-investment project, they found that the shared-investment strategy would generate $1 mil-

Table 5–13 Valuation Summary for Home Phones Division—Strategy 2, Five-Year Forecast ($ in millions)

Cumulative present value of cash flows	$ (5.176)
Present value of residual value	128.878
Shareholder Value	$123.702
Less: Prestrategy shareholder value	70.714
Value created by strategy	$ 52.988

lion less value. Moreover, Biz Phones is reluctant to undertake such a project because it perceives that the benefits would accrue to Home Phones, while Biz Phones would only lose control over its production process without getting much credit for contributing to Home Phones' success.

Corporate management is considering two alternatives:

1. Turning down the project, consistent with current policy of assessing the operating divisions' plans on a stand-alone basis (i.e., Home Phones cannot justify the $25 million investment solely on the benefits that would accrue to itself)
2. Evaluating the investment decision in terms of its contribution to shareholder value of the overall company

The issue is whether the benefits to Home Phones of the shared investment would more than offset the detriment to Biz Phones by improving the shareholder value of the corporation as a whole. In this case the value created for the overall company is about $16.5 million higher under Strategy 2 compared to Strategy 1. Thus, it would benefit the corporation to have Home Phones and Biz Phones jointly build and use the new production process.

The treatment of the subsidiaries as autonomous business units (as reflected in Strategy 1) would result in sacrificing opportunities offered by potential synergies between the businesses. The shared-investment strategy would help the Home Phones division but would not be as favorable for the Biz Phones division. By applying the shareholder value approach to evaluation of a funding allocation decision, one could assess what the overall impact of the shared-investment strategy would be on the corporation as a whole in order to select the strategy that would maximize overall shareholder value creation. Exploiting the opportunity to share activities in the value chain by related divisions is an essential aspect of strategies that seek to gain competitive advantage.

Product-Line Value Creation

A manufacturer of personal computers sells through its own sales force to major corporate accounts and also sells to retail computer stores. While there is general agreement that direct sales to corporations and the retail channel of distribution are complementary rather than competitive, there is a keen interest in analyzing the relative contributions of the two segments. The most recent year's contribution statements for the corporate and retail segments are presented in Table 5–14.

The computers sold directly to corporations and those sold to retail dealers are identical. In both markets discounts from list price have averaged about 25 percent. Thus, the manufacturing contribution ratio for each segment is also an identical 60 percent. Due to relatively greater selling expenses (e.g., the direct sales force) and order processing costs, the contribution margin ratio for the corporate segment is just 40 percent compared to 46 percent for the retail segment. Other expenses directly traceable to the respective segments such as advertising and promotion were 18 percent of sales last year. As a consequence, the segment operating contribution ratio for retail (28 percent) remains a significant six percentage points greater than corporate (22 percent). On the basis of the contribution statement, management concluded that even though each segment generated the same level of sales, the retail segment was clearly more profitable, with an operating contribution of $70 million versus $55 million for the corporate segment. Indeed, this analysis along with some pressure from retail chains has moved management to consider the possibility of distributing exclusively through the retail channel.

There are several limitations associated with the foregoing contribution statement. First, it is historical rather than forward-looking. Second, it ignores the investments in working and fixed capital needed to generate the sales. Finally, it does not consider the possible differences in risk related to the corporate versus retail segments. To transform the conventional contribution analysis to a shareholder value creation analysis the three limitations listed above must be overcome.

Assume the following constant projections over the five-year forecast period:

	CORPORATE	RETAIL
Sales growth rate	18%	18%
Operating profit margin	22	24
Incremental working capital investment	12	30
Cost of capital	14	15

The projected operating profit margin for retail of 24 percent continues to be better than the 22 percent margin projected for the

Table 5–14 Contributions of Corporate and Retail Segments ($ in millions)

	Corporate	%	Retail	%	Total	%
Sales	$250	100	$250	100	$500	100
Variable manufacturing costs	100	40	100	40	200	40
MANUFACTURING CONTRIBUTION MARGIN	150	60	150	60	300	60
Variable selling and administrative expenses	50	20	35	14	85	17
CONTRIBUTION MARGIN	100	40	115	46	215	43
Other expenses directly traceable to segments	45	18	45	18	90	18
SEGMENT OPERATING CONTRIBUTION	$ 55	22	$ 70	28	$125	25
Unallocated common expenses					45	9
EARNINGS BEFORE TAXES					$ 80	16

corporate segment. Retail's incremental working capital requirements of 30 percent, however, are two and a half times greater than those of the corporate segment. This is due, in part, to the substantially slower inventory turnover realized in the retail segment particularly for smaller dealers. In addition, the company has used liberal collection policies as a competitive vehicle in gaining acceptance among dealers. As a result, retail averages sixty days of outstanding receivables in contrast to forty days for the corporate segment. The higher cost of capital, 15 percent, assigned to retail is based on a relatively higher expected variability in demand in response to economy-wide factors than might be expected for sales to corporations. Furthermore, because the company is not yet well established in the extremely competitive retail channel, management believes it to be a relatively risky business at this time.

Tables 5–15 and 5–16, in sharp contrast to the earlier analysis, show that the corporate segment will create about $36 million more value than the retail segment, that is, $353.864 million versus $317.440 million. The reversal in results is due to the higher working capital requirements and relatively higher risk associated with the retail channel. These results have strongly altered management's view of possibly distributing exclusively through the retail channel.

If management wishes to estimate the combined value creation of the two segments, then unallocated common expenses as well as fixed capital investment in shared production and warehouse facilities must be incorporated into the analysis. At this consolidated level, income taxes need also to be considered.

Operating profit margins are projected to decrease by four percentage points when unallocated common expenses are considered. The income tax rate is expected to approximate 46 percent. Incremental fixed capital investment is projected at 15 percent. With these additional forecasts, the value created by the combined segments totals $188 million compared to $671 million (see Table 5–16) before consideration of capital investment, common expenses, and income taxes.

Implementation Issues

Ultimately the performance of the business rests not only on available sources of competitive advantage and the strategies employed to exploit these sources, but also on the execution or implementation

Table 5–15 Cash Flows and Shareholder Value for Corporate Segment (Cost of Capital = 14%) ($ in millions)

Year	Cash Flow	Present Value	Cumulative Present Value	Present Value of Residual Value	Cumulative PV + Residual Value	Increase in Value
1	$ 59.500	$52.193	$ 52.193	$406.642	$458.835	$ 65.977
2	70.210	54.024	106.217	420.910	527.127	68.292
3	82.848	55.920	162.137	435.678	597.816	70.689
4	97.760	57.882	220.019	450.965	670.985	73.169
5	115.357	59.913	279.932	466.789	746.721	75.736
						$353.864

Table 5–16 Cash Flows and Shareholder Value for Retail Segment (Cost of Capital = 15%) ($ in millions)

Year	Cash Flow	Present Value	Cumulative Present Value	Present Value of Residual Value	Cumulative PV + Residual Value	Increase in Value
1	$ 57.300	$49.826	$ 49.826	$410.435	$460.261	$ 60.261
2	67.614	51.126	100.952	421.142	522.094	61.833
3	79.785	52.460	153.412	432.128	585.540	63.446
4	94.146	53.828	207.240	443.401	650.641	65.101
5	111.092	55.232	262.472	454.968	717.440	66.799
						$317.440
	Total shareholder value created					$671.304

of strategy. The best conceived strategy without an organization capable of implementation is largely worthless. Successful implementation requires strategic *management*. Collier[8] lists eight principles that are the foundation for a well-working strategic management system:

1. A committed CEO
2. A properly organized company
3. Credible plans
4. Supportive functional action plans
5. Realistic resource allocations
6. Culturally compatible strategies
7. A good strategy monitoring system
8. Compensation linked to strategy

Collier suggests that the CEO need not only be committed to strategic planning, but must also be committed to strategic management. This more active role means that his decisions about resource allocations to business units must be consistent with the strategic plans. Further, he will seek genuine commitment to the plan from line managers by insisting that they, rather than the staff planners, develop the strategic plans.

The second principle, a properly organized company, is critical to implementation. As discussed at the outset of this chapter, a central task of strategic management is to identify individual businesses as strategic business units so that a unified strategy can be developed and carried out for each unit. As Collier observes, "trying to carry out incompatible strategies—for instance, trying to be the low-cost producer in one market while at the same time producing a custom-engineered product for another—in the same organization usually results in inferior performance in both markets."[9]

Plans that are not credible undermine both the planning process and the motivation by line management to implement. Plans that are continually blindsided by unanticipated events such as inflation, technology changes, and strategic moves by competitors are damaging not only to the company but also to the credibility of the managers responsible for developing the strategic plans. Thus, plans need to be based not only on well-grounded competitive analysis, but must also incorporate responses in the event that contingencies arise that could negate the current strategy.

It is important that the focus of the major functions within the business unit such as manufacturing, marketing, and R&D be fully compatible with the strategy. For example, if the strategic plan calls for market share gains with superior products, the R&D function must have a program to develop them, manufacturing must incorporate the technology and quality control to produce them, and marketing needs to develop programs to introduce the products to customers. All of this activity requires first-class communications and coordination between functional heads and line managers. Of course, resource allocation must be supportive of chosen strategy.

Collier's sixth principle, culturally compatible strategies, is gaining increasing recognition with the growing interest in corporate culture. It can be assumed that a general manager will build an organization that is compatible with his own orientation. It is both frustrating to the manager and dysfunctional to the company to place an aggressive, growth-oriented manager in charge of a business unit that needs to be "harvested." The reverse would be an equally poor fit. In each case the manager would likely seek opportunities to move away from the established plan. Many companies have apparently found this to be an implementation nightmare.

A well executed strategy monitoring system is critical to achieving successful implementation. Performance reports serve as the prime feedback source in the planning process. Collier, formerly the officer in charge of strategic planning at Borg-Warner, describes the monitoring of strategic implementation as follows:

> At Borg-Warner, the strategy implementation of the limited number of units that should be monitored by the CEO is done through a strategic issue system. During the annual resource allocation procedure, the planners at the corporate level identify as "critical" about twenty to thirty of the 100 SBU plans that are submitted. A critical SBU is one whose impact—positive or negative—on the corporation's overall performance or resource requirement is important or where there is a serious question about its strategy. The corporate central management selects ten or twelve of these critical SBU plans to be made strategic issues.
>
> For the limited number of SBUs that have been made strategic issues, corporate management withholds allocation judgment until it is given a detailed presentation and discussion, the corporate central management decides whether to accept or modify the strategy and makes a capital allocation appropriate to that decision. This decision goes back to the affected management both verbally and in writing,

> together with the reasons therefore. Both this response and the original strategic issue report outlining the questions that the CEO would like addressed in the presentation are made by the planners for approval by the CEO.
>
> Following the strategy response by the corporate central management to the affected SBU, the chief operating officer is given a set of questions to raise at his regular quarterly operating reviews to test whether the strategy is being implemented in the way the central corporate response is directed. These questions are prepared by the corporate planning staff. If the answers indicate that the strategy is being implemented in line with the response, no action is required on the part of the CEO. If the answers indicate a deviation is occurring, the COO brings this to the attention of the CEO if, in the COO's judgment, the deviation cannot be corrected. At that point, the CEO decides whether to permit the deviation, change the allocation, or call for a new presentation of strategy to be followed with a new decision. The quarterly checking continues until the strategy outlined in the response is fully implemented.[10]

Finally, to ensure that management throws its full weight in carrying out strategic plans, compensation needs to be linked to strategic objectives. The enthusiasm in companies for strategies that will create shareholder value would increase substantially if incentives were directed toward implementing such strategies. A means of linking performance evaluation and compensation to strategies will be presented in Chapter 8.

The shareholder value approach has much to offer in ensuring successful implementation of complex strategies. The shareholder value approach provides organizations with a consistency of analysis across functions, levels, and types of business decisions. In this way, those who are competing for resources in a company will share the same framework for analyzing their businesses and can also speak to other business units in the same "language." In addition, this approach is not more difficult to implement because it requires only a modest amount of new data (such as the cost of capital). It also offers the benefit of overcoming the limitations of traditional accounting-based financial statements.

In a broad sense, the steps required in introducing the shareholder value approach will generally include the following:

1. Educate managers about the approach and how to use tools effectively in implementing the approach.

2. Use the approach "passively" in evaluating a completed plan.
3. Use the approach "actively" to develop the current plan.
4. Develop performance measures that are consistent with the strategy.

By providing a common framework for analysis, the shareholder value approach can substantially enhance organizational communication, which in turn improves management productivity by contributing to more efficient and more effective decision making.

Chapter 6

Financial Feasibility of Strategies

Assuming that management has satisfied itself that the proposed strategic plan will create shareholder value, then it must address the question of whether the proposed plan can be funded. This latter question concerning financial feasibility is often approached with what has become known as the "sustainable growth" model. This chapter presents the limitations of the sustainable growth model and offers a superior alternative, the affordable sales growth approach.

Sustainable Growth Versus Sustainable Value Creation

In many companies sales or earnings growth targets are established at the beginning of the strategic planning process. In the shareholder value approach, growth is not a target, but a consequence of the strategic planning process which attempts to maximize shareholder value. Treating growth as a target is incompatible with the shareholder value approach because growth per se does not necessarily lead to value creation. Moreover, companies that develop strategies from preset growth targets may forego significant value-creating opportunities. They may reject investment opportunities yielding rates of return above the cost of capital in order to maintain growth rates in line with established targets. The second, and more prevalent, danger is that investment opportunities yielding *less* than the cost of capital will be accepted in order to achieve the targeted growth rate. In brief, strategic plans should not be developed by first setting growth targets. Instead, planned growth should proceed from a comprehensive planning process seeking to maximize creation of shareholder value.

The notion of a "sustainable growth rate" has gained some currency among corporate planners. The idea was popularized over the past fifteen years by the Boston Consulting Group (BCG) and others. The sustainable growth rate is the maximum growth rate in assets a company can sustain without issuing new equity. The sustainable growth rate is used by some companies as an index of the economic desirability of a strategy as well as the financial feasibility of the plan. As will be shown shortly, *the sustainable growth rate is neither reliably linked to value creation nor is it an accurate measure of the fundable rate of growth*.

The BCG growth rate model begins with the assumption that the maximum rate of growth (assuming no new equity) is equal to the firm's return on equity if no dividends are paid.[1] For example, assume a company earned $10 million on a beginning equity of $50 million during the year just ended. If last year's 20 percent return on beginning equity (ROE) is repeated during the next year, the company's earnings will grow by 20 percent to $12 million, that is, 20 percent return on this year's beginning equity of $60 million. This growth rate will continue as long as the company earns 20 percent on each year's beginning equity and pays no dividends.

Dividend payments will naturally reduce the sustainable growth rate. The rate is simply the product of ROE times the earnings retention rate, that is, 1 minus the dividend payment ratio. Returning to the prior example, assume that 40 percent of earnings is paid as dividends and thus the earnings retention rate is 60 percent. The sustainable growth rate is then the 20 percent ROE times the 60 percent earnings retention rate or 12 percent. Six million of last year's $10 million of earnings are reinvested. This year's earnings will grow by 12 percent to $11.2 million, that is, 20 percent return on this year's beginning equity of $56 million.

I will now go on to demonstrate that sustainable growth is not a reliable measure of sustainable value creation and therefore not a desirable measure of sustainable competitive advantage. Table 6–1

Table 6–1 Sustainable Growth with Value Creation—Base Case ($ in millions)

	Years					
	1	2	3	4	5	6+
Sales	$110.00	$121.00	$133.10	$146.41	$161.05	$161.05
Earnings before taxes	$ 22.00	$ 24.20	$ 26.62	$ 29.28	$ 32.20	$ 32.20
Income taxes	11.00	12.10	13.31	14.64	16.10	16.10
Earnings after taxes	11.00	12.10	13.31	14.64	16.10	16.10
+ Depreciation	1.00	1.10	1.21	1.33	1.46	1.61
– Investment in fixed and working capital	6.00	6.60	7.26	7.98	8.78	1.61
Cash flow from operations	$ 6.00	$ 6.60	$ 7.26	$ 7.99	$ 8.78	$ 16.10
Present value at 15%	5.22	4.99	4.77	4.57	4.36	
Cumulative present value of cash flows						$ 23.91
Present value of residual value						53.36
Shareholder value						77.27
Less: Prestrategy shareholder value						66.67
Value created by strategy						$ 10.60
Beginning equity	$ 50.00	$ 55.00	$ 60.50	$ 66.55	$ 73.20	$ 80.52
+ Earnings after taxes	11.00	12.10	13.31	14.64	16.10	16.10
– Dividends	6.00	6.60	7.26	7.99	8.78	16.10
Ending equity	$ 55.00	$ 60.50	$ 66.55	$ 73.20	$ 80.52	$ 80.52
Return on equity (ROE)[a]	22%	22%	22%	22%	22%	
Sustainable growth rate[b]	10%	10%	10%	10%	10%	
Threshold spread[c]	7%	7%	7%	7%	7%	

[a]$\text{ROE} = \dfrac{\text{Earnings after taxes}}{\text{Beginning equity}}$

[b]Sustainable growth rate = ROE (1 – Dividend payout ratio)
= 22% (1 – 54.5%)
= 10%

[c]Threshold spread = Forecasted operating profit margin – Threshold margin
= 20% – 13%
= 7%

illustrates a case in which sustainable growth is accompanied by value creation. For purposes of simplicity, an all-equity capital structure is assumed. Forecasts for the value drivers are as follows:

Sales growth rate	10%
Operating profit margin	20
Incremental fixed plus working capital investment	50
Cash income tax rate	50
Residual value income tax rate	50
Cost of equity capital	15

The above forecasts result in total shareholder value of $77.27 million. Deducting the prestrategy shareholder value of $66.67 million, that is,

$$\frac{\text{Year 0 cash flow before new investment}}{\text{Cost of capital}} = \frac{\$10.00}{.15}$$

results in $10.6 million of value created by the five-year plan. This value creation is the product of forecasted margins above the threshold margin and projected sales growth.

The ROE is 22 percent throughout the forecast period. Any cash flow remaining after investments in fixed and working capital is paid out as dividends. Multiplying the 22 percent ROE by the 45.5 percent earnings retention rate yields a sustainable asset growth rate of 10 percent. Since the return on assets and equity is projected at a constant 22 percent, the sustainable earnings growth rate will be equal to the asset growth rate of 10 percent.

Table 6–2 shows that impressive sustainable growth rates can be accompanied by shareholder value decreases rather than value creation. Only one forecast is revised from the previous case. The incremental fixed plus working capital investment is increased from 50 percent to 110 percent. This change has several consequences. First, the higher investment requirements reduce each year's cash flows from operations to zero. This, in turn, leads to a value decrease of $13.31 million for the five-year plan in contrast to a $10.6 million value increase in the previous case. The negative threshold spread of 8.7 percent indicates investment at substantially below the cost of capital rate. Second, the greater capital intensity without any change in operating profit margin leads to a period-by-period decline in ROE from 22 percent in year 1 to 15.9 percent in year 5.

Finally, the magnitude of investment requirements allows for no dividends. Since the retention rate is now 100 percent, the sustainable asset growth rate is equal to ROE. Most importantly, observe that the sustainable growth rates starting at 22 percent in year 1 and ending at 15.9 percent in year 5 are systematically greater than the 10 percent sustainable growth rate in the previous example. Despite this, value is created with the lower growth rates and value is destroyed with the higher growth rates. Indeed, both the value decrease and the higher sustainable growth rate in the second case are triggered by the increased investment requirements. In brief, these two case examples demonstrate that sustainable growth is not reliably linked to shareholder value creation. The results of these two cases are summarized below:

	BASE CASE	SCENARIO A
Sustainable growth rates	10%	15.9–22%
Value created by strategy ($ in millions)	$10.6	($13.31)

Not only is sustainable growth rate an unreliable indicator of value creation, but in addition it is not a reliable measure of the fundable rate of growth. To illustrate this latter point a third case is presented in Table 6–3. This case maintains all the assumptions of the second case (Table 6–2) except that now 40 percent of the income tax expense is assumed to be deferred income tax.[2] Since the deferred portion of the income tax expense is not currently payable and may never have to be paid, it should not be a deduction in computing cash flow from operations. As a result, cash flow from operations is increased each year by the increase in deferred income taxes. This leads to a value contribution of $4.22 million versus a value decrease of $13.31 million in the second case where all taxes were assumed to be currently payable.

The ROE for this deferred tax scenario is the same as the previous case because the deferral does not affect the total income tax expense amount on the income statement. Thus, the same earnings after taxes amount is added to equity each year in both cases. Since no dividends were paid in either case, the sustainable growth rate is equal to ROE. However, the sustainable growth rate clearly underestimates the growth rate in assets in the deferred tax case. For example, in the first year investment (net of depreciation) was $11

Table 6–2 Sustainable Growth with Value Decrease—Scenario A ($ in millions)

	Years					
	1	2	3	*4*	5	6+
Sales	$110.00	$121.00	$133.10	$146.41	$161.05	$161.05
Earnings before taxes	$ 22.00	$ 24.20	$ 26.62	$ 29.28	$ 32.20	$ 32.20
Income taxes	11.00	12.10	13.31	14.64	16.10	16.10
Earnings after taxes	11.00	12.10	13.31	14.64	16.10	16.10
+ Depreciation	1.00	1.22	1.46	1.73	2.02	2.34
– Investment in fixed and working capital	12.00	13.32	14.77	16.37	18.12	2.34
Cash flow from operations	$ 0	$ 0	$ 0	$ 0	$ 0	$ 16.10
Cumulative present value of cash flows						$ 0
Present value of residual value						53.36
Shareholder value						53.36
Less: Prestrategy shareholder value						66.67
Value created by strategy						$(13.31)
Beginning equity	$ 50.00	$ 61.00	$ 73.10	$ 86.41	$101.05	
+ Earnings after taxes	11.00	12.10	13.31	14.64	16.10	
Ending equity	$ 61.00	$ 73.10	$ 86.41	$101.05	$117.15	
Return on equity (ROE)	22.0%	19.8%	18.2%	16.9%	15.9%	
Sustainable growth rate	22.0%	19.8%	18.2%	16.9%	15.9%	
Threshold spread[a]	(8.7%)	(8.7%)	(8.7%)	(8.7%)	(8.7%)	

[a]Threshold spread = Forecasted operating profit margin – Threshold margin
= 20% – 28.7%
= (8.7%)

Table 6–3 Sustainable Growth Versus Affordable Growth—Scenario B ($ in millions)

	Years					
	1	2	3	4	5	6+
Sales	$110.00	$121.00	$133.10	$146.41	$161.05	$161.05
Earnings before taxes	$ 22.00	$ 24.20	$ 26.62	$ 29.28	$ 32.20	$ 32.20
Income taxes	11.00	12.10	13.31	14.64	16.10	16.10
Earnings after taxes	11.00	12.10	13.31	14.64	16.10	16.10
+ Depreciation	1.00	1.22	1.46	1.73	2.02	2.34
– Investment in fixed and working capital	12.00	13.32	14.77	16.37	18.12	2.34
+ Increase in deferred income taxes	4.40	4.84	5.32	5.86	6.44	
Cash flow from operations	$ 4.40	$ 4.84	$ 5.32	$ 5.86	$ 6.44	$ 16.10
Present value at 15%	3.82	3.66	3.50	3.35	3.20	
Cumulative present value of cash flows						$ 17.53
Present value of residual value						53.36
Shareholder value						70.89
Less: Prestrategy shareholder value						66.67
Value created by strategy						$ 4.22
Beginning equity	$ 50.00	$ 61.00	$ 73.10	$ 86.41	$101.05	
+ Earnings after taxes	11.00	12.10	13.31	14.64	16.10	
Ending equity	$ 61.00	$ 73.10	$ 86.41	$101.05	$117.15	
Return on equity (ROE)	22.0%	19.8%	18.2%	16.9%	15.9%	
Sustainable growth rate	22.0%	19.8%	18.2%	16.9%	15.9%	

million plus the $4.4 million of cash flow available from operations. The total investment of $15.4 million on a beginning asset base of $50 million represents a 30.8 percent increase compared to the calculated sustainable growth rate of 22 percent. The fundable rate of asset growth is greater than the sustainable growth rate which is tied to accounting numbers rather than cash flows.

A principal focus of this section has been to demonstrate that sustainable growth does not necessarily lead to sustainable value creation. The shareholder value approach to strategic planning does provide a measure of sustainable competitive advantage, that is, sustainable value creation. Once the investment requirements and risk characteristics of a strategy have been established, sustainable value creation is determined by three essential factors: (1) sales growth rate, (2) threshold spread, that is, the amount by which the forecasted operating margins exceed the threshold margin, and (3) the duration over which threshold spreads are expected to be positive or equivalently the period over which investments are expected to yield rates of return greater than the cost of capital—that is, the value growth duration.

Strategies can be expected to contribute value only if the business operates above the threshold margin. Therefore, the most reliable indication of "value sustainability" can be found in sustained performance above the threshold margin. Once management has identified a sustainable competitive advantage, it will also wish to determine how large an advantage can be achieved. The size of its advantage or value creation potential is jointly determined by the sales growth rate, threshold spread, and duration. This idea is portrayed in Figure 6–1. The index of value creation potential is calculated and plotted for each of a company's four business units. The product of the forecasted sales growth rate and threshold spread is represented on the vertical axis. The duration, in years, is depicted on the horizontal axis. The growth rate times the threshold spread may be thought of as the average "units" of value created per period. When this amount is multiplied by the duration a rough index of value creation potential is generated. The index is characterized as "rough" because it is based on long-term averages for sales growth rates and threshold spreads. While the index is not intended as a substitute for more detailed calculations of value creation, it does serve as a reasonable first approximation of relative value creation potential for top management. In this particular example, business unit A is clearly expected to be the star performer and business unit D is a candidate for divestiture.

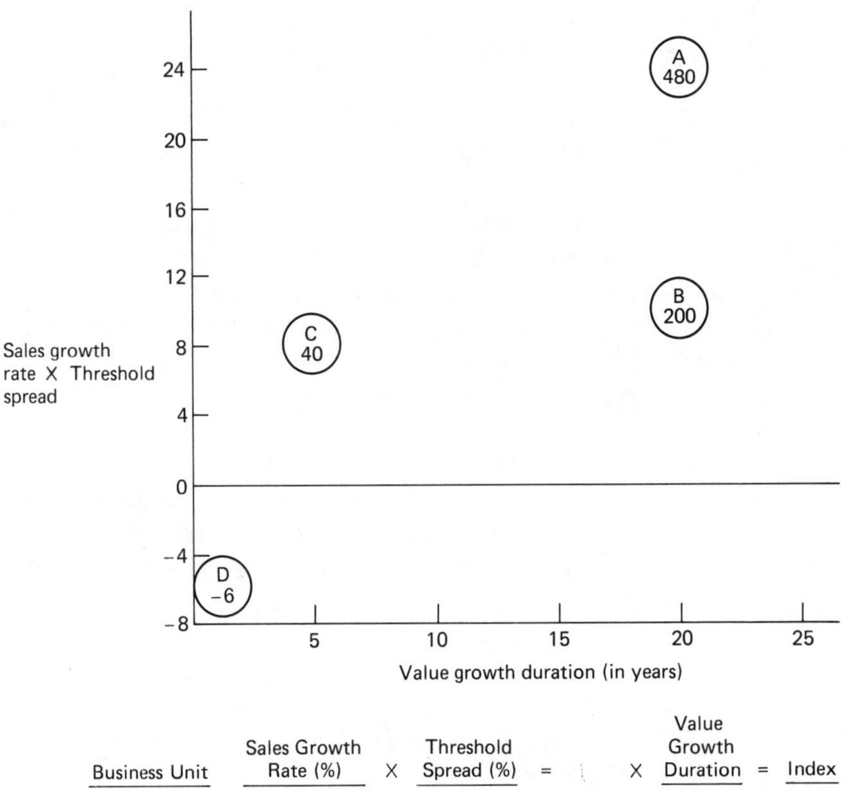

Business Unit	Sales Growth Rate (%)	X	Threshold Spread (%)	=		X	Value Growth Duration	=	Index
A	12		2		24		20		480
B	10		1		10		20		200
C	8		1		8		5		40
D	6		-1		-6		1[a]		-6

[a] Company expects to sell or liquidate the unit within one year.

Figure 6–1 Index of Value Creation Potential for Four Business Units

Once strategies are formulated, their financial feasibility must be tested. In the next section, the affordable sales growth rate approach will be presented as a superior analytical tool to the sustainable asset growth rate approach.

Affordable Sales Growth

After management has identified a plan that will create value for shareholders, the question turns to the financial feasibility of the plan. The sales growth rates projected in the plans can be compared with the business unit's or company's affordable sales growth rate.[3] The affordable sales growth rate is the maximum annual percentage increase in sales a business can afford without issuing new equity, given its forecasted operating profit margins, investment requirements per dollar of sales increase, target debt-to-equity ratio, and target dividend payout rate. If sales grow at a greater rate, the business must improve operating performance, increase financial leverage, decrease dividends, or sell new shares.

It is important to keep in mind that the affordable sales growth rate when compared with the planned growth rate is a measure of the financial feasibility of the plan and not a measure of its potential contribution to shareholder value. As established earlier, a strategic plan should not be developed by first setting sales growth targets. Instead, planned sales growth should be the outgrowth of a comprehensive value creation planning process.

To illustrate the affordable sales growth rate approach, consider the case of a relatively capital-intensive steel products manufacturing company.[4] "Most likely" strategic scenarios were developed by each business unit. These forecasts were then consolidated at the corporate level with the following results:

Net income/sales	6.12%
Incremental fixed capital investment	25.00
Incremental working capital investment	30.00
Dividend payout rate	35.00
Target debt-to-equity ratio	30.00
Cash income tax rate	49.00
Book income tax rate	49.00

The affordable sales growth rate for the above forecasts is 10.378 percent. That is the growth rate at which cash inflows will be equal to cash outflows. Cash inflows arise from net income plus depreciation of $1 million plus any increase in debt capacity. Cash outflows result from investments in fixed and working capital and the payment of dividends. Assume sales last year were $100 million. If sales grow at the affordable rate of 10.378 percent then current year's sales will be $110.378 million.

$$\text{Cash inflows} = \text{Net income} + \text{Depreciation} + \text{Increase in debt capacity}$$

$$\begin{aligned}\text{Net income} &= (\text{Sales})\left(\frac{\text{Net income}}{\text{Sales}}\right)\\ &= (\$110.378)(6.12\%)\\ &= \$6.755 \text{ million}\end{aligned}$$

$$\text{Increase in debt capacity} = (\text{Target debt/Equity})\,(\text{Net income} - \text{Dividends})$$
$$= (30\%)\,(\$6.755 - 2.364)$$
$$= \$1.317 \text{ million}$$[5]

$$\text{Cash outflows} = \text{Incremental fixed and working capital investment} + \text{Depreciation} + \text{Dividends}$$

$$\text{Incremental fixed and working capital investment} = (\text{Incremental sales}) \left(\begin{array}{c}\text{Incremental fixed + Working} \\ \text{capital investment rates}\end{array}\right)$$
$$= (\$110.378 - 100.000)\,(25\% + 30\%)$$
$$= \$5.708 \text{ million}$$

$$\text{Dividends} = (\text{Net income})\,(\text{Dividend payout rate})$$
$$= (\$6.755)\,(35\%)$$
$$= \$2.364 \text{ million}$$

Therefore:

$$\text{Cash inflows} = \text{Net income} + \text{Depreciation} + \text{Increase in debt capacity}$$
$$= \$6.755 + 1.000 + 1.317$$
$$= \$9.072 \text{ million}$$

$$\text{Cash outflows} = \text{Incremental fixed and working capital investment} + \text{Depreciation} + \text{Dividends}$$
$$= \$5.708 + 1.000 + 2.364$$
$$= \$9.072 \text{ million}$$

Suppose management believes it can grow (and create value as well) at a rate greater than the indicated 10.4 percent affordable rate. The projected growth might be made affordable by judicious changes in product-market strategy, financial leverage, dividend policy, or improved asset management. To explore some of these possibilities the affordable growth rate matrix presented in Table 6–4 can be particularly useful. For example, the affordable growth rate can be increased from 10.4 percent to 12.3 percent if some combination of product-market strategies were able to increase net income/sales from 12 to 14 percent. Alternatively, by decreasing the dividend payout from 35 to 30 percent and increasing the target debt-to-equity ratio from 30 to 35 percent, the company could increase its sales growth rate to 11.8 percent. Increasing operating

Table 6–4 Affordable Sales Growth Rate Analysis

		Incremental Fixed Plus Working Capital Investment Rate								
		50%			55%			60%		
		Dividend Payout			Dividend Payout			Dividend Payout		
		30%	35%	40%	30%	35%	40%	30%	35%	40%
Net income / Sales										
10%										
	25%	9.8	9.0	8.3	8.8	8.1	7.5	8.0	7.4	6.8
Debt/Equity	30%	10.2	9.4	8.6	9.2	8.5	7.8	8.4	7.7	7.1
	35%	10.7	9.8	9.0	9.6	8.9	8.1	8.7	8.1	7.4
12%										
	25%	12.0	11.0	10.1	10.8	9.9	9.1	9.8	9.0	8.3
Debt/Equity	30%	12.5	11.5	10.6	11.3	10.4	9.5	10.2	9.4	8.6
	35%	13.1	12.0	11.0	11.8	10.8	9.9	10.7	9.8	9.0
14%										
	25%	14.3	13.1	12.0	12.8	11.8	10.8	11.6	10.7	9.8
Debt/Equity	30%	14.9	13.7	12.5	13.4	12.3	11.3	12.1	11.2	10.2
	35%	15.6	14.3	13.1	14.0	12.9	11.8	12.7	11.7	10.7

margins is not always feasible and changing leverage and dividend policies is not necessarily prudent. Under such circumstances, the affordable sales growth analysis may simply suggest to management that the company is growing too fast for its own good.

Corporate management can conduct this type of analysis in terms of affordable dividends as well as affordable sales growth.[6] The affordable dividend payout rate is the maximum payout rate the company can afford without issuing new equity, given its forecasted sales growth, operating profit margins, investment requirements, and target capital structure. For managements that believe that maintaining or increasing the current dividend level is important, the affordable dividend analysis often raises some concerns. One concern would be that this year's dividend is larger than next year's projected affordable dividend. For a company with a relatively low affordable dividend payout rate, this analysis highlights the company's vulnerability to decreased operating profit margins or increased investment requirements.

Chapter 7

Stock Market Signals to Management

IN CONTRAST TO EARLIER CHAPTERS, where strategies were assessed on the basis of management forecasts, now our interest centers on what the price of the shares tell us about the *market's* expectations concerning the company's future performance. As will be demonstrated, estimating shareholder return requires insight into *both* corporate plans and the current assessment of these plans by the market as reflected in the current stock price. Chapters 4 and 5 established the link between the competitive analysis process and the shareholder value approach to assessing strategies. Throughout the discussion, it was emphasized that value would be created only if corporate investments were made at above the market-required rate of return, that is, the cost of capital. If the company successfully invests at above the cost of capital rate, will shareholders also earn a rate of return exceeding the cost of capital? The short answer to this question is that it depends on the expected level of performance implied by the stock price when the investor purchases the shares. This chapter will focus on a more detailed answer to this and related questions about corporate performance and shareholder returns. This analysis impacts major management issues such as the selection of hurdle rates for corporate investments, the design of performance evaluation and executive compensation systems, as well as investor communications.

Corporate Versus Shareholder Rate of Return

Investors and corporate managers are each involved in investment decisions aimed at achieving maximum economic returns for a chosen level of risk. In both cases, the economic rate of return is calculated taking into account the required investment and the forecasted cash flows associated with the investment. Additionally, we know that hurdle rates for corporate investments are governed by the risk-adjusted returns demanded by investors in the capital markets. Despite the fact that investors and managers both use the same discounted cash flow (DCF) model to estimate prospective returns, the rate of return that must be earned by corporate investments to produce the required investor rate of return is ordinarily significantly higher than the investor-required rate itself. This is the case because the relevant investment amount as well as forecasted cash flows for the investor and manager are different. Investment for a prospective shareholder (or opportunity investment for a current shareholder) is simply the current market price of the stock. The current stock price represents the discounted present value of all cash flows expected from prospective as well as past corporate investments.

Shareholders invest in rights to financial claims, that is, dividends and capital appreciation. Managers, in contrast, make real investments in fixed and working capital. Unlike the shareholder who makes his entire investment when he purchases shares, the investments in corporate strategies are made over a period of time. The company's beginning investment is the capitalized value of its currently sustainable cash flow stream, that is, its prestrategy value. It represents the value of the business today if no additional value were created. Unlike market value, the prestrategy value does not anticipate the economic value to be created by future investments. Recall that shareholder value is the sum of prestrategy value and the value created during the forecast period.

Just as there are differences in the investments made by the shareholder and the company, the same is true for cash flows. The shareholder has a claim to all cash flows—those due to past as well as prospective investments. In contrast, the corporate manager investing in future strategies is concerned only with the incremental cash flows associated with prospective investments, since past investments are sunk costs.

The foregoing may be summarized as follows:

	SHAREHOLDER PERSPECTIVE	COMPANY PERSPECTIVE
Investment	Current market price of shares	Prestrategy value
Return	Cash inflows due to past and future corporate investments minus expenditures for future corporate investments	Cash inflows due to future corporate investments minus expenditures for future corporate investments

If management and the market have identical forecasts, then the following will be true:

Market price = Prestrategy value + Value created by strategy = Shareholder value

Whenever the market price is greater than prestrategy value, the market is expecting management to invest *above* the cost of capital or investor-required rate of return. If management were investing at exactly the cost of capital, then there would be no value created by the strategy. One important implication of the above is that if, after the shareholder makes his investment, the market comes to believe that management will invest at (rather than above) the cost of capital rate, the price of the shares will decline and the shareholder will earn less than his required rate.

To illustrate the relationship between corporate and shareholder returns, consider the following simplified example. Evanston Corp. achieved total sales of $100 million last year and a pretax operating profit of $14 million. The company pays income taxes at a rate of 50 percent of operating profit. For purposes of keeping the illustration simple, Evanston is assumed to be totally financed by equity. Management is currently considering the possibility of expanding capacity which would enable the company's sales to increase from $100 million to $120 million while retaining its operating profit margin at 14 percent. The expansion requires an outlay of $8.4 million for fixed and working capital. Management estimates the cost of equity capital to be 14 percent.

Next year's cash flow is as follows:

	($ IN MILLIONS)
Sales	$120.00
Cost of sales	103.20
Operating profit	16.80
Income taxes	8.40
Operating profit after taxes	8.40
Incremental investment	8.40
Cash flow from operations	$ 0

The residual value at the end of the first year is equal to the capitalized value of the sustainable cash flow or cash flow before new investment, that is, $8.40/.14 = $60 million. To compute shareholder value, the residual value of $60 million must be discounted back one period (i.e., $60/1.14) to obtain a value of $52.63 million. The prestrategy value or residual value at the beginning of the first year is the capitalized value of the cash flow before new investment of $7 million (on sales of $100 million), that is, $7 million/14 percent = $50 million.

The value created by this strategy is calculated as follows:

	($ IN MILLIONS)
Shareholder value	$52.63
Less: Prestrategy shareholder value	50.00
Value created by strategy	$ 2.63

$$\text{Corporate rate of return (CROR)} = \frac{\text{Increase in shareholder value}}{\text{Prestrategy shareholder value}} = \frac{\$60 - 50}{\$50} = 20\,\%$$

Because the strategy did create value, the *corporate* rate of return on the strategy must be greater than 14 percent. The shareholder value at the end of the year of $60 million represents a $10 million increase over the prestrategy investment base of $50 million or a 20 percent rate of return. This 20 percent corporate return is based only on corporate investment and related cash flows and is not directly affected by movements in the company's share price.

The shareholder rate of return (SROR), however, is affected both by the level of today's share price and subsequent movements in price. To demonstrate, consider the following three possibilities for the current market price of Evanston's shares:

	PRICE PER SHARE AT BEGINNING OF YEAR
1. Market is pessimistic and does not anticipate management's strategy. Instead the market assumes that the company will continue to invest at the 14% cost of capital rate. Market price is thus equal to the pre-strategy value.	$50.00
2. Market fully anticipates management's strategy. Market price is thus equal to shareholder value.	52.63
3. Market is more optimistic than management about prospective strategy. Market price is thus greater than shareholder value.	57.00

Now suppose management's forecast materializes and the market price of Evanston at the end of the year is $60 per share. The SROR for each of the three scenarios, assuming shares are purchased at the beginning of the year and no dividends are paid during the year, is summarized below:

SCENARIO	CURRENT MARKET PRICE PER SHARE	YEAR-END PRICE	SHAREHOLDER RATE OF RETURN (SROR)	REALIZED CORPORATE RATE OF RETURN (CROR)
Market pessimistic	$50.00	$60.00	20%	20%
Market anticipates	52.63	60.00	14	20
Market optimistic	57.00	60.00	5.26	20

The above table illustrates four broad principles:

1. When the market anticipates and impounds management's strategy in the current stock price, investors who purchase shares today will earn the required rate of return for equity (as shown by the 14 percent SROR in the "anticipated" scenario). Stated in another way, if an investor purchases shares and there is no change in expectations between the

date he purchases the shares and the date he chooses to sell the shares he will earn the market rate of return for equity.

2. When the current market price reflects anticipations that the company will invest at only the cost of capital rate (i.e., the company is valued at its prestrategy value), the SROR will be identical to the corporate rate of return. This is illustrated in the "market pessimistic" scenario in which the $50 price anticipates a 14 percent CROR rather than the realized 20 percent rate of return on corporate investment.
3. When the current market price reflects too much optimism, the SROR will be below the cost of capital rate even though the company may be investing at rates well above the cost of capital. This situation is illustrated by the "market optimistic" scenario in which the current $57 price enables the investor to earn only about 5.25 percent return while the company is generating a 20 percent yield on its investment.
4. Finally, the above table illustrates once again the principle that the corporate rate of return is based on corporate investment and related cash flows and is independent of the stock price.

An intriguing application of this concept is that it can be used to look at the three scenarios and identify the rate of return the company must achieve for shareholders to earn their 14 percent required rate of return on their investment. We already know that the corporate return must be 20 percent for shareholders to achieve a 14 percent yield at the price ($52.63) that fully anticipates management's strategy. Results for all three scenarios are presented below:

	Current Market Price Per Share	Shareholder Rate of Return (SROR)	Required Corporate Rate of Return (CROR)
Market pessimistic	$50.00	14%	14%
Market anticipates	52.63	14	20
Market optimistic	57.00	14	30

The "market pessimistic" price of $50.00 per share is consistent with a 14 percent return on corporate investment. Thus, if the company achieves and is expected to continue to achieve a 14 percent return, the SROR will also be 14 percent. As expected, the required rate of return on corporate investment for the "optimistic" price of $57.00 per share is higher (30 percent) than either of the other two cases. To justify this price and achieve a 30 percent return on corporate investment, Evanston's expected operating profit margin would have to increase from 14 to 15 percent.[1] In summary, the more optimistic the market is about the company's future value creation opportunities, the higher the corporate rate of return must be for today's investor to realize his required return.

The shareholder's rate of return depends on the expected level of performance implied by the stock price at date of purchase and any subsequent revisions in market expectations prompted by company performance as well as changes in industry or macro prospects. Clearly, shareholders are affected by the degree to which expectations are revised over time or by what economists refer to as elasticities of expectation. The central issue is to what extent does the reporting of an unanticipated event such as better or worse company performance impact expectations. Elasticities of expectations typically range from 0 to 1. An elasticity of expectation of zero means that expectations are not revised when reported performance in the current period is different from earlier expectations. By contrast, an elasticity of 1 means that expectations are revised by the same percentage as the percentage change between reported and expected performance for the current period.[2]

The elasticity of expectations concept can be simply illustrated by returning to the prior example. Suppose that Evanston is currently selling at $57.00 per share which implies an expected operating profit margin of 15 percent. If Evanston management reported margins of 14 percent for the year and elasticity of expectations were zero, then the stock price at the end of the year would continue to reflect the original expectations of a 15 percent margin for all subsequent years. In this event, shareholders would earn the 14 percent required rate less any current period cash flow reduction due to the decrease in operating profit margin. They would, in fact, earn 12.8 percent.[3] If elasticity of expectations were 1, then the stock price would reflect a full revision of expectations to 14 percent margins for all subsequent years. This, in turn, would provide shareholders with only a 5.26 percent rate of return for the year.

To gain an idea of the sensitivity of SROR to changes in market expectations after the investor purchases shares, Table 7–1 displays returns to the investor who purchased shares at $52.63 per share (elasticity of expectations assumed to be 1). If the 20 percent sales

Table 7–1 Sensitivity of Shareholder Rate of Return to Sales Growth Rate and Profit Margin

		Sales Growth Rate		
		18.0	20.0	22.0
Profit Margin	13.0	4.3	4.7	5.1
	14.0	13.4	14.0	14.6
	15.0	22.6	23.3	24.0

growth rate and 14 percent margin impounded in the $52.63 current price materialize, the shareholder will earn 14 percent. A plus or minus one percentage point change in expected profit margin can affect SROR by over 9 percent (dropping to 4.7 percent or increasing to 23.3 percent), while a two percentage point change in the expected sales growth rate affects SROR by only 0.6 percent (dropping to 13.4 percent or increasing to 14.6 percent). If the elasticity of expectations were less than one, the sensitivity of the shareholder's rate of return would be correspondingly lower. The above analysis as well as earlier analysis in this section reinforce what insightful investors have known all along—extraordinary returns are generated by investors who can correctly anticipate generally unanticipated events. More importantly, management can use this analysis to establish the level of corporate performance expected by the market and compare this with its own planning projections. As will be shown, this comparison has important implications for selecting hurdle rates, the design of executive compensation systems, and investor communication programs.

Reading the Market

Publicly held companies are constantly engaged with the stock market in mutual signaling and monitoring. The process is depicted in Figure 7–1. The company provides information to the markets via published reports and a variety of other communications. The market takes this information, as well as information from other sources, and impounds its view of the company's future prospects in the market price. The market price, in turn, is a signal to the company about the level of expected company accomplishments needed if shareholders are to earn their required rate of return on the company's shares.

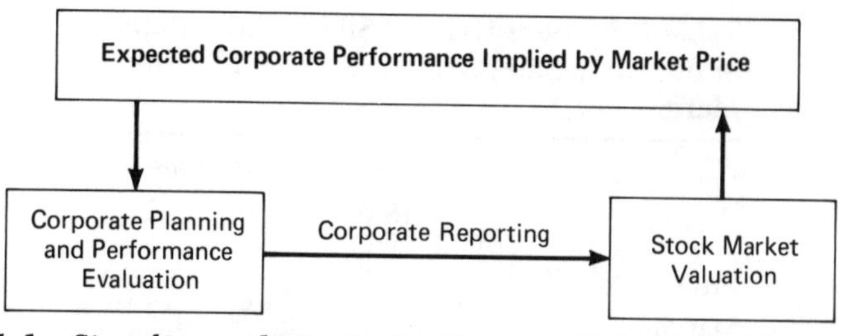

Figure 7–1 Signaling and Monitoring Between Publicly Held Companies and the Stock Market

Historically, the emphasis of academicians and practicioners alike has been on how information made available to the market is impounded in stock prices. The focus here is on how management can "read" market expectations about its company from stock price. IBM will be used as a case example to illustrate the approach I have found to be most effective in reading the market. The IBM case represents a more detailed application of the basic concepts introduced in the last section.

The Value Line Investment Survey report dated August 9, 1985 was used for purposes of approximating the market's expectations about IBM's future performance. Value Line makes projections for key financial parameters such as revenues, cash flow, earnings, dividends, operating profit margins, and capital expenditures for next year as well as projections for the period three to five years from today. Thus, for example, in August 1985, Value Line presents estimates for the current year (1985), projections for 1986, and projections for the 1988 to 1990 period. Using these Value Line projections, value driver estimates for IBM are as follows:

Sales growth rate	14%
Operating profit margin	25
Incremental fixed capital investment	40
Incremental working capital investment	9
Cash income tax rate	45
Residual value income tax rate	45
Cost of capital	14

To simplify the example, the above rates are assumed to be constant for the entire forecast period.

IBM's total debt was about $4 billion which represented less than 5 percent of the market value of its stock. The debt was also offset by a similar amount of marketable securities. Because IBM is almost entirely equity financed, the cost of equity and overall cost of capital are nearly identical. At the time of this analysis IBM was selling at $128 per share.

What is the $128 price per share saying about the market's expectations about IBM's performance? If one accepts Value Line projections as reasonably representative of market expectations, then to justify the price of $128 IBM must be expected to perform at these projected levels for a period of seven years and thereafter it is assumed that IBM will invest in strategies that yield the cost of capital rate of 14 percent. Stated in another way, the present value of a seven-year cash flow projection using the above value driver estimates plus the present value of the residual value at the end of seven years amounts to $128 per share. This analysis helps answer several important questions about the signals emanating from stock market prices.

How sensitive is shareholder rate of return to changes in expectations for various value drivers? Table 7–2 depicts the sensitivity of SROR to changes in two value drivers—the sales growth rate and operating profit margin. If expected margins increase or decrease by one percentage point from their currently expected level of 25 percent, SROR will correspondingly increase or decrease by just under one percentage point. If market expectations for IBM's sales growth were to decrease from 14 to 12 percent, investors could expect to see their returns move from 14 to 12.6 percent.

How sensitive is the shareholder rate of return to fluctuations in the current price? If a shareholder continues to share the market ex-

Table 7–2 Sensitivity of IBM Shareholder Rate of Return to Changes in Sales Growth Rate and Profit Margin

		Sales Growth Rate		
		12.0	14.0	16.0
Profit Margin	24.0	11.6	13.0	14.4
	25.0	12.6	[14.0]	15.4
	26.0	13.5	15.0	16.4

pectations implied by IBM's current price of $128 per share, the expected returns for various prices for IBM stock are as follows:

PRICE PER SHARE	SROR
$108	17.5%
118	15.7
128	14.0
138	12.5
148	11.2

The lower the price of IBM shares that can be purchased for a given set of expectations, the greater the rate of return to the investor.

A third question can be posed. *If the current share price changes, what expected changes in value drivers must materialize if the investor is to earn his required rate of return?* To illustrate, listed below are the sales growth rates required at five different prices for IBM which will enable the investor to earn the 14 percent rate of return.

PRICE PER SHARE	SALES GROWTH RATE REQUIRED FOR SROR OF 14%
$108	9.1%
118	11.7
128	14.0
138	16.1
148	18.0

What corporate rate of return is required by the current stock price for the investor to earn his required rate of return? If the investor is to earn his 14 percent rate of return at the $128 per share price, the *corporate* rate of return at IBM must be 24.5 percent. The 10.5 percent difference between the corporate versus the shareholder rate of return, the *market expectations premium*, is not surprising. IBM's prestrategy value of $74 per share represents about 58 percent of its $128 market price. The remaining 42 percent of the current market price represents expectations that IBM will be able to invest at *above* the cost of capital over the next seven years. In effect, 42 percent of the current market price may be seen as a purchase of a "value growth option" by the investor.

Table 7–3 Sensitivity of IBM Corporate Rate of Return to Changes in Sales Growth Rate and Profit Margin

		Sales Growth Rate		
		12.0	14.0	16.0
Profit Margin	24.0	22.0	23.3	24.5
	25.0	23.2	24.5	25.7
	26.0	24.3	25.6	26.9

How sensitive is the corporate rate of return to changes in expectations for various value drivers? The sensitivity of the corporate rate of return to changes in expectations for sales growth and profit margins is presented in Table 7–3.

The sixth and final question that can be asked is: *If the current stock price changes, what expected changes in the corporate rate of return must materialize for the investor to earn his required rate of return?* Listed below are the corporate rates of return required for five different prices of IBM shares.

Price Per Share	Corporate Rate of Return Required for SROR of 14%
$108	20.5%
118	22.5
128	24.5
138	26.2
148	28.0

The principal market and corporate statistics developed for the IBM case are summarized below:

Market price per share	$128
Value growth option	42.0%
Value growth duration (Years)	7
Cost of capital	14.0%
Required corporate rate of return	24.5%
Shareholder rate of return	14.0%
Market expectations premium	10.5%

Table 7–4 Required Corporate Rate of Return Implied by Market Versus Cost of Capital for Computer Companies

	Required Corporate Rate of Return	Cost of Capital	Market Expectations Premium[a]
Burroughs	14.7%	12.0%	2.7%
Digital Equipment	26.0	14.1	11.9
Honeywell	31.1	12.9	18.2
IBM	24.5	14.0	10.5
NCR	21.1	14.3	6.8
Sperry	17.5	12.8	4.7

[a]The market expectations premium is the excess of the required corporate rate of return over the cost of capital. Therefore the premium represents the market's assessment of the company's competitive advantage potential.

Table 7–4 presents a comparison of cost of capital versus the required corporate rate of return for IBM as well as other computer companies. These calculations are based on September 30, 1985 market prices and Value Line projections available at that date. The large market expectations premiums are due, as was the case with IBM, to the robust value growth option as a percentage of market value.

The framework for reading the market presented here also provides some insights for the continuing debate about the market's time horizon. One of the most destructive canards in business is the notion that the stock market has a short time horizon. This belief has led many companies to a preoccupation with short-term financial results, particularly current-period reported earnings per share, and as a consequence has discouraged attention to research and development and capital investment with long-term payoffs. It is the most commonly cited justification for executive compensation and incentive systems that focus on short-term performance. But it simply isn't true. An examination of stock prices reveals that the market looks well into the future.

The financial community is obsessed with its own short-term performance. Portfolio managers compete frantically for the best ninety-day returns. They are constantly moving in and out of the market, in and out of individual stocks, often trying to outguess what other investors are about to do. This can lead to short-term fluctuations in the stock price that, in the view of management, have little connection with a company's long-term opportunities and prospects.

But it is important to distinguish between the daily scurrying of investors and the forces that determine market prices. Any reasonable reading of the market shows that prices behave as if the market cares most about companies' long-term prospects, even though the financial community appears to emphasize short-term financial results.[4] The most plausible explanation of this seeming paradox is that investors often see long-term implications in current information, including reported earnings, and use the latest results to reassess a company's prospects.

For example, an announcement of a major writedown in earnings may lead to a significant increase in share price, if it results from a decision by management to cut its losses and abandon an unprofitable line of business (such as Lockheed's L-1011 program and RCA's videodisk business). In such situations, the market doesn't appear to be reacting to the unexpected decrease in current earnings per se, but rather to the projected longer-term consequences of redeployment of corporate resources.

There is evidence that the market discriminates between changes in earnings per share that are and are not expected to affect future cash flow. The market isn't fooled by changes in accounting methods—for instance, studies have shown that a switch from accelerated to straight-line depreciation, which alters reported EPS but not expected cash flows, does not affect stock prices.

In a world of economic, technological, and political uncertainty, some might question how the market can reasonably assign so much value to expectations beyond five years. But a high value growth option as a percent of the current market price of a stock is a signal of the market's confidence that well-managed companies with strong current competitive positions and an ability to adapt are likely to do well in any future product-market scenario. This interpretation is consistent with the widely held view that the market pays a premium for companies providing evidence of a sustainable competitive advantage.

Management Implications

Having distinguished between corporate versus shareholder rate of return and also having provided a systematic approach to reading the market, we now turn to the management implications of this analysis for setting hurdle rates for investment, developing performance standards for executive compensation, and investor communications.

Hurdle Rates

To calculate present value, cash flows are discounted by the rate of return available to investors for comparable investment alternatives. This rate of return is commonly referred to as the "hurdle rate" in corporate capital budgeting systems. A comprehensive study of the cost of capital practices of major U.S. firms was recently conducted by Gitman and Mercurio.[5] They sent a questionnaire to the chief financial officer of each firm in the 1980 Fortune 1000 listing. Nearly 95 percent of the 177 respondents were involved in manufacturing.

The study found more than 87 percent of the firms use a weighted average cost of capital as a hurdle rate for making financial decisions. Of the firms using a cost of capital approach, the majority use target capital structure weights. The most frequently used approach to calculating the cost of equity is the "return required by investors." At a time (October 1980) when the yield on government bonds was about 12.4 percent, most companies estimated their cost of capital to be in the 13 to 17 percent range. Finally, a majority of the respondents differentiate between the risk of capital projects by developing various hurdle rates.

The Gitman-Mercurio study provides evidence that major U.S. companies develop cost of capital estimates along the lines described in Chapter 3 as hurdle rates for capital budgeting decisions. Recall that if the stock market expected the company to invest *at* the cost of capital or hurdle rate, the shares would be priced at their prestrategy value. When the company's shares are priced above the prestrategy value, the market is signaling its expectation that the company will have opportunities to invest at above the hurdle rate. In this situation, investment at only the hurdle rate level will presumably lead to a lowering of expectations and will not enable present shareholders to earn their required rate of return. For example, if IBM set its hurdle rate at its 14 percent cost of capital and its investment projects typically yielded near the hurdle rate, then its present price would be difficult to justify. Recall that if the investor is to earn his 14 percent rate of return on the current price of IBM shares, then

IBM's corporate rate of return must be 24.5 percent. Nonetheless, investment above the cost of capital rate, even at a rate below the corporate rate of return implied by the market price, is preferable to the alternative of distributing the investment funds as dividends. This is true because shareholders who would then invest in similar risk opportunities elsewhere can be expected to earn no more than the cost of capital rate.

The disparity between the hurdle rate and the required corporate rate of return implied by the market price of a company's shares can pose a genuine dilemma for management. On the one hand, one can argue that a 14 percent hurdle rate for a company whose price implies investment opportunities yielding on average 24.5 percent is simply too low. However, if the hurdle rate is properly viewed as the *minimum* acceptable return and management believes that collectively its investments will yield approximately the rate implied by the market price, then the 14 percent hurdle rate becomes much more reasonable. In setting hurdle rates, management needs to consider the following questions:

- Are market expectations reasonable in light of the company's long-term plans and other information available to management?
- At what level should hurdle rates be set so as to maximize value creation potential?

If management believes market expectations are unduly pessimistic or optimistic, then the required corporate rates of return implied by these market prices are correspondingly low or high as well. For example, as shown in Table 7–3, if market estimates of the sales growth rate and profit margin are 2 percent and 1 percent too high, respectively, then IBM's required corporate rate of return decreases from 24.5 percent to 22.0 percent. Once management has developed an estimate of the market implied corporate rate of return and then its own forecast, it is in a better position to choose a reasonable target rate of return. Then the issue shifts to choosing a level of hurdle rates that will provide the best opportunity to achieve the target corporate rate of return and more generally maximize the company's value creation potential.

Hurdle rates need to be evaluated in terms of whether they have a desirable effect on managers' behavior. To what extent will altering a hurdle rate affect managers' efforts devoted to searching out investment opportunities in new products, additional capacity, cost-reduction projects and replacement projects? Do hurdle rates set at the cost of capital rate limit managers' motivation to seek extraordinary but more risky opportunities that can earn substantially above the hurdle rate? Would setting hurdle rates above the cost of capital rate exclude from consideration value-creating projects that are important to the firm's future? Or would setting hurdle rates above the cost of capital simply induce some managers to forecast more robust returns for these lower return projects?

Regardless of how an organization answers the above questions, understanding market expectations is an essential part of the process of setting reasonable internal performance standards. This is also a good time to emphasize once again that investing in projects that yield rates of return above the hurdle rate provides no guarantee of corporate value creation because projects reviewed under capital budgeting systems account for only a fraction of a company's total expenditures. Recall my earlier plea to invest in strategies, not projects. If investors are to earn their required rates of return, then the corporate rate of return on *strategies* must be at a level consistent with the present market price of the company's shares. The appropriation requests to fund individual projects coming from operating units should meet at least two tests. First, each expenditure should be consistent with the previously approved strategy. Second, the project should have the greatest value creation potential among all realistically competing options. In brief, projects should support strategies in the most productive available manner.

Performance Evaluation

Because Chapter 8 will be devoted to a more detailed analysis of performance evaluation and executive compensation, the present discussion will be relatively brief. The framework for reading the market does have some important implications for designing performance evaluation and executive incentive systems. As depicted in Figure 7–2, three rates of return are relevant to assessing the performance of a business—the cost of capital, the corporate rate of return implied by the current price of the company's shares, and management's forecast of the corporate rate of return. The difference between the corporate rate of return implied by the stock price and the cost of capital represents a market expectations premium. In the

IBM case, for example, the required corporate rate of return of 24.5 percent compared to its 14 percent cost of capital leads to a market expectations premium of 10.5 percent. If IBM management, based on its strategic plan, were to forecast a 20 percent corporate rate of return, a planning shortfall of 4.5 percent from market expectations would materialize. The difference between the market expectation premium of 10.5 percent and the planning shortfall of 4.5 percent represents the portion (6 percent) of the market expectations premium that management expects to satisfy.

The central issue is by what threshold standard should the business and its managers be evaluated? The rates of return depicted in Figure 7–2 offer three alternative standards: the cost of capital, the corporate rate of return implied by the market price, or the corporate rate of return forecast by management. One possibility is to evaluate and reward managers on the basis of value creation. This approach would reward managers for investing at above the cost of capital. The argument in favor of this approach is simply that the essence of corporate strategy is to develop sustainable value creation and managers who contribute to its accomplishment should be rewarded commensurately. Others might argue that using the cost of capital as a hurdle rate ignores the market expectations premium and thereby rewards managers for a level of performance which is below that needed for shareholders to realize their required return.

This brings us to the second possibility, the corporate rate of return implied by the market price, which does fully incorporate market expectations. Those who favor this standard would undoubtedly argue that managers' interests should be aligned with those of present shareholders and therefore managers should be rewarded only when they meet or exceed market expectations. One immediate

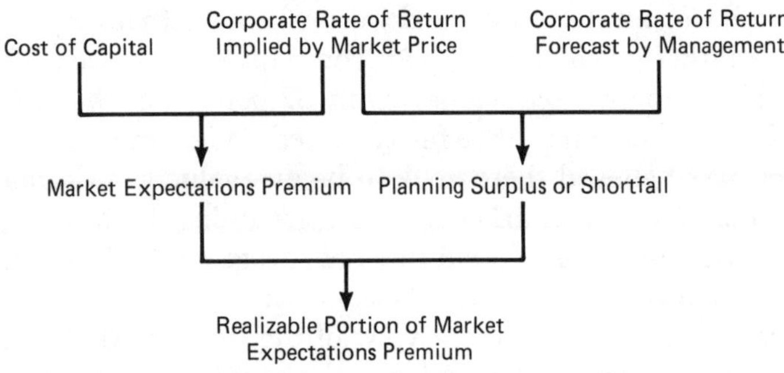

Figure 7–2 Market Expectations Versus Management Forecast

problem is that management may possess proprietary information not presently available to the market. Stated in more general terms, management may believe that market expectations are either too robust or too modest and, in either case, should not serve as a foundation for internal performance evaluation.

The third and final possibility is the corporate rate of return forecast by management. This approach would essentially use the plan as the threshold standard of performance. Those who favor this approach might argue that a sound plan emerging from a comprehensive competitive analysis process is not only the most logical standard, but most importantly the standard to which managers have made an organizational commitment. Critics of this standard would assert that either it fails to incorporate market expectations or that managerial rewards should be made for value creation per se and not for either a higher or lower standard. These issues and some suggested resolutions will be discussed in Chapter 8.

Investor Communications

In Chapter 5 the importance of conducting a corporate financial self-evaluation as part of the strategic planning process was emphasized. Estimating the value of the company based on management projections is critical to decisions such as selling new shares, stock repurchases, divestments, and financing of major investments including acquisitions. Reconciling management valuations with market prices becomes particularly important when there are significant disparities between the two.

In a survey conducted in January 1984 by Louis Harris & Associates, top executives of more than 600 companies drawn from *Business Week*'s Corporate Scoreboard were asked whether they believed that the market price of their own company's stock accurately reflected the company's real value.[6] Only 32 percent of the executives believed that their shares were fairly valued. While only 2 percent of the executives believed their stock to be overvalued, a dramatic 60 percent believed the market was undervaluing their company's stock. In addition, more than a third of this group believed that the market "seriously" undervalued the company.

How can this management view of the stock market be reconciled with the evidence gathered over the past twenty years that the market is reasonably efficient?[7] In an efficient market, prices reflect available information. Furthermore, when unexpected information that affects the prospects of the firm becomes available the stock price will respond quickly and without bias to this information. Users may differ about the significance of the new information, but the price arrived at in an efficient market would represent the best *current* interpretation of the information. An important implication of the efficient market is that investors should not expect to earn consistent above-average returns from analyses of published information.

Many readers may well believe that markets are not nearly as efficient as many academic studies suggest. My intent is not to introduce the controversy over efficient markets, but rather to demonstrate that management's view that the market undervalues its shares can be due to reasons that do not negate the idea that the stock market is efficient. There may be several reasons for disagreement between management and the stock market. First, in many companies management has not conducted a detailed corporate self-evaluation and consequently the belief that the market is undervaluing its stock is intuitive rather than being supported by analysis. Second, management may possess information, relevant to the future prospects of the firm, that has not been communicated to the financial markets. Recall, that in an efficient market prices reflect *available* information. Third, even though management and the market may have essentially the same information, management may well have a systematically more optimistic set of projections than those implied by the current stock price. None of these three reasons provides a basis for making judgments about market efficiency. In the first case management simply has no substantive basis for its belief about undervaluation. In the second case, the market does not have the relevant information to process. And finally, in the third case, valuation disagreements evolve from management optimism.

What role can investor communications play in a reasonably efficient market? The fundamental purpose of investor communications is to provide information, within competitive limits, that enables security analysts and investors to make soundly based forecasts of the value drivers. Sharpening an analyst's ability to forecast cash flows entails:

- Explaining the business and the environment in which the business operates so that the market does not discount the stock for something it does not understand.

- Emphasizing future prospects rather than historical performance. The past is relevant only to the extent that it helps an investor assess future prospects.
- Focusing on strategies and opportunities for long-term value enhancement rather than the outlook for the near term. Long-term values usually carry more weight than short-term performance.
- Avoiding the creation of over-expectations, because when actual results fall short of expectations the reaction usually more than offsets any benefit that may have been gained by a temporary run up of market values.
- Facing bad news openly so that investors are not left with the impression that management does not understand their problems.[8]

There are arguably more limited benefits for investor communications in an efficient market. Nonetheless if, after conducting its analysis, management believes its company's shares to be undervalued, a genuine opportunity may exist. This is the case because management-perceived undervaluation in an efficient market is most likely due to a failure clearly to communicate corporate strategies and prospects to the market. Certainly undervaluation is not in the best interests of present shareholders.

Management is not the only group that has come to believe that corporate shares are undervalued. So-called corporate raiders such as Carl Icahn, Irwin Jacobs, and T. Boone Pickens have also discovered "undervaluation." Unlike many managements who see undervaluation to be a failure on the part of the stock market, the raiders or "takeover entrepreneurs" see these same prices as an indictment of incumbent management and as an opportunity to buy companies and implement substantially improved value-creating strategies. In many cases, the question is simply whether the needed restructuring will be done by incumbent management or by new management after a takeover. If incumbent management intends to pursue a new value-creating strategy, a critical role of investor communications is to share this information with the financial community. Indeed, if the strategy is seen to be credible, the rise in the company's share price may provide an opportunity for current management, rather than a new management team, to execute the strategy.

PART ***III***

Additional Shareholder Value Applications

Chapter 8

Performance Evaluation and Executive Compensation

PROPERLY DESIGNED PERFORMANCE MEASURES and executive incentive compensation schemes are central to the value creation process. Their purpose is straightforward—to motivate managers to create value by rewarding them for value created. A fundamental requirement for successful planning and performance evaluation systems is that performance measurements be consistent with those established in the planning process. When performance evaluation and incentives differ from measurement standards employed in planning, decision making will be motivated by the performance evaluation system and not the planning system. Performance evaluation and compensation affect *implemented* strategy. For example, companies that employ long-range planning, but tie performance incentives largely to short-term performance will motivate a short-term emphasis in management decision making.

This chapter reviews some of the major shortcomings in existing executive compensation plans. Incentive compensation is then viewed as an essential instrument for integrating the interests of management and shareholders. After developing the basis for selecting performance standards, alternative approaches such as stock market versus corporate financial measures and relative versus absolute standards are assessed. In all of this discussion, care is taken to distinguish between designing value-creating motivational systems at the business unit versus the corporate level. Finally, a detailed application of the shareholder value approach to performance evaluation and executive incentives is presented.

Shortcomings of Existing Systems

Executive compensation has come under increasing attack during the past few years. According to a 1984 Louis Harris poll 76 percent of the American public believes that top corporate executives are not worth the salaries and bonuses they receive.[1] Peter Drucker contends that resentment over top-management compensation is by no means confined to unions and rank-and-file employees, but extends up in the ranks of professionals and managers as well. Drucker recommends that executives limit their compensation package to some multiple of the total compensation package of the rank and file.[2]

The focus here will be the relationship between compensation and performance rather than on the level of executive compensation. Indeed, in my judgment, much of the rhetoric on "excessive" compensation is based on a perception of inadequate performance by management rather than excessive compensation per se. Graef Crystal, a well-known compensation consultant, expressed this viewpoint as follows:

> Boards of directors, individual shareholders, and large institutions have got to clean up their own acts with respect to corporations that have poor performance and then make that performance even poorer by offering outrageous amounts of compensation to demonstrably incompetent executives.[3]

The concept of "pay-for-performance" is widely accepted by board members, top management, compensation consultants, and stockholders. Nonetheless, executive compensation continues to come under increasing criticism. Citing a 10 percent real dollar increase from 1971 to 1981 in total compensation of senior management in the Standard & Poor's 400, while total shareholder value (stock price change plus dividends) decreased 2 percent in real dollars, the head of Booz Allen & Hamilton's executive compensation practice has commented that "executive compensation programs in too many U.S. corporations have rewarded executives handsomely for performance that has not benefited shareholders equally."[4]

Shareholder and management interests were more closely tied during the 1950s and 1960s when stock option plans that enabled corporate-level executives to benefit from share price increases were a more significant part of executive compensation packages. The stock market's performance during much of the 1970s made options substantially less valuable. Indeed, many options were never exercised. Beginning in the early 1970s, many companies shifted their emphasis from stock options to performance plans that reward executives for the accomplishment of three- to five-year financial performance goals. By 1981, 82 of the 200 largest industrial companies had adopted performance plans. All use accounting numbers for establishing performance standards, either earnings-per-share growth, accounting return on investment, or some combination of the two. All but six of the companies have made grants to executives.[5]

The apparent lack of association between shareholder returns and increases in executive compensation raises the essential question of whether existing compensation programs motivate executives to pursue strategies that promise to create economic value for shareholders. Existing compensation programs often incorporate three major roadblocks to the selection and execution of value-creating strategies by corporate executives:

- The increased-pay-for-increased-size phenomenon
- The relatively heavy weighting attached to short-term performance in incentive compensation packages
- The invariable reliance on such accounting measures as earnings and return on investment rather than economic performance measures for both short- and long-term incentive plans.

The relatively high association between firm size and executive compensation can only further fuel managements' natural inclination to grow businesses as fast as possible. There is no economic virtue in growth per se. "Bigger" does not automatically lead to "better." Economic value will be created only if the company is investing at a rate of return greater than that demanded by investors in the securities market.

Despite the recent introduction of multiyear performance plans, in many companies they are not likely to offset the more immediate short-term pressures because typically fewer than one third of the managers participating in annual bonus plans are included in the long-term performance incentive plans. Additionally, the annual bonus usually constitutes a greater percentage of total compensation than long-term incentives for chairmen, CEOs, and profit center managers. Given the pervasiveness of annual bonus plans, which reward executives primarily for one-year earnings results, it should come as no surprise that short-term earnings have become an essential, if not the dominant, criterion in decision making.

The dysfunctional consequences introduced by the increased-pay-for-increased-size philosophy and the overemphasis on short-term results are exacerbated by the universal use of accounting numbers for assessing both short- and long-term performance. As shown in Chapter 2, earnings growth can be achieved not only when management is investing at a rate of return above that demanded by the market, but also when it is investing below the market rate and thereby decreasing the value of the common shares. As previously discussed, many companies achieved impressive double-digit, annual earnings-per-share growth rates during the 1970s, while providing their shareholders minimal or negative rates of return from dividends plus share price changes. In sum, the problem associated with performance measurement is not only the undue emphasis on the short term, but also the more fundamental problem of measurements based on an inappropriate bottom line.

Selecting Performance Measures

The separation of ownership and control in large, publicly held corporations has contributed to some conflicts of interest between management and shareholders. Executive compensation tied to shareholder value performance represents an important means of reducing such conflicts. A well designed compensation system in itself represents a source of value by aligning management incentives more closely with shareholder interests.

Lambert and Larcker[6] list three principal kinds of conflicts. First, executives may derive nonpecuniary benefits from corporate jets or other expenditures that have a higher value to management than to shareholders. Some evidence of this phenomenon becomes apparent when management takes a public company private via a leveraged buyout. With a substantially greater ownership stake, management often introduces "mean-and-lean" cost control tactics that did not exist under public ownership.

A second source of potential conflict is due to different attitudes toward risk by managers and shareholders. It is reasonable to expect that corporate executives, acting only as economic agents, have a lower tolerance for risk than do stockholders. Why? Because managers generally operate under an "asymmetrical reward function"—that is, the penalties of failing to meet some minimum performance standard appear to be much greater than the uncertain rewards for exceeding that standard. Moreover, if the company invests in a risky project, shareholders can always balance this risk against other risks in their presumably diversified portfolios. The manager, however, can balance any project failure only against the other activities of the division or the company. Thus a manager may reject a strategy that would benefit shareholders because the perceived personal risks are too high.

The third potential conflict materializes from differences in decision-making time horizons of managers and shareholders. For example, a CEO's investment decision may be evaluated by the board over a shorter time period than that used by shareholders for evaluating the same investment decisions. This perception may well compel the CEO to place undue weight on short-term earnings rather than assess value creation potential over the full life of the investments.

In subsequent discussions of performance measures, it will be useful to consider to what extent each alternative measure is likely to reduce these three major conflicts—nonpecuniary benefits, risk, and decision-making time horizons.

Criteria for Performance Measures

Successful performance measures should meet a number of fundamental criteria. First and foremost, they must be valid (i.e., the measures should be consistent with basic economic theory of value). Without this critical criterion, there is no assurance that executives are "making the right numbers." Second, performance measures should be verifible, that is, they should be calculated unambiguously from readily available data and therefore not easily manipulated. Third, if a performance measure is used to assess an executive, he or she should have a reasonable degree of control over the results being measured. Fourth, the measures should be global. They should be relevant to the performance of the company's various operating units, the company as a whole as well as the comparative performance of competitors. Finally, the measures need to be communicable, that is, easily explained both inside the organization and to the company's external constituencies.

The focus at this point is on two of the foregoing criteria—validity and controllability. There are two essential sources for valid measures of value creation—the stock market and the company. As will be demonstrated, the choice of market versus corporate measures is largely dictated by the controllability criterion. For example, individual business unit managers have little impact on the company's stock price. Another major issue that must be resolved in designing executive incentives is whether performance will be judged in absolute or relative terms.

Limitations of Market-Based Incentives

Why not simply tie executive incentives to shareholders' return as measured by dividends plus market appreciation? Certainly that method would be the most direct means of linking top management's interests with those of shareholders. But exclusive reliance on market returns has its own limitations. First, movements in a company's stock price may well be greatly influenced by factors beyond management control, such as the overall state of the economy and stock market. Second, market returns may be materially influenced by what management believes to be unduly optimistic or pessimistic expectations at the beginning or end of the performance measurement period. And third, divisional and business unit performance cannot be directly linked to stock price. The same limitation applies to private companies.

Some would assert that executives should bear not only the company-specific risks but also the systematic risks of the overall market that investors cannot diversify away. Others believe that general economic conditions beyond management's control should not determine the level of executive incentives because such incentives fail to communicate clear performance objectives to management. Tying incentive compensation to the company's stock price also increases the executive's exposure to risk. This increased risk exposure may cause the executive to become more conservative than the shareholders who can balance risky investments against other investments in their diversified portfolios. In addition, the exposure to market risk reduces the value of the compensation package and therefore would require some commensurate increase in total compensation. The market's lackluster performance during the 1970s appreciably diminished the value of stock options and other incentives tied to stock price and thereby set the stage for accounting-based performance plans. Booz Allen reports that the proportion of total CEO compensation attributable to option gains declined from 35 percent in 1966 to 6 percent in 1981. A number of compensation consultants assert that the shift from options to performance plans that reward managers for meeting three- to five-year earnings goals represents an unfortunate movement toward pay delivery and away from shareholder value creation.[7]

It is possible to estimate the portion of a stock's price movement that is attributable to company performance rather than to general market movements. One approach is to characterize deviations from a company's expected stock price volatility relative to the market as an approximation of the company-specific impact on stock price. Ubelhart[8] has applied this approach to a market-indexed stock option plan with the following example. Assume the company provides options at its current market value of $100 per share. Suppose that over a specified duration the overall market increases by 20 percent. The company's historical and expected volatility index (e.g., beta) relative to the market is 1.25. Thus, if the market goes up by 20 percent, the stock is expected to go up by 25 percent (i.e., 20 percent times 1.25). The new option price is then the original price of $100 plus the market-indexed change of $25 or $125. Option holders would only gain if the stock sold for more than $125. If the market decreased by 20 percent, the new option price would be $75. The option holders would benefit even in the face of a stock price decline as long as the price was greater than the $75 option price. Of course, this approach can be modified to permit overall market changes to affect incentives by various degrees. In summary, market returns for factors generally beyond management control can be adjusted for, but such quantification does require subjective judgments.

The problem that market-based incentives can be affected by unduly optimistic or pessimistic expectations is more difficult to resolve. Management's belief that the market is over- or undervaluing its company's shares does not negate "market efficiency." The most widely accepted form of market efficiency states that prices quickly reflect all publicly available information relevant to an assessment of a company's activities and prospects. In contrast, management's expectations are based not only on publicly available information, but also on more detailed inside knowledge of the company's operations.

For example, suppose the chief executive officer is offered a multiyear performance plan based on stock market appreciation in the company's future. If the CEO believes the shares to be overvalued, the incentive may seem unattractive because of the expected limitations of the future rate of stock appreciation. The CEO may well argue that revision of investor expectations about the current state of the business rather than performance over the next few years will dominate the expected stock price change. If the CEO believes the company is currently undervalued rather than overvalued, a multiyear incentive based on stock appreciation may be seen as a potential "windfall" gain.

The third problem associated with stock market-based incentives is the difficulty of linking divisional performance to the stock price, which assesses the company's consolidated performance and not that of individual operating units. This poses no problem for incentives at the corporate level, but does for executives at the divisional and business unit levels.

In summary, linking executive incentives directly to the market performance of the company's stock can tie management's interests more closely with those of shareholders. However, the acceptance of stock market risk may move management to become more risk averse than is desirable from the standpoint of shareholders. Market-based incentives are primarily relevant to corporate-level executives. For executives of private companies and individual business units within publicly held companies, long-term incentives based on financial performance objectives such as value creation offer a more meaningful and direct link for supporting business strategies.

Absolute Versus Relative Performance

Relative performance approaches to executive compensation are based on how well the company performs relative to a selected peer group. Relative performance measures remove macroeconomic and industry-related factors which are beyond management's control and thereby separate out management's distinctive contribution.

There are two essential issues. The first issue involves the merits of absolute versus relative plans, while the second issue relates to the alternative measures that need to be considered in developing relative performance plans.

Some of those who oppose relative performance plans assert that shareholders are best served when management is subject to the same risks and rewards as shareholders themselves. Jude T. Rich, a well-known compensation consultant, states this viewpoint emphatically:

> As a shareholder I would say that for every dollar I get in stock appreciation plus dividends, I'll give you—the manager—so many cents. During depressions shareholders lost fortunes and employees were thrown out of work. Why should executives make a lot of money in such a situation? The fact that circumstances are beyond their control is not an issue. If a company doesn't do well, executives shouldn't.[9]

Another concern associated with relative performance plans is that they may dilute management's incentive to exit from unattractive businesses that offer returns below the cost of capital. By removing industry-related factors, management's performance relative to its peers in the industry may well be strong, but any new strategic investments may at the same time decrease shareholder value. Relative performance measures in structurally unattractive industries such as the steel industry may thus provide unwarranted signals of optimism to management and more significantly may provide improper incentives for strategic decision making.

Relative performance plans based on shareholder return do overcome one of the principal limitations of stock market-based incentives discussed earlier. When a relative measure is employed, economy and industry factors beyond management control are excluded. Furthermore, a relative shareholder return target reinforces management's primary objective of creating value for shareholders.

Johnson Controls recently initiated a particularly innovative relative shareholder return plan as a long-term incentive for two of its senior executives. The seven-year plan began October 1, 1983. Each executive has a designated "plan base amount" ($300,000 and $100,000, respectively). The annual award is an amount equal to a percentage of the plan base amount. The percentage can vary from zero to 150 percent depending upon a comparison of the company's average annual total shareholder return (stock price appreciation plus total dividends per share) for the most recent ten years and the average annual total shareholder return of a number of similar Fortune 500 companies. The seven-year performance period extends approximately three years beyond the retirement of the two executives.[10] This plan thus not only removes market risk, but also attempts to reduce differences in decision-making time horizons of managers and shareholders by extending the performance period beyond the executives' retirement dates.

One of the greatest difficulties in designing relative performance plans is finding an appropriate peer group. For companies operating in well-defined industries such as banking, pharmaceuticals, and oil the task is relatively straightforward.[11] However, the diversification of so many companies into unrelated products and markets has substantially increased the problem of finding a relevant peer group of competitors. While the fundamental idea of gaining a sustainable competitive advantage is based on improving performance relative to peer companies, it can be argued that ultimately every management competes against the broader spectrum of the shareholders' market opportunities. Those who subscribe to this view would choose a broader market index such as Standard & Poor's index of 400 industrial companies as a benchmark for performance. Clevepak Corp., a manufacturer of industrial machinery and construction materials, recently adopted a plan for its top thirteen officers which awards bonuses after three years only if Clevepak's stock outperforms the index. If the stock does better than the index by 10 percent or more each year on average, the officers will receive up to 300 percent of their annual base salaries.[12]

The differences that can materialize in management evaluations when using a market index rather than a more delineated peer group of competitors is well illustrated in the case of Walter Wriston's 1970–1984 tenure as chairman and CEO of Citicorp. Callard Madden & Associates estimated the returns to Citicorp shareholders over the 1970–1984 period to be almost identical to the return on the Standard & Poor's 500 index. Wriston's critics point to this record as evidence that despite his aggressive leadership shareholders did not materially benefit. Wriston's supporters would point out that running a bank during that period was not a particularly lucrative business. Further, during Wriston's term Citicorp shareholders did considerably better than shareholders of other large U.S. banks—about

50 percent better than shareholders of Bank America, Manufacturers Hanover, and Chemical Bank and nearly 100 percent better than Chase Manhattan shareholders.[13]

The focus thus far has been on relative performance plans with market-based (shareholder return) measures of performance. As discussed earlier, market-based plans are primarily relevant to senior executives at the corporate level rather than business unit executives. Relative performance plans can, of course, use financial as well as market measures of performance. When financial measures used in relative performance plans are short-term or accounting-based such as earnings-per-share growth or accounting return on investment, the shortcomings are the same as in absolute performance plans—the performance targets are not reliably linked to the creation of shareholder value. Ranking at the top of a peer group in earnings-per-share growth, for example, provides little satisfaction to shareholders if such growth is accomplished with investments yielding less than the cost of capital. In the next section, the application of the shareholder value approach to performance evaluation and executive incentives using the same value drivers employed in the strategy valuation process will be presented.

Linking Strategy and Performance[14]

In Chapter 5, I demonstrated how, by estimating the future cash flows associated with each strategy, executives can assess the economic value to shareholders of alternative strategies at the business unit and corporate levels. This shareholder value approach provides a valid and consistent framework for not only evaluating strategic plans, but for measuring subsequent performance as well. After all, performance measurement needs to be tied directly to strategic plans to motivate effective implementation. Without this linkage, planning becomes an exercise with minimal organizational impact. An illustration will be used to present the concept and its detailed application.

Alpha Specialty Chemicals, Inc. manufactures and sells a wide range of products from plastic packaging, catalysts, and container sealant chemicals to graphic arts–related products. Three years ago, Alpha management developed a three-year plan. (The planned cash flows are presented as part of Table 8–1. The actual cash flows are

Table 8–1 Actual Versus Planned Three-Year Cash-Flow Statement ($ in millions)

	YEAR 1		YEAR 2		YEAR 3		TOTAL	
	Actual	*Plan*	*Actual*	*Plan*	*Actual*	*Plan*	*Actual*	*Plan*
Sales	$220.00	$230.00	$255.20	$264.50	$296.03	$304.17	$771.23	$798.67
Operating expenses[a]	191.40	195.50	216.92	224.83	251.63	258.55	659.95	678.88
Depreciation	6.90	6.90	7.83	7.93	9.20	9.12	23.93	23.95
	$198.30	$202.40	$224.75	$232.76	$260.83	$267.67	$683.88	$702.83
Operating profit	21.70	27.60	30.45	31.74	35.20	36.50	87.35	95.84
Income taxes on operating profit[b]	8.68	11.04	12.18	12.70	14.08	14.60	34.94	38.34
Operating profit after taxes	13.02	16.56	18.27	19.04	21.12	21.90	52.41	57.50
+ Depreciation	6.90	6.90	7.83	7.93	9.20	9.12	23.93	23.95
– Capital expenditure	14.90	15.90	18.39	18.28	21.45	21.02	54.74	55.20
– Increase in working capital	5.00	6.00	7.04	6.90	8.17	7.93	20.21	20.83
Cash flow	$ 0.02	$ 1.56	$ 0.67	$ 1.79	$ 0.70	$ 2.07	$ 1.39	$ 5.42

[a]Expensed investments such as for research and development are excluded from this "operating expense" category. They should be classified as an investment along with capital expenditures and incremental working capital. In this example, we assume the company has no significant expensed investments.

[b]Taxes currently payable, i.e., excludes deferred taxes.

presented as well and will be discussed subsequently.) In the year preceding the plan, Alpha's sales totaled $200 million, and its operating profit before interest and taxes was 12 percent of sales or $24 million. The three-year plan is based on the following assumptions:

Sales growth rate = 15%
Operating profit margin = 12%
Cash and residual value income tax rate = 40%
Incremental fixed capital investment = 30%
Incremental working capital investment = 20%

The planned shareholder value contribution of Alpha's strategy is calculated in Table 8–2. The cash flows for each of the three years are taken directly from Table 8–1 and are discounted at Alpha's 14 percent cost of capital. The residual value assumes that after the planning period the company's return on incremental investments will be equal to the risk-adjusted rate of return required by the market (i.e., the cost of capital). Recall that the value of a company is unaffected by growth when it is investing at the cost-of-capital rate. Thus, the assumption of no growth in cash flows after the planning period will yield an identical result. Stated in another fashion, the company's investment strategies after the forecast period are expected to have a net present value of zero. The residual value is then the present value of the cash-flow perpetuity beginning one year after the end of the planning period. The prestrategy value is calculated the same way except that it capitalizes the sustainable cash-flow level achieved during the year preceding the plan (period zero). Alpha's strategy creates value of $6.87 million: the present value of its forecasted cash flows ($4.15 million) plus its residual value of $105.58 million, less its prestrategy value of $102.86 million.

As stated earlier, successful performance measures must first and foremost be valid. Ideally, this means that the performance evaluation model is a mirror image of the company's value-oriented strategic planning model. Simply stated, performance incentives should be linked to corporate and business unit strategies. To estimate the value created by a plan, forecasted cash flows are discounted back to the present. In contrast, performance evaluation takes place at the end of the period and thus focuses on value created at that time. The transformation from a planning perspective to a performance evaluation perspective can be achieved with relative ease. To accomplish this I have converted the present value created

Table 8–2 Present Value Created by Strategy ($ in millions)

YEAR	CASH FLOW	PRESENT VALUE
1	$1.56	$1.37
2	1.79	1.38
3	2.07	1.40
		$4.15
Plus: Residual value		105.58[a]
Less: Prestrategy value		102.86[b]
Present value created by strategy		$6.87

[a] $\dfrac{\text{Year 3 cash flow before new investment }(1 - \text{Residual value tax rate})}{\text{Cost of capital }(1 + \text{Cost of capital})^3}$

$= \dfrac{36.50\ (1 - .40)}{.14(1 + .14)^3} = 105.58$

[b] $\dfrac{\text{Year 0 cash flow before new investment }(1 - \text{Residual value tax rate})}{\text{Cost of capital}}$

$= \dfrac{24.00\ (1 - .40)}{.14} = 102.86$

by Alpha's three-year plan (Table 8–2) to future value terms in Table 8–3 by simply compounding all cash flows forward to the performance measurement date. Thus, the future value creation is simply the present value creation compounded at the cost of capital rate for the length of the planning period. This approach provides a direct linkage between strategic planning and performance measurement and a sound benchmark for assessing performance.

Before elaborating further on the use of the future value approach to performance measurement, it would be useful to examine the relationship between this value creation measure and the expected rate of return to shareholders. If the market fully anticipates management's strategy and there is no change in the market's expectations, then next period's market value will be equal to the current market value compounded by the discount rate less any dividends. For purposes of simplicity, assume that Alpha has no outstanding debt and thus its discount rate is its cost of equity capital.

$$\text{Next period's market value} = \text{Current market value }(1 + \text{Cost of equity capital}) - \text{Dividends} \quad (1)$$

Under the assumption of no change in market expectations, shareholders will earn a rate of return from dividends plus capital gains of exactly the discount rate. From equation (1) we obtain:

$$\text{Shareholder rate of return} = \frac{(\text{Next period's market value} - \text{Current market value}) + \text{Dividends}}{\text{Current market value}} \quad (2)$$

If market expectations were identical to Alpha plan presented in Table 8–2, then the current market value of Alpha would be the present value of the next three years' cash flows ($4.15 million) plus the residual value ($105.58 million), or $109.73 million.[15] If the first year's results materialize as planned and expectations hold, Alpha's market value at the end of year 1 can be calculated as follows:

Year	Cash Flow	Present Value at the End of Year One
2	$1.79	$1.57
3	2.07	1.59

$$\text{Residual value} = \frac{\text{Year 3 cash flow before new investment } (1 - \text{Residual value tax rate})}{\text{Cost of capital } (1 + \text{Cost of capital})^2}$$

$$= \frac{36.50\,(1 - .40)}{.14\,(1.14)^2} \qquad \underline{120.37}$$

$$\underline{\underline{\$123.53}}$$

As expected, the application of equation (1) yields an identical result:

$$\begin{aligned} \text{Next period's value} &= 109.73\,(1 + .14) - 1.56 \\ &= \$123.53 \text{ million} \end{aligned}$$

And again, as expected, employing equation (2) the rate of return earned by Alpha shareholders is identical to the 14 percent discount rate.

$$\begin{aligned} \text{Shareholder rate of return} &= \frac{(123.53 - 109.73) + 1.56}{109.73} \\ &= 14\% \end{aligned}$$

If the market fails to recognize the value creation potential of prospective management strategies, then the current market price

Table 8–3 Future Value Created by Strategy
($ in millions)

Year	Cash Flow	14% Compounding Factor	Future Value
1	$1.56	1.30	$2.03
2	1.79	1.14	2.04
3	2.07	1.00	2.07
			$6.14
Plus: Residual value			156.43[a]
Less: Compounded prestrategy value			152.39[b]
Future value created by strategy			$10.18[c]

[a] $\frac{\text{Year 3 cash flow before new investment (1 − Residual value tax rate)}}{\text{Cost of capital}}$

$= \frac{36.50\,(1 - .40)}{.14} = 156.43$

[b] $\frac{\text{Year 0 cash flow before new investment (1 − Residual value tax rate)} \; (1 + \text{Cost of capital})^3}{\text{Cost of capital}}$

$= \frac{24.00\,(1 - .40)\,(1 + .14)^3}{.14} = 152.39$

[c] Future value creation = Present value creation $(1 + \text{Cost of capital})^3$
$10.18 = 6.87\,(1/14)^3$

may well be closer to the prestrategy value than the internally calculated value. When this is the case and the company subsequently demonstrates value by investing in strategies that yield more than the market discount rate, the market can be expected to revise its expectations upwards and shareholders will earn more than the discount rate. The reverse will be true if the company invests in strategies yielding less than the market discount rate. In summary, there is a sound economic basis for using internal value creation measures as a basis for assessing both strategies and subsequent performance.

Table 8–1 presents the actual compared to planned cash flows for the three-year planning period. The differences result in an unfavorable value creation variance of $10.22 million for the three-year period as calculated in Table 8–4. For purposes of effective feedback, management needs to know not only the amounts of the value variances, but also their essential causes if corrective steps are to be initiated. With this in mind, a more detailed analysis of the first year's value creation variances is developed in Table 8–5. The

Table 8–4 Value Creation Variance for Three-Year Strategy ($ in millions)

	Cash Flow			14%	Future
Year	*Actual*	*Planned*	*Variance*	Compound Factor	Value Variance
1	$0.02	$1.56	$1.54U	1.30	$2.00U
2	0.67	1.79	1.12U	1.14	1.28U
3	0.70	2.07	1.37U	1.00	1.37U
Poststrategy value	150.86	156.43	5.57U	1.00	5.57U
Total					$10.22U

U—Denotes unfavorable variance

first three columns depict the actual, planned, and variance in value created by major account classifications. Of the $26.83 million unfavorable variance, $1.54 million is due to a cash flow shortfall during the forecast period, while the remaining $25.29 million is due to an unfavorable variance in Alpha's residual value.

In the next three columns variances are categorized into three underlying causes: sales, margins, and investment. Of the $26.83 million unfavorable variance, $5.33 million is attributable to not achieving planned sales and $21.50 million to failure to achieve planned margins. The variances due to investment expenditures are offsetting. The detailed variance analysis in Table 8–5 follows the same approach used in more conventional profit variance analyses except here the focus is on shareholder value creation rather than profit.

Value Performance Incentive Plan

Value creation serves not only as an economically attractive measure of performance, but it can be used directly as a basis for executive incentives as well. Before outlining the structure of a value performance plan, a value creation table is presented in Table 8–6. The value creation table provides useful strategic insights as well as a basis for awarding incentives.

Alpha's target (future) value creation of $10.18 million for its three-year plan is based on projected 15 percent sales growth and 12

Table 8–5 Analysis of Year 1 Value Creation Variances ($ in millions)

	Value Creation			Variance Due to		
	Actual	*Plan*	*Variance*	*Sales*	*Margins*	*Investment*
Sales	$220.00	$230.00	$10.00U	$10.00U		
Operating expenses	191.40	195.50	4.10F	8.50F[d]	$ 4.40U[e]	
Depreciation	6.90	6.90	—			
	198.30	202.40	4.10F			
Operating profit	21.70	27.60	5.90U	1.50U	4.40U	
Income taxes on operating profit	8.68	11.04	2.36F	.60F[f]	1.76F[g]	
Operating profit after taxes	13.02	16.56	3.54U	.90U	2.64U	
+ Depreciation	6.90	6.90	—			
– Capital expenditures	14.90	15.90	1.00F			$1.00F
– Increase in working capital	5.00	6.00	1.00F	2.00F[h]		1.00U[i]
+ Residual value	93.00[a]	118.29[b]	25.29U	6.43U[j]	18.86U[k]	$0
– Compounded prestrategy value	117.26[c]	117.26[c]				
Value creation	$ (24.24)	$2.59	$26.83U	$5.33U	$21.50U	$0

[a] $\frac{\text{Actual cash flow before new investment (1 − Residual value tax rate)}}{\text{Cost of capital}} = \frac{21.70(1-.40)}{.14} = 93.00$

[b] $\frac{\text{Planned cash flow before new investment (1 − Residual value tax rate)}}{\text{Cost of capital}} = \frac{27.60(1-.40)}{.14} = 118.29$

[c] $\frac{\text{Operating profit (1 − Residual value tax rate)(1 + Cost of capital)}}{\text{Cost of capital}} = \frac{24(1-.40)(1+.14)}{.14} = 117.26$

[d] $(\text{Actual sales} - \text{Plan sales}) \times \frac{\text{Plan operating expenses}}{\text{Plan sales}} = (220.00 - 230.00) \times \frac{195.50}{230.00} = 8.50\text{F}$

[e] $\text{Actual operating expenses} - [(\text{Actual sales}) \times \frac{\text{Plan operating expenses}}{\text{Plan sales}}] = 191.40 - [(220.00) \times \frac{195.50}{230.00}] = 4.40\text{U}$

[f] (Sales variance on operating profit) × (Plan tax rate on operating profit) = 1.50 × .40 = .60F

[g] (Margin variance on operating profit) × (Plan tax rate on operating profit) = 4.40 × .40 = 1.76F

[h] (Actual sales − Plan sales) × (Plan working capital per dollar of sales increase) = (220.00 − 230.00) × (.20) = 2.00F

[i] (Actual increase in working capital) − (Actual sales increase) × (Plan working capital per dollar of sales increase) = 5.00 − (20)(.20) = 1.00U

[j] $\frac{\text{Sales variance on operating profit (1 − Residual value tax rate)}}{\text{Cost of capital}} = \frac{1.50(1-.40)}{.14} = 6.43\text{U}$

[k] $\frac{\text{Margin variance on operating profit (1 − Residual value tax rate)}}{\text{Cost of capital}} = \frac{4.40(1-.40)}{.14} = 18.86\text{U}$

U—Denotes unfavorable variance

F—Denotes favorable variance

Table 8–6 Value Creation Tables[a]

Value Creation ($ in millions)

		Sales Growth Rate				
		10%	14%	15%	16%	22%
Operating	11.75%	2.40	4.91	5.56	6.23	10.44
Profit	12.00%	6.49	9.42	[10.18]	10.95	15.86
Margins	12.25%	10.59	13.93	14.80	15.68	21.29

Performance Index (%)

		Sales Growth Rate				
		10%	14%	15%	16%	22%
Operating	11.75%	24	48	55	61	103
Profit	12.00%	64	93	[100]	108	156
Margins	12.25%	104	137	145	154	209

Value Creation Variances ($ in millions)

		Sales Growth Rate				
		10%	14%	15%	16%	22%
Operating	11.75%	−7.78	−5.27	−4.62	−3.95	0.26
Profit	12.00%	−3.69	−0.76	[0]	0.77	5.68
Margins	12.25%	0.41	3.75	4.62	5.50	11.11

[a]Assumed cost of capital = 14%; income tax rate = 40%; capital expenditures per dollar of sales increase = 30%; working capital investment per dollar of sales increase = 20%.

percent operating profit margin. Note that a 1 percent increase or decrease in sales growth—to 16 percent and 14 percent respectively—affects the value creation by approximately $0.75 million. In contrast, a 0.25 percent change (to 12.25 percent and 11.75 percent, respectively) in margins affects value by $4.6 million. The substantially greater value leverage from margin improvements relative to sales growth increases is motivating Alpha management to reconsider its current strategy, which is dominated by increasing market share. As an additional insight into the tradeoff between sales growth and margins, note that the $10.18 million value creation could also be achieved with less than 10 percent sales growth if margins were increased to 12.25 percent. Alternatively, if margins were to decrease to 11.75 percent, the sales growth rate would have to increase to about 22 percent to achieve the same value creation.

The value creation table in Table 8–6 is based on assumed rates of 30 percent and 20 percent per dollar of sales increase for investment in fixed and working capital, respectively. To provide further insights into strategic tradeoffs, value creation tables with various levels of investment intensity can be easily developed. For example, the target value creation would be affected by about $1.2 million for a 1 percent change in working capital required per dollar of sales.

The translation of value creation tables from performance evaluation guidelines to executive incentives is straightforward. Performance plans are one of the most popular forms of long-term incentives. The amount of incentive paid is contingent on the achievement of three- to five-year earnings-per-share or accounting ROI goals. These plans are of two types—performance units or performance shares. Under the performance unit plan, the dollar amount of compensation per unit is assigned at the beginning of the award period. In a performance share plan, the compensation per share is set by the company's market price per share at the end of the performance or award period. By substituting value creation for earnings-per-share or ROI as the reward criterion, performance plans can become an important motivational tool in directing management to develop strategies in the best long-run interests of the company and its shareholders. I will refer to this new incentive plan as a *value performance plan*. The development of a value performance plan involves the same steps required for conventional performance plans:

- Establish performance targets at the beginning of the award period
- Allocate to each executive a fixed number of units or shares at the beginning of the award period
- Develop an "earn out" formula for number of units or shares to be awarded based upon the degree to which performance goals are met during the award period

Returning to the Alpha case, the value creation target for the three-year plan was $10.18 million. Assume the board of directors approves a specified number of units or shares to eligible executives. One approach to determining the number of units or shares to be awarded is to award them on the basis of actual to target value creation. To facilitate this, each value creation entry is converted to a performance index with the target value assuming an index of 100 percent (see Table 8–6). For example, if margins were 12 percent and sales growth 14 percent, the resulting value of $9.42 million would be 92.5 percent of the target $10.18 million. Assuming 10,180 shares would be awarded for target level performance, in this example the executive would earn 92.5 percent of those shares, or 9420 shares. Alternatively, the award may be calculated as 10,180 shares plus or minus a specified number of shares, say 1000 shares, per $1 million of variance from targeted performance. Applying this formula to the $9.42 million value creation outcome, we have:

SHARES AWARDED IF TARGET LEVEL ACHIEVED		VALUE CREATION VARIANCE	SHARES PER $1 MILLION OF VARIANCE
10,180 shares	+	($9.42 – $10.18) = 9,420 shares	(1,000 shares)

One of the most difficult organizational challenges is to induce executives to share their true beliefs about prospects for the business. Business unit managers, for example, will often exaggerate longer-term product-market projections with the hope of competing more successfully in the intracompany capital allocation process. This is particularly true when incentives are based on the absolute performance targets rather than on the relationship between actual versus targeted performance. On the other hand, when incentives are tied to some predetermined performance targets, executives will normally be motivated to set relatively modest performance goals. Value performance plans have the desirable property of providing executives with little positive motivation to be misleading in their planning projections. Unlike earnings-based performance plans, more optimistic growth projections under a value performance plan are offset by the incremental investment requirements associated with faster growth. If such strategies are also judged more risky, the discount rate may rise as well. Thus, the idea of exaggerating prospects to gain more capital is substantially less attractive. If the participating executives were unduly pessimistic in their projections, they would run the active risk of not having strategies fully funded and perhaps even inviting serious consideration for redeploying their assets to more productive business opportunities.[16]

To provide a consistent framework for dealing with different investment risks and thereby increasing shareholder value, funds should be allocated to business units on a risk-adjusted return basis. Estimating a business unit's risk-adjusted cost of capital necessarily involves a substantial degree of judgment. While cost-of-capital judgments are critical to strategy assessment, awards under value performance plans can be designed to be largely independent of the chosen risk-adjusted discount rate. This is an important feature because if awards earned could be materially influenced by subjective estimates of the discount rate, the effectiveness of the plan could be seriously diminished by protracted controversy over the appropriate rate.

Suppose that Alpha's discount rate is estimated to be 15 percent rather than 14 percent. The value creation table in the top panel of Table 8–7 shows that the value of planned performance is now $6.19 million compared to $10.18 million for a 14 percent discount rate (Table 8–6). Assume that, as before, 10,180 shares are awarded for target level performance and also that the percent of award earned is based on the performance index. A comparison of the performance index results for 15 percent (see Table 8–7) and 14 percent (see Table 8–6) discount rates shows that the larger the discount rate the greater the volatility in the performance index. For the executive willing to entertain relatively more risk, the greater upside potential may well justify the greater downside risks. Indeed, if the market discount rate is estimated to be 15 percent, a full sharing of risk by executives would call for awards to be based on value creation numbers based on this same 15 percent rate.

Table 8–7 Value Creation Tables[a]

Value Creation ($ in millions)

		Sales Growth Rate		
		14%	15%	16%
Operating	11.75%	1.42	1.78	2.14
Profit	12.00%	5.73	[6.19]	6.66
Margins	12.25%	10.04	10.60	11.17

Performance Index (%)

		Sales Growth Rate		
		14%	15%	16%
Operating	11.75%	23	29	35
Profit	12.00%	93	[100]	108
Margins	12.25%	162	171	181

Value Creation Variances ($ in millions)

		Sales Growth Rate		
		14%	15%	16%
Operating	11.75%	−4.77	−4.41	−4.05
Profit	12.00%	−0.46	[0]	0.47
Margins	12.25%	3.85	4.41	4.98

[a]Assumed cost of capital = 15%; all other parameters are the same as in Table 8–6.

Many corporate executives may, however, have a lower tolerance for risk than their shareholders. If the company invests in a risky strategy, shareholders can balance this risk against other risks in a diversified portfolio. The corporate executive can ordinarily balance this risk only against the other activities of the company while the division-level executive ordinarily has no diversification potential.

By employing value creation *variances* for calculating performance plan awards, the awards become largely independent of the risk-adjusted discount rate selected. While the discount rate will certainly affect the size of the value created, the value creation variances are relatively insensitive to the choice of a discount rate. In fact, in most cases the value variances will be less rather than more for higher discount rates. This modestly reduces the incentive risk for executives operating relatively risky business units with higher discount rates. Suppose that, once again, Alpha's actual results were 12 percent margins and 14 percent sales growth; the value creation variance assuming a 15 percent discount rate is $ – 0.46 million (see Table 8–7). The number of shares to be awarded is then the 10,180 shares for target performance less 1000 shares per $1 million of unfavorable variance. This is equal to 10,180 less 460, or 9720 shares. This compares with $ – 0.76 million variance and an award of 9420 shares for a 14 percent discount rate.

To reinforce the importance of sustaining value beyond the long-term planning period, new value performance plans with new performance targets can be introduced annually or every second or third year. The introduction of a new value performance plan discourages executives from introducing nonstrategic, short-term decisions near the end of the plan to inflate residual value. This is the case because the "inflated" residual value of the current plan becomes the prestrategy value of the next plan. To further reinforce strategic plans and related value performance plans, intermediate targets for market share, productivity, product quality, and other strategic factors can be established for annual bonus plans.

Let us now evaluate briefly value performance plans versus conventional performance plans based on the five basic criteria presented earlier. Value performance plans clearly dominate accounting-based conventional performance plans on the criterion of *validity*. Value performance plans are based directly on the economic model of value, while earnings and accounting return on investment each provide, at best, an unreliable basis for estimating changes in the economic value of the firm. The shortcomings of conventional plans should not, however, be interpreted as a failure of accounting. The essential problem lies in the use of accrual accounting numbers, developed for *ex post* external reporting, for unintended, inappropriate purposes such as strategic planning, performance evaluation, and executive incentives. The role of top management is directly to assess the relationship between today's investments and the magnitude and timing of uncertain future cash flows and not to be influenced by arbitrary income determination conventions that do not affect cash flows. After all, in the final analysis, economic value is created by cash flows, not accounting conventions.

Value performance plans are also superior on the *verifiability* criterion. They are based solely on verifiable cash flows and thereby avoid the discretion and resulting controversy often associated with accounting numbers. The greater objectivity of cash flow measurement minimizes the discrepancy between performance and reward, thereby reinforcing the accomplishment of preestablished targets. Value performance plans require no data, except cost of capital estimates, not already required under conventional performance measurement systems. Thus the incremental data costs should be relatively modest.

The third criterion is *controllability*. The degree of control over the results being measured can be both greater and lesser in conventional systems compared to value performance plans. By judicious use of accounting choices (e.g., capitalization vs. expensing, changes in depreciation, or other accounting methods) executives can sometimes produce results that have little or no relation to what is going on strategically at the product, market, and technology levels. March says it particularly well:

> Executives in American industries make reputations by managing accounts rather than managing technology, service, or products. The statement is overdrawn. There are some important constraints. But there is a very real risk that our incentive schemes encourage too much attention to the management of accounts and too little attention to the management of the fundamental concerns of business.[17]

Interestingly, there are other circumstances where executives exercise less control under accounting-based performance plans. This is the case when performance plans are based on *reported* earnings and the Financial Accounting Standards Board has promulgated a new standard, say, in the area of foreign exchange. If an executive's award can be affected by decisions of an external accounting policy-making body that are unrelated to his strategic performance, the motivational effect is likely once again to be dysfunctional.

Value creation is a *global* measure that is equally relevant to executives whether they are at the corporate level or with one of the company's operating units. Indeed, value creation can serve as the economic objective that enables management to coordinate business unit planning with corporate planning. Effective value performance plans can therefore be developed for operating unit executives as well as for the top corporate officers.

Finally, there is the criterion of *communicability*. Value creation and the related executive incentive plan, the value performance plan, can be explained in an intuitively appealing and relatively easy manner to various levels of management and the company's constituencies including the financial community. To introduce the concept first internally and subsequently in his letter to shareholders appearing in the annual report, the CEO may communicate along the following lines:

> The company's primary financial objective is to provide shareholders with a rate of return on their investment which is at least equal to, and hopefully exceeds, the rate available on investments of comparable risk. Shareholders earn their return from the realization of cash from two sources—dividends and available proceeds from sale of their shares. The economic value of a shareholder's investment is the anticipated cash flow discounted by the minimum acceptable rate of return demanded to compensate for risk.
>
> During the past year, we have adopted the identical discounted cash flow approach for estimating the value created by any and all investments made by management in behalf of shareholders. We have for several years used this approach for assessing the economic attractiveness of major capital investment projects as well as for valuing prospective acquisition candidates. This year we have extended the shareholder value approach to incorporate the company's entire strategic plan. Management focuses on three essential questions: How much value will be created by the corporate plan? Which business units are expected to contribute value and which are not? How might alternative strategies affect shareholder value?
>
> To ensure that management at all levels is properly motivated to develop and implement value-creating strategies, long-term executive

> incentives tied directly to value creation targets will be introduced this year. These value performance plans will provide cash and stock awards to top corporate officers and business unit executives for the accomplishment of value creation targets.
>
> I believe that the introduction of value creation as the essential basis for assessing strategic plans and subsequent performance represents an important milestone in your company's continuing efforts to maximize its strategic opportunities and more closely link the interests of management with those of shareholders.

The supply of value-creating strategies developed in major corporations would increase if corporate incentives were directed toward their implementation. As long as the present emphasis on short-term accounting numbers persists, we can only speculate about the foregone opportunities of individual companies and the economy attributable to undeveloped strategies in search of compatible incentives. Value performance plans present a promising approach for motivating executives to make decisions consistent with the long-term interests of the company and thereby respond to shareholders who rightfully demand a reasonable return on executive incentives.

Chapter 9

Mergers and Acquisitions

SINCE THE MID-1970s we have been in the midst of a major wave of corporate acquisitions. In contrast to the 1960s, when acquirers were mainly freewheeling conglomerates, the merger movement of the 1970s and the 1980s includes such long-established giants of U.S. industry as Du Pont, Exxon, General Electric, General Motors, IBM, and U.S. Steel. Today acquisitions and divestitures are broadly considered to be a normal part of corporate strategy. The volume of transactions and the dollar value of mergers and acquisitions have risen to record levels (see Table 9–1). Moreover, the number of acquisitions involving a purchase price in excess of $1 billion has also increased substantially over the past few years. In 1984 and 1985 alone, there were 45 acquisitions with price tags exceeding $1 billion. These mega-mergers attest to the fact that very few companies are safe from a potential takeover.

The current merger movement also involves two relatively new players—the so-called raiders and the leveraged-buyout (LBO) firms. Raiders such as Carl Icahn, Sir James Goldsmith, Irwin Jacobs, and T. Boone Pickens look for undermanaged companies where changes in strategic direction could dramatically increase the value of the stock, and companies with high break-up values relative to their current stock price. LBO investment firms such as Wesray,

Table 9–1 Merger and Acquisition Statistics, 1980–1985

Year	Number of Transactions	Total Dollar Value (in billions)	Number of Transactions Over $1 Billion
1980	1,583	$ 36.3	4
1981	2,314	73.2	9
1982	2,321	66.1	11
1983	2,339	51.9	7
1984	3,064	125.2	19
1985	3,165	139.1	26

Source: The M&A Data Base, Philadelphia, PA.

Clayton and Dubiller, Forstmann Little, and Kohlberg, Kravis, Roberts have purchased divisions of public companies as well as major public companies and taken them private. Recent LBOs include such well-known companies as Beatrice, R. H. Macy, Northwest Industries, Levi Strauss, and Denny's. Both raiders and LBO firms have access to large pools of debt financing which enable them to take on highly leveraged capital structures. There is a growing concern that the rising tide of leveraged acquisitions and buyouts places an undue burden on cash flow to service debt and may restrict some companies from making future investments needed to remain competitive. The ultimate fear is that ambitious debt levels by acquiring companies can lead to bankruptcy as was the case for Baldwin-United, Saxon, Wickes, and others.

Finally, the recent merger movement involves the frequent use of tender offers that often lead to contested bids, and to the payment of substantial premiums above the pre-merger market value of the target company. It is not uncommon for acquisitions to be completed at premiums ranging from 50 percent to as much as 100 percent over pre-merger market price. To pay such a premium, management of the buying company must establish that the market is undervaluing the target or that it can dramatically change the target company's prospects. In most cases, this will prove to be a challenging assignment.

The need for careful deliberation by management and the board of directors rather than hastily improvised valuations developed in a feverish atmosphere was underscored in the recent landmark Trans Union case. In that case, the Delaware Supreme Court held Trans Union's directors personally liable for breaching their fiduciary duties when they voted to sell the company to the Marmon

Corporation for $55 per share in 1980. The directors' decision was made during a two-hour meeting without the benefit of an independent valuation. Despite the fact that the $55 per share price was considerably above Trans Union's trading price, the court ruled that the directors "lacked valuation information adequate to reach an informed business judgment."

More than a few of the recent acquisitions will fail to create value for the acquirer's shareholders. After all, shareholder value creation depends not on pre-merger market valuation of the target company but on the actual acquisition price the acquiring company pays compared with the selling company's cash-flow contribution to the combined company. Only a limited supply of acquisition candidates is available at the price that enables the acquirer to earn an acceptable economic return on investment. A well-conceived evaluation program that minimizes the risk of buying an economically unattractive company or paying too much for an attractive one is particularly important in today's seller's market. The dramatic increase in premiums that must be paid by a successful bidder calls for more careful analysis by buyers than ever before.

Because of the competitive nature of the acquisition market, companies not only need to respond wisely but often must respond quickly as well. The growing independence of corporate boards and their demand for better information to support strategic decisions such as acquisitions have raised the general standard for acquisition analysis. Sound analysis, convincingly communicated, also yields substantial benefits in negotiating with the target company's management or, in the case of tender offers, its stockholders.

In this chapter I will show how management can estimate the value a prospective acquisition will, in fact, create. I will present a comprehensive framework for acquisition analysis that has been profitably employed in practice. The analysis provides management and the board of the acquiring company with information for both making a decision on the candidate and formulating an effective negotiating strategy for the acquisition. The chapter begins with a framework for assessing the value created by the acquisition and the value created for the buyer. This is followed by a discussion of operating, financial, and tax benefits that can materialize in a merger. The discussion then turns to the empirical evidence available about who actually has benefited from mergers and acquistions. The following section outlines the five essential stages of the acquisition process. Finally, a recent transaction, the Quaker Oats acquisition of Stokely–Van Camp, is used to illustrate the shareholder value approach to acquisition analysis.

Value Creation Framework

The basic objective of making acquisitions is identical to any other investment associated with a company's overall strategy, namely, to develop a value-creating sustainable competitive advantage. The shareholder value approach enables management to evaluate all investments, whether they be dedicated to internal growth or to external growth such as merger and acquisitions, with an economically sound and consistent measurement system. Indeed, mergers and acquisitions may be seen as a special case of a strategy or perhaps more realistically as an important component of a company's corporate and business strategies.

As one would expect, there are striking similarities between the analysis of strategies presented in Chapters 4 and 5 and acquisition analysis. The three basic steps of competitive analysis—to assess industry attractiveness, to evaluate the business's competitive position within the industry, and to identify sources of competitive advantage—are equally relevant for evaluating presently owned businesses and businesses that are candidates for purchase. After all, immediately following the acquisition, the target company becomes part of the "presently owned businesses" of the buyer. As will be shown later in this chapter, the basic calculations for valuing acquisitions closely parallel those for valuing strategies. There are, however, two distinct features associated with mergers and acquisitions that need to be acknowledged.

First, when a company makes capital investments in connection with its internal development, it is adding real assets to the productive capacity of the industry and may well be affecting the competitive structure. In contrast, a merger per se does not alter productive capacity, but simply transfers ownership rights from one set of shareholders to another. While there are often substantial advantages associated with acquisitions when compared to internal development, the price of an acquisition is set in a highly competitive market for companies, which tends to limit extraordinary value-creating opportunities.

This leads to the second distinct feature of mergers and acquisitions. Investments such as machines and plant made in connection with a company's internal development are typically purchased in relatively active markets with quoted prices. While publicly traded companies also have quoted trading prices, the price required to obtain a controlling interest in the target company will ordinarily be materially higher than the trading price. Thus, price is more negotiable in acquisitions than in the normal process of directly acquiring real assets. Integrating the organizational assets, particularly the commitment of employees, is by far a more compelling task in the case of acquisitions than for expansion via internal development.

While mergers and acquisitions involve a considerably more complex set of managerial problems than the direct purchase of ordinary assets, the economic substance of these transactions is the same. In each case, there is a current outlay made in anticipation of a stream of future cash flows.

To estimate the value creating potential of an acquisition to the buying company's shareholders, assessments must be made of the stand-alone value of the seller, the value of acquisition benefits, and the price required to gain control of the seller. The respective roles of the above factors in the value creation framework can be gleaned from the following three fundamental equations.

$$\text{Value created by acquisition} = \text{Value of combined company} - \left(\text{Stand-alone value of buyer} + \text{Stand-alone value of seller}\right) \quad (1)$$

$$\text{Maximum acceptable price to pay for seller} = \text{Stand-alone value of seller} + \text{Value created by acquisition} \quad (2)$$

$$\text{Value created for buyer} = \text{Maximum acceptable price to pay for seller} - \text{Price required to gain control of seller} \quad (3)$$

The value created by acquisition depicted in the first equation is the difference between the post-merger value of the combined company and the sum of the stand-alone values of the buyer and seller. This difference represents the acquisition benefits generated by operating, financial, and tax synergies. These synergies will either increase cash flow returns or decrease the riskiness of the cash flow stream. It is important to emphasize that this is the *total* value created by combining the two companies and not the value created for the buyer. The respective amounts of value transferred to the buyer and seller ultimately will be determined by the purchase price paid for the seller.

The stand-alone value of the selling company would ordinarily be the seller's minimum acceptable, or floor, price because it usually has the option of continuing to operate the business. In this event it would be reasonable for the seller to expect the price to be greater than the present value of continuing to operate the business. In most cases it will take a substantial premium over the stand-alone price to persuade the target company to sell. As the premium increases, more of the value created by the acquisition goes to selling shareholders and the more difficult it becomes for the buyer to achieve a rate of return exceeding the minimum acceptable rate.

At this point, two questions need to be answered. What measure ought to be used in establishing the seller's stand-alone value? Under what circumstances will the seller depart from stand-alone value as a floor price?

When the target company is publicly traded, market value is the best basis for establishing stand-alone value. The rationale for market value is presented succinctly and compellingly by Salter and Weinhold.

> Stated in terms of the concept of present value, market value can be understood as an equilibrium point balancing buying and selling prices for future returns among investors with differing perceptions of present value. It is useful to emphasize the mundane point that investors typically have different perceptions of an asset's present value. Indeed, investors trade assets precisely because they have a differing judgment than the marketplace of the current worth of future values. Thus, the effect of a market transaction is to establish a compromise measure of investors' estimates of an asset's present value. Since buyers and sellers are presumably acting in their basic self-interest, the "bloodless verdict of the market" is a practical expression of present value that should be preferred to more subjective, individual expressions of value.[1]

For some companies market value may not be a particularly good proxy for stand-alone value. These are companies whose stocks have been bid up in anticipation of a takeover bid. To estimate stand-alone value, the "takeover premium" impounded in the current market price should be deducted from the current market price.

We now turn to the question of when the seller is likely to depart from using stand-alone value as a floor or minimum acceptable price. The seller's floor price is determined by the attractiveness of his alternative opportunities. If the seller already has a credible offer above the current market price, then this competing offer will in fact be the floor price. On the other hand, if the seller is not optimistic about the future prospects of the business or perceives major capital or managerial constraints in realizing the company's potential, the floor price likely will be lower. To negotiate effectively, buyers need to recognize that the floor price depends on the seller's perceptions and not those of the buyer.

The second equation defines the maximum acceptable price to pay for the seller as the sum of the stand-alone value of the seller plus the value created by the acquisition. The maximum price may be equivalently characterized as the difference between the post-merger value of the combined firm and the pre-merger stand-alone value of the buyer. If the maximum price is actually paid then all value created by the acquisition goes to the seller. Thus, from the buyer's perspective, the maximum price is an economic break-even price, that is, the investment is expected to yield the risk-adjusted cost of capital rate. Ordinarily this price will truly represent the maximum offering price. There are, however, circumstances in which the buyer may be willing to pay even more and also circumstances in which alternative opportunities enable the buyer to set the maximum acceptable price at a considerably lower level.

There are times when an acquisition is simply a necessary investment as part of a more global long-term strategy to attain a competitive advantage in a selected product market. The relevant entity for analysis would thus be the total strategy or organizationally the business unit. The acquisition can be viewed as a project which is an integral part of the strategy. What is important is that the *overall* strategy create value and that the supporting projects represent the most efficient and effective means of implementing the strategy. In such a situation an acquisition per se may not meet conventional discounted cash-flow hurdle rates, but it simply may be the only feasible way to execute the long-term strategy. Such an acquisition represents not an end in itself, but rather it provides the means to participate in the uncertain future opportunities in the industry.[2] IBM, for example, purchased Rolm in 1984, its first major acquisition in twenty years, as an essential step toward making IBM competitive in the fast-growing telecommunications market. If Rolm represented the best means of entry to participate in this market, IBM's willingness to pay a large premium comes as no surprise. The real danger lies in management applying the "strategic opportunity" rationale indiscriminately and thereby either making poor acquisitions or paying too much for others.

There are circumstances under which a buying company's maximum acceptable price would be considerably less than the sum of the stand-alone value of the seller and the value created by the acquisition. All of these circumstances involve the availability of less costly alternatives. In the simplest case, there is an equally attractive seller available at a lesser price. Alternatively, the strategic imperatives can be achieved by other collaborative means such as these: operating ventures (e.g., Tri-Star Pictures, a venture among CBS, Home Box Office, and Columbia Pictures to produce and distribute motion pictures), cooperative ventures (e.g., Dow Jones and Teleprompter who offer the Dow Jones News Retrieval Service through cable systems), research and development ventures (e.g., Microelectronical and Computer Technology Corp. in which fifteen major U.S. electronics firms are partners), and a minority equity investment to establish an informal working relationship and exchange of technology.[3] Finally, there is the alternative of internal development. When this is a viable choice, management is essentially engaged in a make (internal development) versus buy (acquisition) decision. The increasing tilt toward acquisitions reflects several important advantages of acquisitions over internal growth.

- Entry in a product market via acquisition may take weeks or months while internal development typically takes years.
- Acquiring a business with a strong market position is often less costly than a competitive battle to achieve market entry.
- Strategic assets such as brand image, distribution channels, proprietary technology, patents, trademarks, and experienced management are often difficult, if not impossible, to develop internally.
- An existing, proven business is typically less risky than developing a new one.

The third equation defines the value created for the buyer as the difference between the maximum acceptable price and the actual price required to gain control of the seller. In light of the competitive nature of the market for corporate control, an acquisition is likely to create value for the buyer only if the buyer has a distinctive ability to generate significant economic benefits as a result of the combination.

It is important to establish that valuations in the market for corporate control are invariably higher than day-to-day stock market values. The most tangible evidence of this phenomenon is the large premiums, averaging in the neighborhood of 50 percent, that have been paid to selling shareholders during recent years. How can a company's stock be actively traded among well informed investors at a price of, say, $50 per share and then suddenly be worth $75 per share to the acquiring company? One possibility is that corporate buyers overpay for acquisitions. While this is undoubtedly true in some cases, it would be unreasonable to suggest systematic irrationality on the part of managements of acquisitive firms. If this were the case, such behavior would eventually cause these companies to lose their competitive viability. Similarly, there is evidence that the daily trading market is reasonably efficient and the $50 per share price fairly reflects investors' estimates of the present value of the company's future cash flows.

There is a reasonable explanation for the disparity between the $50 per share and $75 per share prices. The $50 per share reflects the value set by investors who exercise no direct control over the company's decision-making process. In contrast, the $75 per share is based on the value of exercising control over the future operations of the business. The $25 per share premium is paid because the buyer is seeking a majority, if not all, of the seller's shares. When a passive investor purchases a small block of shares, he will not upset the balance between the supply and demand for the company's shares. In contrast, when all or a majority of the shares are demanded, one would expect an increase in price. The buyer, in turn, can afford to pay the market premium as long as the value created by the acquisition is greater than the premium.

Can value be created for the buyer even if no value is created by the merger? Yes, but only if the buyer believes the market is undervaluing the stand-alone value of the seller. To illustrate, consider the following example.

	Per Share
Stand-alone value of buyer	$60
Stand-alone value of seller	25
Value of combined company	85

There is no value created by this merger and the maximum acceptable price would ordinarily be the stand-alone value of the seller of $25 per share. Suppose, however, that the current *market* value of the seller is $18 per share, well below the buyer's stand-alone assessment of $25 per share. If the buying company made a successful bid at $23 per share, it would create $2 per share of value despite the fact that the merger itself creates no value. In this case, the buying company is not betting on synergies, but on undervaluation by a normally efficient market.

Merger Benefits

Because the price of an acquisition is set in a highly competitive market for companies, the buyer's value creation potential will depend importantly on the distinctive benefits of the merger. If the benefits are not distinctive, then other prospective buyers with similar economic prospects will bid up the price to a level at which value creation potential is likely to be modest or even negative. Merger benefits providing value creation potential can be classified into three principal categories: operating, financial, and tax. As is the case for any other strategy, the ultimate test of these benefits is whether they will help provide a sustainable competitive advantage for the business via cost leadership, differentiation, or some other strategic means.

Operating

Operating benefits are most likely to materialize in situations in which the merging businesses operate in closely related product markets. A horizontal merger involves two firms whose products are identical or close substitutes and therefore belong to the same market. A vertical merger links firms operating in different stages of the production process for some final product. Vertical integration can move in two directions—forward in the direction of the company's customers or backward to the company's suppliers.

There are several potential sources of value due to post-merger improvements in operations. These operating benefits may be classified into the following broad categories:

Economies of scale
Technical and managerial skill transfer
Asset restructuring

Economies of scale in production, marketing, distribution, and research and development are important benefits, particularly in mergers involving firms in the same or related industries. The effect of economies of scale is to reduce the long-run average cost of the company.

The "brand-name mergers" among consumer goods companies are excellent examples of mergers motivated by economies of scale prospects. The substantial costs and high risk associated with trying to create a well-known and accepted consumer product have influenced the recent wave of acquisitions of companies with strong brand names. Examples would include Philip-Morris's purchase of General Foods, Procter & Gamble's acquisition of Richardson-Vicks, the R. J. Reynolds purchase of Nabisco Brands, and Nestle's acquisition of Carnation. Procter & Gamble expects to be able to improve operating profit margins on Richardson-Vicks products (e.g., Nyquil, Vicks cold remedies, and Oil of Olay skin lotion) by combining sales forces, taking advantage of discounts on higher volume advertising, and by using Richardson's overseas distribution channels to expand P&G's international presence. Procter & Gamble has had a long history of making aquisitions and then using its superior marketing expertise to build up best-selling brands. During the 1950s and 1960s, P&G acquired Charmin Paper, Duncan Hines cake mixes, and Folger's coffee and proceeded not only to build up brand name identity, but put these names on a large number of products.

In the early 1980s, the promise of synergies, largely economies in marketing, led Prudential Insurance, American Express, and Sears, Roebuck to acquire major retail stock brokers—Bache, Shearson Loeb Rhoades, and Dean Witter Reynolds, respectively. The idea was to create a "financial supermarket" by providing a full range of financial services to their customers. After several years, there is still little evidence that these marketing synergies are likely to materialize. In large measure this seems to be attributable to the difficulties of integrating the brokerage business into the buyer's other businesses. This illustrates a fundamental axiom of mergers and acquisitions, namely, that recognizing synergy potential is invariably easier than realizing it.

The second type of operating benefit comes when the technical or management skills of one company can be advantageously applied to the business of the other company in the merger. Salter and Weinhold[4] cite the Heublein acquisition of Vintner in 1968 as a good illustration. Heublein's basic strategy was to market premium-priced liquor products (e.g., Smirnoff vodka), beer, and specialty foods that would provide the high operating profit margins needed to support its advertising-intensive marketing. Vintners, which owned two of California's wine brands, provided the opportunity for Heublein to apply its skill in introducing and promoting speciality products. Heublein helped Vintner identify and then exploit the shift in consumer tastes toward lighter-bodied, slightly flavored drinks by launching two extraordinarily successful products—Cold Duck, a champagne and sparkling burgundy combination, and Bali Hai, a fruit flavored wine. Interestingly, Heublein discovered that aggressive advertising was not the key success factor in its subsequent and less successful acquisitions of Hamm's beer and Kentucky Fried Chicken.

The concept that management can apply the skills acquired in one business and successfully apply them to another has great appeal. But, once again conceptual synergies do not always translate readily to realized synergies. Philip Morris, for example, was not able to apply the brand management skills it employed so successfully in its cigarette business to broaden the appeal of 7-Up after its acquisition, so in 1986 7-Up was sold to Pepsico. As formidable a force as it is, Coca-Cola found it difficult to transfer its marketing skills effectively from the soft-drink business to three wine companies it acquired in the late 1970s.

It is important to emphasize that the skill transfer in a merger need not necessarily be from the buyer to the seller's product market environment. For example, the motivating force in the IBM acquisition of Rolm was the potential to link Rolm's telecommunications technology to IBM's computer technology. In fact, the IBM-Rolm combination is an excellent example of two companies with complementary resources, that is, each has what the other needs.

The third, and last, major operating benefit comes from asset restructuring. The market value of a firm reflects the strategies that investors expect management to pursue. These strategies may not always be value maximizing. Thus, the current share price may not reflect the value of the firm's assets shifted to higher valued uses. The boldest example of this phenomenon is the disparity between "going concern" market values and breakup value which is the total estimated price the market would place on a company if the component parts were sold separately. In short, the market value of the sum of the parts is often worth more than the whole as reflected in the company's stock price. The lure of major networks such as ABC and CBS as takeover targets is explained by the fact that stock market values were not reflecting the considerably higher liquidating values. By some Wall Street estimates the price of their television stations alone, without including the network, radio stations, and other businesses, approximated the total prevailing stock market value. A similar situation exists in the oil industry where the market value of the oil and gas reserves account for a large part and sometimes exceed the total market value of integrated oil companies.[5]

The disparity between going-concern market values and breakup value places a premium on gaining a controlling interest of a company. Control is significantly more valuable than the passive investment of an ordinary investor because asset restructuring is viewed as a genuine value-creating possibility. A buyer who gains controlling interest has an opportunity to realize a major windfall by liquidating key parts of the company.

Asset restructuring or the shifting of a firm's assets to their highest valued use can be performed either by incumbent management or by means of a takeover. Indeed, as management signals its intention to engage in asset restructuring, the market price of the company's shares can be expected to rise to reflect this favorable expectation.[6] This, in turn, makes the company a less attractive takeover candidate.

Financial

Financial benefits represent the second broad category of potential value-creating merger benefits. Several financial justifications have been proposed for mergers and acquisitions. These include diversification to reduce risk and thereby the firm's cost of capital, lower interest rates available to the merged firm, and exploiting increased debt capacity. As will be demonstrated, each of these reasons should be viewed with caution.

The shareholder benefits of corporate diversification are likely to be more limited than commonly perceived by management. Diversification per se should not be expected to lead to higher share price because shareholders can achieve diversification themselves by investing in a diversified portfolio of stocks or a mutual fund. Moreover, shareholders only have to pay the current market price while the acquiring company must pay a takeover premium. Not surprisingly, investors are unwilling to pay a premium for diversified firms. The risk reduction rationale for corporate diversification is valid only if the merger would lower the probability of the buyer defaulting or going into bankruptcy. Even here, however, the benefits are likely to be modest. Franks, Broyles, and Carleton[7] provide a good illustration. Assume that two companies, A and B, each have an estimated probability of default of 5 percent and that their cash flows are perfectly negatively correlated. If a company defaults, the creditors may, for example, have to liquidate some assets and incur legal, advertising, and selling costs. If either company defaults, the costs are, say, 20 percent of each company's current market value. Therefore, the expected cost of default for each company is 1 percent of company value, that is, 5 percent times 20 percent. Because cash flows are assumed to be perfectly negatively correlated, the probability of default falls to zero after the merger. In the absence of any other benefits, how value creating is the merger? While the decreased cost of default increases the value of the combined firm by 1 percent, the required market premium to gain control would undoubtedly be substantially higher than 1 percent. If the seller were already in financial distress and would clearly default without the merger, then the default cost might be significant enough to justify the merger, particularly if there were other benefits as well.

The second financial rationale for mergers and acquisitions is the potential for lower borrowing costs. When the cash flows of the buyer and seller are imperfectly correlated, a merger reduces the variability of the combined company's cash flow stream. This reduction in risk will also enable the merged firm to borrow at lower interest rates than they could individually as independent companies. Despite the lower interest rates, the merger does not necessarily create *shareholder* value.

Before the merger the firms did not guarantee each other's debt. However, after the merger if either one of the entities defaults on its debt, the resources of the other are used to satisfy the claims. This so-called coinsurance effect means that the merger reduces the riskiness of the debt and thereby also increases its value. If corporate value (i.e., the value of debt plus equity) is not affected by the merger, then any increase in the value of debt must be offset by a corresponding decrease in the value of the equity. After all, the lower default risk on debt is accomplished only because shareholders of the respective firms have provided bondholders unexpectedly better protection on previously outstanding debt directly as a result of the merger.[8] Since shareholders received no compensation for this, bondholders will gain at the expense of shareholders. For new debt issued after the merger, the shareholder gain due to paying lower interest rates to bondholders is offset by the better protection provided to bondholders and the merger per se should not be expected to increase shareholder value.

The third, and final, financial justification claimed for mergers is exploiting increased debt capacity. Here there are two possibilities. First, the seller may have unused debt capacity, that is, it could lower the cost of capital by introducing more leverage in its capital structure. If a target company has unused debt capacity that can be exploited by other buyers, the required takeover price should reflect this and tend to eliminate any extraordinary rates of return due to underleveraging by the seller.

The second possibility offers more value creation potential. In choosing an optimal debt level, management must weigh the essential tradeoff between the present value of the savings from the tax-deductibility of interest versus the present value of the costs of financial distress due to carrying too much debt. Insofar as a merger decreases the probability of financial distress, it enables the combined company to increase its level of borrowing without increasing the present value of the costs of financial distress. The value created by this incremental debt capacity depends on the value of the additional interest tax shield made available. The value of the interest tax shield to the buyer, in turn, depends on several factors. Firms facing high marginal tax rates will recoup the greatest benefit. Interest tax shields will be worth more to profitable, relatively stable firms that are likely to have taxable income to shield, than to firms with accumulated tax losses or uncertain prospects. Companies with other ways to shield taxable income such as by investment tax credits and accelerated depreciation on facilities will value the interest tax shield less highly than those without alternative shields.

Finally, the value of the interest tax shield also depends on the personal tax rates of bondholders and shareholders. As the effective tax rate on equity decreases or the effective rate paid by bondholders on interest income increases, the value of the interest tax shield decreases. A company that pays no dividends and attracts investors with a long-term capital gains orientation will have a shareholder clientele with a relatively low effective tax rate. Pension funds and other institutional shareholders may have a tax-exempt status. Similarly the personal tax rate on debt may range from zero to the top marginal tax rate. To illustrate the effect of personal tax rates on the value of using additional debt, Piper and Weinhold[9] developed the following estimates for the change in value if a company in the 48 percent tax bracket were to substitute $1 million of debt for $1 million of equity.

		Personal Tax Rate for Bondholders		
		0 %	35 %	50 %
Personal	0 %	$480,000	$200,000	($40,000)
Tax Rate for	10 %	530,000	280,000	60,000
Shareholders	20 %	580,000	360,000	170,000

In summary, if a merger does in fact reduce risk, debt capacity is increased and its value to the buyer depends on how well it can exploit the resulting tax shield on interest payments.

Before concluding this discussion about leverage, it is important to distinguish between combining the operations of two companies versus an acquisition of a company by an investment organization. Leveraged buyouts accomplished by Wall Street investment firms and takeovers organized by investors such as Carl Icahn are clear examples of changes in ownership without combining the operations of two companies. Thus the argument that a merger reduces risk and thereby creates additional debt capacity is simply not relevant to LBOs and takeovers by raiders. Interestingly, these two types of transactions typically employ the most highly leveraged financing arrangements. This so called "junk bond" financing involves the use of unsecured, high-yield securities sold to pension funds, insurance companies, savings and loan institutions, and wealthy individuals. The buyer is usually a shell company that has no assets other than the stock acquired from the seller, which, in effect, becomes the collateral for the bonds.

In the above situations, the selling company may not have exploited fully its debt capacity, but the acquisition per se is not likely to create new debt capacity. There is growing concern about the burden of servicing the heavy debt loads associated with LBOs and other highly leveraged takeovers. The market concern is revealed whenever there is a decline in bond prices upon the announcement of a takeover. As a recent example, when R. H. Macy & Co. announced its $3.6 billion leveraged-buyout proposal, the market price of its stock rose by some $16 per share while the price of Macy bonds dropped significantly when investors were suddenly faced with the prospect of owning much riskier debt. Clearly there was a loss of wealth by bondholders. For shareholders, the question is to what extent will the apparent gains from aggressive leveraging be offset by the costs of financial distress due to carrying too much debt. As is the case for all risky bets, only time will tell.

Tax Savings

The third, and final, merger benefit category is tax savings. While there are a number of tax provisions that favor mergers, buyers have been particularly attracted by the benefits of net operating loss carryovers and also the additional depreciation allowed when the basis of acquired assets has been stepped up. Both of these provisions have a favorable impact on the buyer's cash flow. In some cases the cash flow benefits are large enough to play a significant role in financing the acquisition itself.

A net operating loss (i.e., the excess of deductions over gross income) of a corporation may be offset against taxable income, either as a carryback to the preceding three years or as a carryforward to the subsequent fifteen years. For example, assume the seller has carryback losses totaling $50 million, and the buyer's pretax income for the coming year is projected to be well above $50 million. At a marginal tax rate of, say, 46 percent the savings amount to $23 million, that is, $50 million times 46 percent. The present value of the savings will be somewhat less since it will not be realized until the end of the year.

In a taxable transaction, the buyer's tax basis for acquired assets is equal to the fair market value of the consideration paid. Thus, if the acquisition price is substantially in excess of the seller's tax basis, the seller's assets are revalued upward. The additional depreciation from this stepping-up of the assets decreases the buyer's tax bill in each year for the remaining life of the assets. The tax savings can be particularly robust when acquiring capital intensive firms during periods of high inflation.

Are these tax savings likely to create value for the buyer? The fundamental principle is the same for any form of merger benefit, whether it be operating, financial, or tax motivated. In each case, the buyer must have a *distinctive* ability to exploit the synergies. If there are other potential buyers with comparable prospects, then one would expect prices to be bid up in the competitive market for corporate control to a level where buyers can expect to earn only a normal rate of return. In light of the above, we may conclude that tax savings could create value for the merger, but they may create little value for the buyer. In the final analysis, the amount of value created for the buyer will be determined by the relative negotiation leverage available to the buyer compared to the seller.

Evidence on Merger Benefits

Thus far this chapter has focused on establishing a value creation framework for mergers and then an assessment of the operating, financial, and tax savings benefits. We now turn to the empirical evidence concerning the actual benefits realized from recent mergers.

Responsible statements about the consequences of mergers and acquisitions should be based on systematic research using objective data rather than ad hoc case examples to support one's prior viewpoint. Fortunately, there is a rapidly growing body of empirical studies on the economic consequences of mergers. Before reviewing the findings of this research, it is essential that the underlying framework of analysis be understood.

How can a researcher evaluate the effect of a corporate merger? Some might argue that the success or failure of a merger cannot be judged until years after the transaction. After a period of, say, five or ten years, a comparative evaluation can be made of the financial results for the combined company and its competitive peer group. Such an *ex post* approach to analyzing merger benefits suffers from several important limitations. First, it relies on accounting numbers such as earnings which may not be reliably associated with the creation of economic value. Second, by looking at results over a number of years, the analysis comingles the financial impact of strategic investments made subsequent to the merger with the results of the merger. In point of fact, once the merger is completed, it becomes impossible to assess what would have happened to the buying company without the merger. Therefore, the incremental benefit of the merger itself cannot be established. Finally, the *ex post* approach overlooks the fact that there are economic gains and losses that materialize at the announcement date of the merger.

One does not need to wait for five or ten years to evaluate the benefits of mergers. The stock market evaluates each acquisition at the announcement of the transaction and when there is information leakage even earlier. The market evaluation is made by generally well-informed investors with very strong incentives in light of the substantial dollars at risk to develop accurate estimates of the likely consequences of the merger. Therefore, in a reasonably efficient market the expected value of the merger to buying and selling shareholders will be reflected by the changes in the share prices of the buyer and seller at the announcement date.

While the market's short-term response to a merger announcement provides a reasonably reliable barometer of the likely consequences of the transaction, there is, of course, the possibility that with hindsight the market assessment will turn out to be incorrect. There is, however, evidence that the market's assesments are unbiased. This means that, on average, the market neither overvalues or undervalues the transaction. There is an approximately fifty-fifty probability that the market assessment will be too low or too high in estimating the eventual value created by the merger. The collective judgment of competitive investors can thus be viewed as an objective assessment of the value of the merger to buying and selling shareholders. In brief, the immediate price reaction is the market's best guess about the long-term implications of the transaction. Should the market err in its assessment of the likely consequences of the merger, the resulting mispricing would offer market participants trading opportunities that would move market prices to a more unbiased outlook.

The evidence regarding changes in the value of selling companies is unambiguous. Although estimates of the value increase may vary, recent studies find that target company abnormal stock price changes average 30 percent in tender offers and 20 percent in mergers. Abnormal stock price changes are stock price changes adjusted to eliminate the effects of marketwide price changes.[10]

The findings concerning changes in the value of buying companies are somewhat mixed. Some studies find very small positive abnormal stock price changes, while others find very small negative changes. The overall evidence supports the idea that, on average, shareholders of buying companies earn little, if anything, from mergers.[11] What is important to emphasize is that the *aggregate* net change in the value of the buyer plus seller is positive. This suggests that the market believes that the combination will create value. Most, if not all, of the value created appears to be captured by sellers.

The finding that shareholders of buying companies reap such minimal rewards is undoubtedly disturbing to managements of acquisitive firms. Perhaps the most comforting way to interpret this phenomenon is to suggest that when average abnormal returns for the buyer are close to zero, the market for corporate control is simply highly competitive and efficient. What is perhaps more troublesome is that some recent studies report that more than 60 percent of the bidding firms experienced abnormal stock price *declines*. In such cases the market has made its judgment that these bids do not serve the best interests of shareholders. How can this outcome be explained?

One possibility is that there exists a conflict between management's best interests and those of the company's shareholders. For example, one might expect that managers would be more likely to undertake mergers which increase pro forma earnings per share when a significant part of their compensation is tied to accounting-based performance. Because earnings-increasing mergers are not necessarily value-increasing mergers, Larcker conducted a study that hypothesized "that as the percentage of remuneration tied to accounting measures goes up, the stock market's reaction to the merger would be more adverse."[12] He did, in fact, find that the more accounting-oriented the compensation plan, the more negative, on average, was the market reaction.

Another plausible explanation for the frequent negative market response to the bidding firm may be that the pre-merger share price often reflects an expectation that the company will invest in strategies, including acquisitions, yielding a rate of return *above* the minimum acceptable or cost of capital rate. Thus, if market participants believe that the acquisition will earn only the cost of capital rate, share price can be expected to decline.

Others might argue that while shareholders of the buying company may incur substantial losses at the time of merger announcement, these losses will be reversed over time as the benefits of the transaction become more apparent. Once again, in a reasonably efficient stock market one would expect the present value of such benefits, even if they be several years away, to be reflected in the buying company's current share price. If this were not the case, then the buyer's shareholders who sell their shares at the merger announcement date would be systematically and unwisely selling for too low a price. There is no evidence of such irrationality.

Milton L. Rock, the publisher of *Mergers & Acquisitions*, offers an articulate and balanced perspective on the role of stock prices as a measure of corporate performance:

> Imperfect though they may be, stock prices enjoy wide acceptance as measurements of corporate performance. Simplistic catch-alls for any economic or financial category are to be opposed, but there is no readily available substitute for the share price as a pervasive barometer of corporate achievement and prospects. This is a fact of life that the corporate chief executive cannot ignore. Indeed, achievement and maintenance of a fair and fully valued stock price should be a key part of the CEO's continuing responsibility. . . . Even the CEO who doesn't accept the efficient-market theory must recognize how important it is to prevent the stock market from erring. Corporate goals, objectives, strategies, and achievements must be adequately communicated so that share price indeed equates with corporate performance.[13]

At the very least, the buying firms' recent record of limited value creation should motivate more demanding standards for acquisition analysis.

The Acquisition Process

Recall from Chapter 5 that strategic planning takes place at both corporate and business unit levels. This dichotomy is relevant for internal development and acquisitions alike. Although corporate and business unit levels are faced with different strategic tasks, they share the common objective of creating shareholder value. At the business unit level, strategy is driven by product-market issues. In contrast, strategic planning at the corporate level has a portfolio orientation. The central concern is with allocating resources among the company's various businesses so that the overall value of the portfolio is enhanced.

Allen, Oliver, and Schwallie,[14] as an example, present the following "business-strategy based" acquisition alternatives for creating value:

- Acquire a synergistic product-market position via scale economies of distribution, production, or technology.
- Acquire position in key international markets and achieve scale economies for global production and technology investments.
- Acquire a "beachhead" in an emerging high-growth market or technology.

They then go on to cite the following "corporate-strategy" based possibilities:

- Acquire a company with underutilized financial strengths, such as unused debt capacity, tax loss carryforwards, foreign tax credits, and so on.
- Acquire an underskilled company in a related industry and apply superior corporate marketing, technology, or production expertise to enhance the competitive position and performance of the acquisition candidate.
- Acquire a company whose portfolio can be profitably restructured by selling losers and redeploying resources to businesses with a competitive advantage.

The acquisition process, whether it be conducted at the business unit or corporate level, involves five essential stages:

Competitive analysis
Search and screen
Strategy development
Financial evaluation
Negotiation.

The essential purpose of the *competitive analysis stage* is to identify synergistic interrelationships between the company's businesses and other businesses which it may wish to enter. These relationships represent opportunities to create a competitive advantage by reducing costs or enhancing differentiation in various value chain activities. If the interrelationships are truly distinctive, the acquisition candidate will be worth more to the buying company than to either the selling shareholders or to other competing bidders who cannot exploit such interrelationships.

Porter believes that horizontal strategy is the essence of corporate strategy.[15] Horizontal strategy, the coordination of strategies of related business units, is relevant not only to the analysis of existing business units, but also to the selection of new businesses to enter (via internal development or acquisition) based on interrelationships with existing units. Horizontal strategy, which aims to identify and exploit interrelationships, is best developed at either the group, sector, or corporate level where presumably management ordinarily will have a more global perspective than at the business unit level.

Porter presents the sharing of value activities, both primary and supporting, as a key interrelationship with both cost leadership and differentiation competitive advantages. A shared brand name, for example, can lower advertising expense and at the same time reinforce a differentiated product reputation. As another example, a shared service network can reduce costs while providing more responsive customer service. It should be pointed out that the analysis of interrelationships provides not only a framework for initially identifying the value creation potential of existing and new businesses, but also for identifying business units that should be divested because they have no important interrelationships with other units. In summary, at the end of the competitive analysis stage the company will have developed a list of business areas it wishes to enter and exit.

In the *search and screen stage* the idea is to develop a list of good acquisition candidates. The search process focuses on how and where candidates may be found, while the screening process involves identifying a few of the best candidates that meet the established criteria. The business areas of interest have already been established during the competitive analysis stage. Additional screens may be established on criteria such as company size, plant locations, current share of market, quality of management, and capital structure.[16] Once the best apparent candidates have been identified, more detailed analysis for each will be initiated.

The third stage of the acquisition process, *strategy development*, involves taking the synergistic interrelationships developed in generic fashion in the competitive analysis stage and examining their implementation potential for each of the identified candidates. It is not enough to have a generic acquisition strategy. Its feasibility must be tested against specific acquisition candidates. The buyer's thinking at this stage must move from conceptual synergies to realizable synergies. Synergies, however, are not likely to be realized unless operational strategies have been developed for systematically exploiting them.

The more an acquisition depends upon synergistic interrelationships, the greater is the need to develop a post-merger integration blueprint *beforehand*. This becomes even more essential in situations in which the two organizations have very different cultures.[17] For example, the success of Sears' attempt to develop a one-stop financial supermarket (Allstate, Dean Witter, and Coldwell Banker) and link it to its traditional retail shopping operations will depend importantly on how well it can integrate vastly different businesses and cultures. Not only is pre-merger strategy development for post-merger integration essential for exploiting synergies, it is also necessary for preserving the stand-alone value of the seller. A company can lose its value quickly when key people leave. An example of this "floating goodwill" problem is Schlumberger's 1979 acquisition of Fairchild Camera & Instrument. Schlumberger, an oil-service company, brought in its own team to manage Fairchild, a Silicon Valley semiconductor company. The new team quickly reduced the payroll significantly and eliminated bonuses and profit-sharing. The result was an exodus of key engineering staff and a substantial decline in product development and Fairchild's position in the industry.

Next, there is the *financial evaluation stage* of the acquisition process. A more detailed illustration of this stage is reserved for the next section. The central issues addressed in this stage include:

- What is the maximum price that should be paid for the target company?
- What are the principal areas of risk?
- What are the cash flow, earnings, and balance sheet implications of the acquisition?
- What is the best way of structuring the acquisition?

The fifth, and last, stage of the acquisition process is the *negotiation stage*. The success of negotiations will depend to a large degree on the quality of the "homework" done in the first four stages. There are a number of excellent books on negotiation. One that I have found particularly useful for merger and acquisition negotiations is *Getting to Yes* by Roger Fisher and William Ury (Boston: Houghton Mifflin, 1981). The authors summarize their approach with four basic rules.

- *Separate the people from the problem.* Because ego and emotion often get entangled with the substantive economic and organizational issues, the "people problem" should be dealt with separately. The buying and selling company negotiators should be positioned to work together, attacking the problem, not each other.
- *Focus on interests, not positions.* The object of the negotiations is to satisfy each party's interests and not its negotiation position which often obscures underlying interests.
- *Invent options for mutual gain.* Searching for a unique solution is dysfunctional. Develop a range of potential solutions that advance shared interests and serve as catalysts for creatively reconciling conflicting interests. For example, if there are irreconcilable differences concerning acquisition price, an earn-out arrangement may well serve both the buyer's and seller's interests.
- *Insist on using objective criteria.* Rather than reaching an impasse or rewarding intransigence, discuss objective criteria (e.g., relative market values, expert opinions) by which an equitable agreement can be reached.

This completes the overview of the five essential stages in the acquisition process. We now proceed to a more detailed examination of the financial evaluation stage.

Valuing the Acquisition

In this section, the shareholder value approach to merger and acquisition evaluation will be demonstrated. This overall methodology has been used extensively by acquisition-minded companies during the past decade. The specific model illustrated here has been employed in some of the largest recent mergers and is actively used by over two hundred major American companies.[18]

The financial evaluation process involves both a self-evaluation by the acquiring company and the evaluation of the candidate for acquisition. Two fundamental questions posed by a financial self-evaluation are: (1) How much is my company worth? (2) How would its value be affected by each of several scenarios? The first question involves generation of a "most likely" estimate of the company's value based on management's detailed assessment of its prospects and plans. The second question calls for an assessment of value based on a range of plausible scenarios that enable management to test the effect of hypothesized combinations of product-market strategies and environmental forces.

Corporate self-evaluation, when conducted as an assessment of the value created for shareholders by various strategic planning options, promises potential benefits for all companies. In the context of the acquisition market, self-evaluation takes on special significance.

First, while a company might view itself as an acquirer, few companies are totally exempt from a possible takeover. Self-evaluation provides management and the board with a continuing basis for responding to tender offers or acquisition inquiries responsibly and quickly. Second, the self-evaluation process might well call attention to strategic divestment or other restructuring opportunities. Finally, financial self-evaluation offers acquisition-minded companies a basis for assessing the comparative advantages of a cash versus an exchange-of-shares offer.

Buying companies commonly value the purchase price for an acquisition at the market value of the shares exchanged. This practice is not economically sound and could be misleading and costly to the buying company as well as the selling company. A well-conceived analysis for an exchange-of-shares acquisition requires sound valuations of both buying and selling companies. If the buyer's management believes the market is undervaluing its shares, then valuing the purchase price at market might well induce the company to overpay for the acquisition or to earn less than the minimum acceptable rate of return. Conversely, if management believes the market is overvaluing its shares, then valuing the purchase price at market obscures the opportunity to offer the seller's shareholders additional shares while still achieving the minimum acceptable return.

To illustrate the above concepts, consider the following example.[19] The buying company management values its own company at $150 million. The buyer's value is $15 per share with 10 million shares outstanding for a total market value of $150 million. The buyer values the target (including synergies) at $45 million. What is the *maximum* number of shares the buyer can issue in exchange for all the seller's outstanding shares? The answer is clearly 3 million shares valued at $15 per share and can be demonstrated as follows:

	SHARES OUTSTANDING (MILLIONS)
Pre-merger	10
New shares issued	3
Post-merger	13
Post-merger: Buyer's shareholders own 10/13 of ($150 million + $45 million)	($ millions) $150
Less: Pre-merger value of buyer	150
Value created for buyer	$ 0

Now suppose all the facts remain the same except that the buyer's market value is $9 per share for a total market value of $90 million. What is the *maximum* number of shares the buyer can issue under these circumstances? The correct answer is once again 3 million shares because the buying company management continues to value itself at $150 million. Management, in fact, believes it is being undervalued by $6 per share. If the shares exchanged were valued at the market price of $9 per share, then the buyer would be willing to exchange up to 5 million shares in exchange for the seller's $45 million value. But this will lead to the buyer overpaying by $20 million for the acquisition as is shown below.

	SHARES OUTSTANDING (MILLIONS)
Pre-merger	10
New shares issued	5
Post-merger	15
Post-merger: Buyer's shareholders own 10/15 of ($150 million + $45 million)	($ millions) $130
Less: Pre-merger value of buyer	150
Value created for buyer	$ (20)

With this background on financial self-evaluation we are now ready to present a case illustration of the shareholder value approach to acquisition analysis.

Quaker Oats Acquisition of Stokely-Van Camp[20]

Chronology of the Deal

In November of 1982 the management of Stokely–Van Camp Inc. formed the SVC Acquiring Corporation and offered Stokely shareholders $50 per share for their stock with the intent of acquiring the company through a leveraged buyout. The shareholders subsequently filed a lawsuit against the management, claiming that $50 per share was not a fair price. In February 1983 the SVC Acquiring Corporation raised its offer to $55 per share.

Although four months later Stokely's board of directors unanimously approved the deal, that agreement was terminated after Pillsbury initiated a tender offer in July for Stokely's shares at $62 per share. At that point Stokely's management went to their investment banker, Goldman Sachs, in order to try to obtain a better price. They decided to use an auction in which the participants had the right to review some internal documents and then had twenty-four hours to settle on a price and make an offer.

In July 1983 Quaker Oats won the auction with its offer to purchase Stokely's common stock for $77 per share in cash. (Quaker outbid seven other potential buyers, two of whose bids were only $1.50 per share less than Quaker's.) By the end of 1983 Quaker had acquired all the outstanding Stokely common stock, paying about $230 million (excluding deal costs and "golden parachutes").

Was value created by this acquisition? From the perspective of Stokely's shareholders, the answer was certainly yes. In the six-month period before the merger the value of Stokely's stock more than doubled, rising from $35 per share to the $77 purchase price. But from the perspective of Quaker's shareholders, the desirability of the deal was not immediately clear. The initial market reaction to this deal was negative, although Quaker's stock recovered subsequently as the favorable aspects of the transaction became known to the market.

How might Quaker have analyzed this deal? What were some of the critical synergies? The shareholder value framework of analysis will be used to address these questions.

Steps in the Financial Evaluation of the Quaker/Stokely Merger

This case analysis will begin with a brief overview of the industry, the companies, and their strategies. The focus of the analysis is to show how the shareholder value approach can be used to answer critical questions about the deal such as these:

- What is an appropriate price for the acquisition candidate?
- How much value is created for Quaker shareholders?
- Which factors have the greatest impact on the value of the deal?
- How would the value created by the deal and the maximum price to pay be affected by alternative scenarios?
- What is the best way to structure the deal?
- What are the implications of the deal for post-merger earnings per share and capital structure?
- Will funding the merger be a problem?

The qualitative information in the case is drawn from publicly available sources. Several simplifying assumptions have been made to clarify the analytical method. An actual analysis would likely be more detailed and would incorporate expert opinions, industry data, analysis of "peer" businesses, and so forth. Also, multiple scenarios would be developed in order to determine a *range* of values for the deal.

Overview of the Industry, the Companies and Their Strategies

KEY COMPETITIVE FORCES IN THE INDUSTRY

Food processing is a highly competitive and mature industry consisting of numerous competitors and products. Although sales had been growing nominally at about 11.6 percent annually in the recent years prior to 1983, industry volume growth was relatively flat. Therefore the growth options available to food processors were either to increase market share, introduce new products or product-line extensions, and/or pursue opportunities overseas or outside of the industry.

Larger companies have many advantages over smaller ones in the food industry. Not only can they attain lower production costs by achieving economies of scale, but they can spend heavily on advertising to help differentiate their brands. Strong brand development is essential for maintaining pricing flexibility and thereby sustaining better margins.

Quaker Oats' Strategies

The Quaker Oats Company is a Chicago-based worldwide marketer of consumer products and services. Its principal businesses included grocery products (e.g., Cap'n Crunch, Life, Aunt Jemima, and Ken-L-Ration), toys (Fisher-Price Toys), food products sold to restaurants and institutions, and various speciality retailing outlets (e.g., Brookstone and Jos. A. Bank Clothiers).

During the 1970s Quaker attempted to diversify into areas outside of the mature food industry. Under the leadership of William Smithburg, who became chief executive officer in 1981 and chairman in 1983, Quaker pursued a "back to basics" strategy by attempting to capitalize on the strengths of its U.S. grocery products.

According to its annual report, Quaker had the following four operating strategies in 1983:

- To be a leading marketer of strong consumer goods and services
- To achieve profitable, better-than-average real volume growth in worldwide grocery businesses
- To improve profitability of low-return businesses or divest them
- To establish a meaningful position in specialty retail businesses

Stokely–Van Camp's Strategies

Stokely–Van Camp is an Indianapolis-based company that is divided into two business groups: (1) the U.S. Grocery Products Group, which includes canned products, frozen seasonal fruits and vegetables, and Gatorade thirst quencher; and (2) the Industrial Products Group, which includes consumer vegetable oil products and vegetable oil-derived chemical specialty products.

Stokely–Van Camp's best known brands include Van Camp's Pork and Beans (market leader with 34 percent share) and Gatorade (an "isotonic beverage" which replenishes lost fluids and restores a person's chemical balance following strenuous exercise). Gatorade held an 8.4 percent share of the "single-strength juice drink" market, which includes HI-C, Ocean Spray, and other juices. However, Gatorade can more accurately be described as a "unique product" with no direct competition.

In 1978 Stokely shifted its strategic focus away from some of its seasonal businesses that were characterized by inefficient capacity utilization and low profit margins. By the beginning of fiscal 1984 (June 1), Stokely had divested all its seasonal products and was able to allocate its capital to the product lines that earned higher profit margins: Gatorade, Pork and Beans, and the industrial products business. (Two less profitable divisions, Pomona Products and Purity Mills, remained unsold after the acquisition.)

After divesting its less profitable divisions, Stokely was in a liquid position with $6 million in cash and $123 million in marketable securities at fiscal year-end 1983. Thus Stokely was capable of handling a sizable capital investment program. In addition, lines of credit totaling $55.6 million (which had been used to finance seasonal inventories) were available to finance short-term projects.

Valuation of Stokely

In assessing the maximum price it would be willing to pay for Stokely, Quaker would want to take into account the synergies that could be realized if the two companies were combined.

Qualitative Discussion of Potential Synergies

Four major potential operating synergies can be identified.

First, Quaker would be able to use its superior marketing capability to increase the sale of Gatorade, which to date had been distributed only regionally and have never been backed with a major advertising campaign. Quaker could integrate Gatorade into its national distribution network and could promote the product more heavily. Quaker could also take advantage of its European network to distribute Gatorade, although it would need to invest in additional production capacity overseas.

Second, expense reduction could come from two sources:

1. By distributing Stokely's products via its own national distribution network and thereby eliminating the food brokerage fees currently incurred by Stokely (almost 8 percent of sales).
2. By consolidating some of Stokely's administrative, R&D, and marketing functions with Quaker's.

Third, Quaker's sales are moderately skewed toward cold weather months, while Stokely sales are heavily skewed toward the summer months. With a product mix that covers all seasons of the year, the combined company could decrease cyclicality and gain greater productivity from its sales and distribution network than either company could independently.

Fourth, Quaker has leverage over retailers. Because of its many market-leading brands, Quaker has strong consumer loyalty which translates into favorable shelf space and cooperation from retailers on promotions. This would make it easier for Quaker to introduce new Gatorade flavors and sizes or roll out some of the Van Camp products nationally.

Stokely's vegetable oils and Pomona and Purity Mills lines offer no sources of synergies to Quaker. It is estimated that these operations and other miscellaneous businesses could be divested for approximately $70 million.

Translating Synergies into Financial Forecasts

In this section the potential synergies discussed above are translated into financial forecasts for the value drivers: sales growth, profit margins, fixed and working capital investment requirements, taxes, and the cost of capital. A forecast period of five years (1984–1988) is used.

Sales

Stokely's sales in fiscal 1983 were $383.1 million (excluding sales from businesses that were divested shortly before the acquisition). Without the merger Stokely's sales can be forecast to continue growing at the current rate of 4.5 percent annually. If the companies merged, Stokely's sales growth could be forecast to drop to 1 percent in the first year (reflecting an assumed divestiture of the vegetable oil business), but could then jump to 7 percent in the next two years and to 8 percent for the final two years as the benefits of Quaker's marketing prowess begin to be realized.

Operating Profit Margins

Without the merger Stokely's margins could be expected to remain at 5.5 percent for two years and then shrink to 5 percent as competitive pressures increase. If the companies merged, Quaker would improve margins by eliminating food brokers' fees, although for the first two years those savings would be offset by heavy marketing expenses as Quaker tries to build national brand awareness for Gatorade. Therefore Stokely's margins are forecast at 5.5 percent and 6.0 percent for the first two years, and then rising in the next three years to 6.5 percent, 7 percent, and 8 percent, respectively.

Fixed Capital Investment

Without the merger Stokely's capital expenditures are expected to remain fairly level for the first three years ($11.2, $11.5, and $12.2, all in millions) and then increase in the last two years ($18.9 million and $17.2 million) to expand capacity. If the companies merged, investment would be more aggressive. In the first two years all Gatorade production lines would need to be expanded, and two Gatorade plants would be built in Europe. We will also forecast investment in a new U.S. plant in the fourth year. The yearly forecasts are as follows: $14.5, $16.2, $14.6, $21.2, and $18.8, all in millions.

Incremental Working Capital Investment

Without the merger Stokely would probably continue to invest about 12 cents in working capital for every dollar of increased sales each year. If the companies merged, Stokely would be able to reduce its investment in working capital to about 10 cents a year as a result of improved inventory turnover and receivables management.

Taxes

If Quaker acquires Stokely, Stokely's book and cash income tax rates would both be lower as a result of the tax shield created by the step-up of assets. The book tax rate would be reduced from 46 percent to 43 percent, and the cash tax rate would decline from 40 percent to 37 percent.

Cost of Capital

Before the merger Stokely's weighted average cost of debt and equity was 13.8 percent. Stokely's post-merger cost of capital of 12.9 percent is based on two assumptions: (1) Stokely's debt would increase if it were part of Quaker (i.e., target debt/equity ratio would change from 28 percent to 38 percent), and (2) Stokely would be able to borrow at Quaker's rate (10.5 percent) instead of its own (14 percent). (We assume here that Quaker's size relative to Stokely and its ability to fully integrate Stokely into itself would enable Stokely to borrow at Quaker's rate.)

Revaluation of Assets and Liabilities

In a taxable purchase, a buyer can elect for tax purposes to "step up" the basis of its assets and liabilities, which entails writing up the value of balance sheet items to the purchase price paid for them. In this case assets were written up $76 million. Quaker also applied a new, more accelerated depreciation schedule to the assets acquired from Stokely. The present value of tax reductions resulting from the step-up of assets and the investment tax credits is estimated to be about $10 million.

Market Value of Other Obligations

After the merger the market value of Stokely's other long-term obligations would be $2.2 million, representing the estimated present value of "golden parachutes" for Stokely's top executives. These "parachutes" consist of salaries and bonuses and would be triggered by the sale of Stokely to Quaker.

VALUATIONS OF STOKELY: STAND-ALONE AND WITH SYNERGIES

The value driver forecasts are used to estimate the cash flows for each year which appear in column 1 of Table 9–2. Column 2 shows each of the cash flows discounted by the 13.8 percent cost of capital. Column 3 presents the cumulative present value of those cash flows. Column 4 takes the capitalized value of the sustainable cash flows at the end of each year and discounts it back to the present. Column 5 is simply the sum of columns 3 and 4.

Next, the current value of investment holdings, Marketable Securities, is added to the $76.8 million cumulative present value of the cash flows and residual value (because these investments are not accounted for in the operating cash flows but do have a value to the firm) to arrive at the total corporate value. Finally, the portion of the company that belongs to debtholders and pension holders is subtracted, which results in the equity holders' poriton. This stand-alone "shareholder value" for Stokely is expressed both in total dollars ($150.3 million) and also on a per-share basis ($54.53).

Table 9–2 Cash Flows and Shareholder Value for Stokely Stand-Alone (Average Cost of Capital = 13.8%) ($ in millions)

YEAR	CASH FLOW	PRESENT VALUE	CUMULATIVE PRESENT VALUE	PRESENT VALUE OF RESIDUAL VALUE	CUMULATIVE PV + PV OF RESIDUAL VALUE
1984	$11.336	$9.962	$ 9.962	$75.712	$85.673
1985	8.942	6.904	16.866	69.524	86.391
1986	8.032	5.450	22.316	58.039	80.355
1987	2.492	1.486	23.802	53.296	77.098
1988	7.744	4.057	27.860	48.940	76.800
		Marketable securities			116.700
		CORPORATE VALUE			$193.500
		Less: Market value of debt			42.800
		Less: Unfunded pension liabilities			0.400
		SHAREHOLDER VALUE			$150.300
		Shareholder value per share			$54.43
		Current stock price			$70.00[a]

[a]Stokely's stock price was close to $70 several days prior to Quaker's tender offer in anticipation of a considerably higher bid than the $62 per share Pillsbury had offered Stokely almost a month before.

Next, the value of Stokely to Quaker is calculated incorporating into the projections the effect of synergies described earlier. The value of Stokely's stock now increases from the stand-alone value of $54.43 to a value of about $88 per share, as shown in Table 9–3. This exhibit indicates that based on the set of assumptions used for this analysis, Quaker would be willing to pay a maximum of $87.81 per share for Stokely before taking into account any costs associated with the deal. As discussed earlier, an actual analysis would, of course, involve analysis of several alternative scenarios in order to determine a *range* of values for the acquisition candidate.

As is so often the case in a mature industry, Stokely's value is particularly sensitive to changes in the operating profit margin. As Table 9–4 reveals, a 1 percent improvement in the profit margin would increase shareholder value by $1.583 million. In examining more closely the sensitivity of shareholder value to changes in the operating profit margin we would find that for every improvement in margins of 0.5 percent, an additional $3.67 of value per share is created.

Table 9–3 Cash Flows and Shareholder Value for Stokely with Synergies (Average Cost of Capital = 12.9%) ($ in millions)

Year	Cash Flow	Present Value	Cumulative Present Value	Present Value of Residual Value	Cumulative PV + PV of Residual Value
1984	$84.064[a]	$74.459	$74.459	$78.905	$153.364
1985	5.149	4.039	78.498	81.580	160.079
1986	9.831	6.831	85.330	83.760	169.090
1987	6.167	3.796	89.126	86.288	175.414
1988	14.305	7.799	96.924	94.335	191.259
		Marketable securities			116.700
		CORPORATE VALUE			$307.959
		Less: Market value of debt			42.800
		Less: Unfunded pension liabilities			0.400
		Less: Market value of other obligations			2.200
		SHAREHOLDER VALUE			$262.559
		Shareholder value per share			$87.81
		Current stock price			$70.00

[a]This large cash flow reflects the divestitures of the vegetable oils business and the Pomona and Purity Mills lines for $70 million.

Table 9–4 Relative Impact of Key Variables on Shareholder Value for Stokely with Synergies ($ in millions)

A 1% INCREASE IN:	INCREASES SHAREHOLDER VALUE BY:	% INCREASE
Sales growth rate	$ 0.048	0.018
Operating profit margin	1.583	0.603
Incremental fixed capital investment	(0.221)	(0.084)
Incremental working capital investment	(0.087)	(0.033)
Cash income tax rate	(0.376)	(0.143)
Residual value income tax rate	(0.804)	(0.306)
Cost of capital	(1.645)	(0.627)

Quaker's Self-Evaluation

If Quaker's estimated shareholder value per share is greater than its current stock price, the company would probably be better off using its debt capacity and offering cash for the seller's shares rather than issuing additional shares. The analysis of Quaker led to the conclusion that its estimated shareholder value and market value were virtually identical. In addition, keep in mind that comparing shareholder value per share and the current stock price provides only one criterion for determining deal structure. Other factors go into making the final determination, including the tax effects of the proposed structure, the funds available from investments and borrowing, capital structure, and whether the buyer wants the seller to participate in the ownership of the new company (which always occurs in a shares deal). Quaker did in fact offer cash. The deal therefore qualified as a taxable purchase and thereby enabled Quaker to step up Stokely's assets.

Value Created for Quaker

How much value is created for Quaker? Is more value being acquired than surrendered? The amount of value acquired consists of the shareholder value of Stokely plus the anticipated synergies that would arise from the proposed merger. The value surrendered consists of the purchase price and the total costs of completing the deal.

All of this is presented in Table 9–5. The shareholder value of Stokely of $150.3 million comes from Table 9–2. After adding to this amount the anticipated synergies of $112.259 million and then deducting the recapture tax and deal costs, the value created for Quaker is just $177,000, or about one cent per share.

Based on the analysis in Table 9–5, the maximum price per share that Quaker would be willing to pay is $77.04 per share. This figure represents the shareholder value acquired including the synergies ($150.3 million plus $112.259 million) less the recapture tax and deal costs ($26.2 million plus $6 million) divided by the number of Stokely's shares outstanding (2.99 million). However, this does not give a definitive indication of the desirability of the deal. Very slight changes in the forecast data could materially affect the analysis.

The next step in the analytical process is to determine which factors have the greatest impact on the value of the deal and evaluate the impact of alternative scenarios on the deal.

The sensitivity matrix in Table 9–6 shows that if Stokely's cost of capital were actually 0.5 percentage points higher (i.e., 13.4 per-

Table 9–5 Value Created for the Quaker Oats Company—Quaker-Stokely Merger (Deal Price: $77 per Share) ($ in millions)

	Amount
Cumulative present value of cash flows: Seller	$ 27.860
Present value of residual value: Seller	48.940
Marketable securities: Seller	116.700
Corporate value: Seller	$193.500
Less: Market value of debt: Seller	42.800
Less: Unfunded pension liability: Seller	0.400
Shareholder value: Seller	$150.300[a]
Seller synergies acquired	112.259[b]
Less: Recapture tax: Buyer portion	26.200
Less: Transaction costs: Buyer portion	6.000
Less: Purchase price	230.182[c]
Value created for Quaker	$ 0.177

[a]This shareholder value was originally calculated in Figure 9–2 using Stokely's cash flows before incorporating synergies.

[b]The value of these synergies is calculated as the difference between the shareholder value of Stokely on a stand-alone basis ($150.3 million; see Table 9–2) and the shareholder value of Stokely with synergies ($262.559 million; see Table 9–3).

[c]This purchase price reflects the acquisition of 2.99 million shares at $77 per share.

Table 9–6 Sensitivity of Maximum Cash Price per Share to Changes in Key Variables—Quaker-Stokely Merger (Deal Price: $77 per Share)

		Operating Profit Margin of Seller		
		– 0.50%	0.00%	0.50%
Cost of	– 0.50%	75.53	79.29	83.04
Capital	0.00%	73.44	77.04	80.65
of Seller	0.50%	71.50	74.97	78.44

cent instead of 12.9 percent) the maximum cash price Quaker would be willing to pay would decline moderately (from $77.04 per share to $74.97). However, a rise in cost of capital coupled with a decline in operating profit margin would have a considerable negative effect on value. Quaker would probably assume that Stokely's cost of capital could not be significantly lower than the projected value of 12.9 percent. Therefore the bottom two-thirds of the matrix is the most meaningful portion. This matrix suggests that the maximum price Quaker would be willing to pay under that range of conditions is between $71.50 and $80.65 per share.

The effect of the same scenarios on the deal's internal rate of return based on a purchase price of $77 per share is shown in Table 9–7.

Note that if the cost of capital were higher but the operating profit margin remained unchanged, the IRR would decline from 12.9 percent (in the center cell) to 12.3 percent. If the same increase in the cost of capital were combined with a 1 percent decline in the operating profit margin, the effect is more dramatic, reducing the IRR to 10.3 percent.

Another set of scenarios deals with sales and operating profit margins, as shown in Table 9–8. Finding the value created under

Table 9–7 Sensitivity of Internal Rate of Return to Changes in Key Variables—Quaker-Stokely Merger (Deal Price: $77 per Share)

		Operating Profit Margin of Seller		
		– 0.50%	0.00%	0.50%
Cost of	– 0.50%	11.6	13.6	15.5
Capital	0.00%	10.9	12.9	14.8
of Seller	0.50%	10.3	12.3	14.2

Table 9–8 Sensitivity of Maximum Cash Price Per Share to Changes in Key Variables—Quaker-Stokely Merger (Deal Price: $77 per Share)

		Sales Growth Rate of Seller		
		– 2%	0.00%	2%
Operating Profit Margin of Seller	– 0.50%	72.21	73.44	74.67
	0.00%	75.55	77.04	78.57
	0.50%	78.89	80.65	82.46

these scenarios would be particularly useful to Quaker analysts because differing expectations about Gatorade's performance would strongly affect total sales and margins.

We can see that even a 0.5 percent improvement in profit margins has a greater impact on value than a 2 percent sales increase. But the combined impact of improvements in both factors is significant. If sales growth is 2 percent higher than expected and those sales are accompanied by a 0.5 percent improvement in margins (as Gatorade's high margins help increase the overall corporate profit margins), then the maximum price to pay for Stokely would rise to $82.46.

We can also analyze the effect of various deal structures on traditional accounting-based measures such as net income, earnings per share, and price/earnings multiples. For example, it is interesting to note that at the $77 per share purchase price, value is being created for shareholders despite the fact that there would be a modest amount of short-term earnings dilution in 1984, as below:

	1983	1984	1985	1986	1987	1988
EPS: with acquisition	$6.68	$6.49	$7.82	$8.84	$9.98	$11.31
EPS: without acquisition	6.48	6.58	7.56	8.48	9.49	10.61

The fundability of the deal is another critical issue to examine. Even a very attractive price means little to the buyer who cannot acquire the funds required to complete the transaction. In Quaker's case, its cash on hand in the form of marketable securities and its unused debt capacity means that while it had to borrow about $140 million to finance the acquisition the company was well within its target capital structure range.

Not surprisingly, the acquisition had a very positive effect on the performance of Stokely's stock. For Quaker, the initial market reaction was quite negative, although the stock did regain some of its post-announcement losses over the subsequent two weeks.

The initial negative market reaction to Quaker's acquisition might be due to several possibilities:

1. Not all the information possessed by Quaker was immediately available to the market (such as the amount of cash that could be obtained by selling some of Stokely's "detachable assets" such as corporate airplanes and real estate).
2. Quaker and the market may have had different assessments of the synergies that could be achieved.
3. The market may have expected Quaker to be investing in strategies (including acquisitions) at a rate of return somewhat *above* their required rate of return rather than exactly *at* their cost of capital.

In the two years after the merger Quaker's overall performance has exceeded that of its peer group (General Foods, General Mills, Kellogg, and Beatrice) as well as the market as a whole (using the Standard & Poor's 400 as a proxy for the market), as is shown in Figure 9–1 by the graph of total returns to shareholders (dividends plus stock price appreciation).

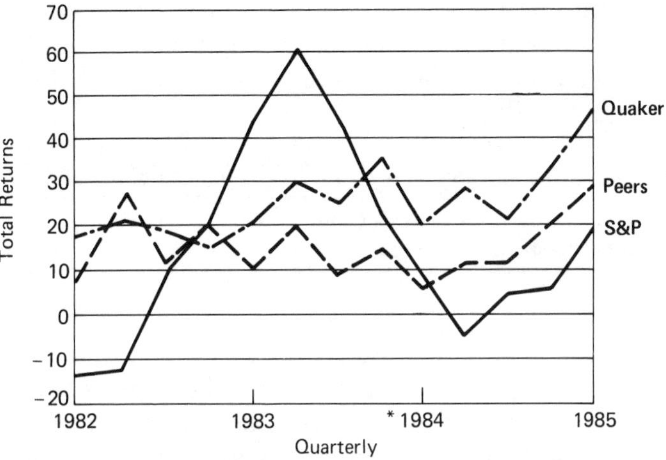

Figure 9–1 Quaker's Total Shareholder Returns Before and After the Merger

The acquisition of Stokely in general and Gatorade in particular has been viewed as a complete success by Quaker's management. As Quaker's chairman and CEO, William D. Smithburg commented in a presentation to financial analysts in October of 1983, "Gatorade is clearly the jewel of the acquisition. It's a profitable, well-organized brand with good growth potential." He also mentioned that although Quaker had bought all of Stokely's businesses, they would follow through on their intention to divest all Stokely units except Gatorade and Van Camp products.

Fortune smiled upon this acquisition in several ways, at least one of which Quaker could hardly have forecast. "As it turned out," Smithburg said in his presentation, "the hot summer gave a major boost to Gatorade's performance." In fact, the summer of 1983 proved to be one of the hottest on record—and nothing could have served as a more effective stimulus to Gatorade's sales.

Stokely also proved to be more cash-rich than the investment community had anticipated. Smithburg reported, "The cash balance turned out to be $123 million." The disclosure of that positive information contributed to the recovery of Quaker's stock price after the merger. As Smithburg concluded at the time of the acquisition, "All in all we believe Stokely is an outstanding value for the price."

The experience of companies that have implemented the foregoing approach to acquisition analysis indicates that it is not only an effective way of evaluating a prospective acquisition candidate, but serves as a catalyst for reevaluating a company's overall strategic plans. The results also enable management to justify acquisition recommendations to the board of directors in an economically sound, convincing fashion. Whether companies are seeking acquisitions or are acquisition targets, it is increasingly clear that they must provide better information to enable top management and boards to make well-conceived, timely decisions. Use of the approach outlined here should improve the prospects of creating value for shareholders by acquisitions.

Notes and References

Chapter 1: Shareholder Value and Corporate Purpose

1. Michael L. Blyth, Elizabeth A. Friskey, and Alfred Rappaport, "Implementing the Shareholder Value Approach," *Journal of Business Strategy*, Winter 1986, pp. 48–58.
2. George S. Kimmel, "Creating Shareholder Value: A Primary Financial Objective," *Forum*, June 1984, p. 14.
3. "Executive Pay: Who Made the Most," *Business Week*, May 6, 1985, p. 89.
4. For a particularly lucid analysis of this argument, see William H. Meckling and Michael C. Jensen, "Reflections on the Corporation as a Social Invention," *Midland Corporate Finance Journal*, Fall 1983.
5. Adolph A. Berle and Gardiner C. Means, *The Modern Corporation and Private Property*, revised edition (New York: Harcourt Brace Jovanovich, 1968).
6. Thomas J. Peters and Robert H. Waterman, Jr., *In Search of Excellence* (New York: Harper & Row, 1982).
7. W. Bruce Johnson, Ashok Natarajan, and Alfred Rappaport, "Shareholder Returns and Corporate Excellence," *Journal of Business Strategy*, Fall 1985.
8. Some executives have used the term "restructuring" to justify almost any strategy that departs from business as usual. *Business Week* hu-

morously (I assume) defines restructuring as "writing down and leveraging up."

9. Jack L. Treynor, "The Financial Objective in the Widely Held Corporation," *Financial Analysts Journal*, March–April, 1981.
10. *Ibid.*, p. 71.
11. *Ibid.*, p. 69.

Chapter 2: Shortcomings of Accounting Numbers

1. This assumes that the change in accounting is for financial reporting purposes and does not affect the computation of income taxes. It is, of course, also possible that an accounting change is seen as a signal for some more fundamental changes in the company's prospects. For example, a change to an income-increasing accounting method (e.g., a switch from accelerated to straight-line depreciation) may be viewed by the market as indicating a downturn in the company earnings prospects. In such a situation the accounting change may trigger a decrease in share price. Note, however, the market value decline is not due to the accounting change *per se*, but rather due to information inferred from management's decision to make an accounting change.
2. The expected value is calculated summing the product of each outcome times the probability of that outcome. The expected value of Strategy A is computed as follows:

PROBABILITY	EARNINGS GROWTH RATE	
.10	6%	0.6%
.25	8	2.0
.30	10	3.0
.25	12	3.0
.10	14	1.4
Expected value		10.0%

3. The standard deviation, σ, is:

$$\sigma = \sqrt{\sum_{i=1}^{n} (g_i - \bar{g})^2 p_i}$$

where g_i = earnings growth rate for the ith possible outcome
$\bar{g}$ = expected value of the earnings growth rate
p_i = probability of g_i occurring

Using the above formula the standard deviations for the strategies are computed as follows:

$$\text{Strategy A} = [(6-10)^2 .10 + (8-10)^2 .25 + (10-10)^2 .30 + (12-10)^2 .25 + (14-10)^2 .10]^{1/2} = \underline{\underline{2.28\%}}$$

$$\text{Strategy B} = [(8-10)^2 .05 + (9-10)^2 .25 + (10-10)^2 .40 + (11-10)^2 .25 + (12-10)^2 .05]^{1/2} = \underline{\underline{0.90\%}}$$

4. As will be discussed more fully in Chapter 3, the overall cost of funds or the firm's cost of capital depends on the mix of debt and equity financing. Because of its prior claim to the firm's assets and because of the deductibility of interest expense for tax purposes, the cost of debt is less than the cost of equity funds. However, as the relative proportion of debt increases so does the cost of equity. The financial manager's challenge is to seek the lowest overall or weighted average cost of funds by examining the tradeoff between introducing lower cost debt and raising the cost of equity.
5. For ease of exposition, but without any loss of generality, assume that the firm has no debt and thus finances all investment via equity.
6. The 1 percent rate of return can be shown by discounting each annual flow by the 1 percent discount factor, summing the resulting present values, and observing that the present value of the cash flows is equal to the $1 million initial investment amount.

Year	Cash Flow	1% Discount Factor	Present Value
1	206,040	.9901	$ 204,000
2	206,040	.9803	201,981
3	206,040	.9706	199,982
4	206,040	.9610	198,004
5	206,040	.9515	196,047
Rounding error			(14)
			$1,000,000

7. The present value (PV) of a cash flow perpetuity which begins one period from now is equal to the cash flow perpetuity (CF) divided by the discount rate (k), that is $PV = \frac{CF}{k}$. This result can be derived as follows:

$$PV = \frac{CF}{(1+k)} + \frac{CF}{(1+k)^2} \cdots \frac{CF}{(1+k)^t}$$

$$PV\,(1+k) = CF + \frac{CF}{(1+k)} + \frac{CF}{(1+k)^2} \cdots \frac{CF}{(1+k)^t}$$

$$PV\,(1+k) = CF + PV$$

$$PV = \frac{CF}{k}$$

8. Alfred Rappaport, "Selecting Strategies That Create Shareholder Value," *Harvard Business Review*, May–June 1981, pp. 139–149.
9. For example, the 1980 Fortune 500 survey reports that forty-eight, or almost 10 percent, of the companies achieved positive EPS growth rates, while shareholders suffered negative rates of return for the 1969–1979 period.
10. James S. Reece and William R. Cool, "Measuring Investment Center Performance," *Harvard Business Review*, May–June 1978, p. 30.
11. *Ibid.*, p. 29.
12. Ezra Solomon, "Return of Investment: The Relation of Book-yield to True Yield," in *Research in Accounting Measurement* (Chicago: American Accounting Association, 1966), reprinted in Alfred Rappaport, *Information for Decision Making* (Englewood Cliffs, N.J.: Prentice-Hall, 1982.)
13. Solomon demonstrates that when the growth rate in investment is identical to the DCF rate of return ROI will also be equal to the DCF rate of return. When investment is growing at less than the DCF rate, ROI will be greater than DCF rate of return. The reverse is true as well.
14. Alfred Rappaport, "Don't Sell Stock Market Horizons Short," Manager's Journal, *Wall Street Journal*, June 27, 1983.
15. Michael Hergert, "Will Corporate Performance Decline in an Improving Economy," *The Journal of Business Strategy*, Spring 1983, p. 101.
16. Barbara S. Thomas, a former commissioner of the SEC, makes the following observation: "I find it somewhat amazing that for over 500 years, indeed until the 1930s, the central focus of accounting and financial reporting was on cash flow and solvency. Yet, for the past 50 years, which includes the entire lifespan of the Commission to date, and the period of greatest development of public external reporting in the United States, the financial community has been obsessed with the income statement and its all-important bottom-line figures—net income and earnings per share." "Deregulation and Cash Flow Reporting: One Viewpoint," *Financial Executive*, January 1983, p. 21.
17. This section is adapted from William H. Beaver and Alfred Rappaport, "Financial Reporting Needs More Than the Computer," Ideas & Trends, *Business Week*, August 13, 1984, p. 16.

Chapter 3: Shareholder Value Approach

1. The market value rather than the book value of debt should be used. During periods of inflation current interest rates may be well above

the interest rates on debt instruments of earlier years. Rising interest rates typically cause market values to fall below book values. In this case, the use of book values would overstate the economic value of the liabilities and therefore understate shareholder value.

2. For valuation purposes, the appropriate way to estimate a company's future working capital investment in inventories is to multiply the additional units of inventory required to support incremental sales by the incremental cost per unit. This approach focuses on the actual cash outlays required for additional inventory and is, therefore, unaffected by a company's inventory valuation method (e.g., LIFO, FIFO) and overhead allocation policies (e.g., depreciation component of inventory).
3. Some financial executives argue against the use of market value weights on the grounds that stock price volatility would result in a volatile cost of capital. This argument is not particularly compelling since cost of capital should be based on target weights rather than capital structure resulting from market price changes. There is no reason to believe that a management-designated target market value structure would be more volatile than a target book value structure.
4. The theoretical foundation for estimating a company's cost of equity capital is provided by the capital asset pricing model (CAPM). The CAPM model is one of the cornerstones of modern finance theory. It provides a methodology for quantifying risk and then using it to estimate the expected return on equity capital. For a particularly lucid exposition of the theory as well as corporate applications see David W. Mullins, Jr., "Does the Capital Asset Pricing Model Work?" *Harvard Business Review*, January-February 1982, pp. 105–114. A comprehensive source of yields on various assets can be found in *Stocks, Bonds, Bills, and Inflation*, a quarterly service of Ibbotson Associates in Chicago.
5. By investing in a portfolio broadly representative of the overall equity market, it is possible to diversify away substantially all of the unsystematic risk—that is, risk specific to individual companies, e.g., the company's president dies unexpectedly, oil is discovered on company property, etc. Therefore, securities are likely to be priced at levels that reward investors only for the nondiversifiable market risk—that is, the systematic risk in movements in the overall market. Beta is a measure of systematic risk.
6. A more detailed discussion can be found in Barr Rosenberg and James Guy, "Prediction of a Beta from Investment Fundamentals," *Financial Analysts Journal*, May-June, 1976, pp. 3–15. Arbitrage Pricing Theory (APT) developed by Professor Stephen Ross of Yale University is attracting increasing interest in the investment community as a po-

tential challenger to the CAPM model. APT maintains the basic CAPM assumption that investors will be rewarded only for systematic risk, i.e., market risk that cannot be diversified away. Unlike CAPM which measures risk solely by the sensitivity of a security's return to movements in a broad market index, APT identifies sources of systematic risk as *unanticipated* changes in key economic factors such as inflation, industrial production, yield curves, and spreads between high-and low-grade bonds.

7. Bradley T. Gale and Ben Branch, "Cash Flow Analysis: More Important Than Ever," *Harvard Business Review*, July-August 1981, pp. 131–136.
8. For a more detailed discussion of product-market imperfections that can give rise to excess returns, see Alan C. Shapiro, "Corporate Strategy and The Capital Budgeting Decision," *Midland Corporate Finance Journal*, Spring 1985, pp. 22–36.
9. To say that the returns from a particular strategy will eventually be driven down to the minimum required rate of return *does not* imply that the company will never be able to earn returns above the cost of capital after the original forecast period. Companies can and do initiate new value-creating strategies on an ongoing basis, and future forecasts will take additional value creation into account. But the value-creating strategies available at any point simply have a limited "life span," and the value of the firm when the strategy is no longer expected to yield excess returns can be estimated by the perpetuity method.

   Not all value-creating strategies have the same life span. Factors such as the rate of technological change, the threat of substitute products, the length of the product life cycle, and the barriers to entry into the industry all affect the life span of a strategy or the period of sustainable competitive advantage. For example, strategies using new technologies typically have relatively long life spans (e.g., ten to fifteen years) because they normally involve a lengthy period of research and development before the products are released. By contrast, strategies involving product-line extensions in mature industries typically have relatively short life spans (e.g., three to five years) due to the intense rivalry among firms in the industry.
10. The perpetuity assumption is a much less aggressive assumption than it might appear initially. This is true because as cash flows become more distant their values in present value terms become correspondingly smaller. For example, a $1.00 perpetuity discounted at 15 percent has a value of $1.00/.15 = $6.67. Below are the present values for annual annuities of $1.00 for periods ranging from five to twenty five years:

Years	Present Value of Annuity	Percent of Perpetuity Value
5	$3.35	50.2%
10	5.02	75.3
15	5.85	87.7
20	6.26	93.9
25	6.46	96.9

Note that by the tenth year 75 percent of the perpetuity value is reached and after another five years 90 percent is approached. As the discount rate is increased, the perpetuity value is approached over a shorter span of time.

11. The perpetuity calculation is based on cash flow before new investment because we do not need to take into account the additional investments in fixed and working capital during the post-forecast period. Although investments in expansion projects in the post-forecast period may help increase the future cash inflows, as long as the investment is earning only the cost of capital rate of return, any increase in cash inflows will be offset by the investment cash outflows required to expand capacity.

    Since investment beyond the forecast period will not affect the value of the firm, in order to calculate the residual value you need only to account for the investment required to maintain existing capacity. In the perpetuity method, it is assumed that the cost of maintaining existing capacity is approximately equal to depreciation expense. If operating profit (before depreciation) in any year is abnormally high or low, it will yield misleading results when serving as a basis for the perpetuity calculation. This problem occurs most frequently with companies in cyclical industries, where the calculated residual value will be abnormally high in "boom" years and abnormally low in "bust" years. To compensate for this it may be necessary to make an adjustment to "normalize" the operating profit.

12. The threshold margin concept was introduced in my article, "Selecting Strategies That Create Shareholder Value," *Harvard Business Review*, May-June 1981, pp. 139-149. For a discussion of how such factors as capital intensity, asset mix, economic life of depreciable assets, income tax rate, risk, and inflation affect the threshold margin; see Bala V. Balachandran, Nandu J. Nagarajan, and Alfred Rappaport, "Threshold Margins for Creating Economic Value," *Financial Management*, Spring 1986, pp. 68–77.

13. In this formulation the residual value income tax is assumed to be equal to the cash income tax rate. This assumption can be easily relaxed by modifying the term.

Chapter 4: Competitive Strategy Framework

1. Michael E. Porter, *Competitive Strategy* (New York: Free Press, 1980).
2. For many businesses research and development represents a third essential investment category. Pharmaceutical companies whose prospects are tied to new product development are an obvious example.
3. Porter provides the following succinct overview: "Buyer power influences the prices that firms can charge, for example, as does the threat of substitution. The power of buyers can also influence cost and investment, because powerful buyers demand costly service. The bargaining power of suppliers determines the costs of raw materials and other inputs. The intensity of rivalry influences prices as well as costs of competing in areas such as plant, product development, advertising, and sales force. The threat of entry places a limit on prices, and shapes the investment required to deter entrants." Michael E. Porter, *Competitive Advantage* (New York: Free Press, 1985), p. 5.
4. *Ibid.*, p. 3.
5. For a more detailed discussion of value activities, see *ibid.*, pp. 33–53.
6. To illustrate, consider a firm evaluating two alternatives for its initial capital structure—leverage and no leverage. The firm requires $10 million and the initial price per share of common stock of $10. The financial leverage alternative calls for selling 500,000 shares and obtaining an equal amount of capital, $5 million, via 6 percent after-tax debt. The no-leverage alternative simply involves the sale of one million shares at $10 per share. Assume that cash flow from operations is projected to be $1 million annually for the most likely case. Optimistic and pessimistic forecasts are $1.5 million and 500,000, respectively. The results of these forecasts are then as follows:

	OPTIMISTIC	MOST LIKELY	PESSIMISTIC
Cash flow from operations	$1,500,000	$1,000,000	$500,000
Interest expense after taxes	60,000	60,000	60,000
Cash flow after interest	1,440,000	940,000	440,000
Cash flow per share—no leverage	1.50	1.00	0.50
Cash flow per share—leverage	2.88	1.88	0.88

For the no-leverage alternative, the percent increase or decrease in cash flow from operations and cash flow per share is identical, while for the leverage alternative the change in cash flow per share is greater than the change in cash flow after interest. In the above case a 50 percent increase or decrease in cash flow from operations leads to a $0.50 change in cash flow per share for the no-leverage alternative. The same percentage change leads to a $1.00 change in cash flow per share for the leverage alternatives.

7. Risk aversion may also manifest itself in unduly conservative estimates of cash flows by overestimating costs or underestimating the magnitude and duration of revenues.
8. Eugene F. Brigham and Louis C. Gapenski, *Intermediate Financial Management* (Chicago: Dryden Press, 1985), p. 214.
9. Porter, *Competitive Advantage*, p. 234.
10. *Ibid.*, p. 238.
11. For a detailed discussion of segmentation variables see *ibid.*, Chapter 7.
12. An excellent source of information about gathering data for an industry or competitive analysis is Appendix B of Porter's *Competitive Strategy*. Also see "How to Snoop on Your Competitors," *Fortune*, May 14, 1984, for a discussion of some of the means currently being employed by companies to obtain information about competitors.
13. Jeffrey R. Williams, "A New Way to Understand Business Competition," working paper, Graduate School of Industrial Administration, Carnegie-Mellon University, May 1985, p. 6.
14. For a detailed discussion of cost leadership and differentiation as sources of competitive advantage see Porter's *Competitive Advantage*, Chapters 3 and 4.

Chapter 5: Value-Creating Business Strategies

1. "The New Breed of Strategic Planner," *Business Week*, September 17, 1984, p. 84.
2. This warning was featured in full-page newspaper advertisements by the investment banking firm of Donaldson, Lufkin and Jenrette.
3. Don Collier, "Strategic Management in Diversified, Decentralized Companies," *The Journal of Business Strategy*, Summer 1982, p. 85.
4. *Ibid.*, pp. 88–89.
5. This section is adapted from my article "Selecting Strategies That Create Shareholder Value," *Harvard Business Review*, May-June 1981, pp. 139–149.

6. Five-year projections are as follows:

	Sales Growth Rate	Operating Profit Margin	Incremental Fixed Investment	Incremental Working Capital Investment	Cash Income Tax Rate	Cost of Capital
Industrial systems	15%	11%	20%	20%	42%	14%
Automotive parts	11	7.5	15	20	44	13

In these analyses different costs of capital (14 percent for industrial systems and 13 percent for automotive parts) were used. The company's cost of capital is not the appropriate rate for discounting the cash flow projection of individual business units. The use of a single discount rate for all parts of the company is valid only in the unlikely event that they are identically risky. Executives who use a single discount rate companywide are likely to have a consistent bias in favor of funding higher-risk businesses at the expense of less risky businesses. To provide a consistent framework for dealing with different investment risks and thereby increasing shareholder value, management should allocate funds to business units on a risk-adjusted return basis.

The process of estimating a business unit's cost of capital inevitably involves a substantial degree of executive judgment. Unlike the company as a whole, ordinarily the business unit has no posted market price that would enable the analyst to estimate systematic or market-related risk. Moreover, it is often difficult to assign future financing (debt and equity) weights to individual business units. One approach to estimating a business unit's cost of equity is to identify publicly traded stocks in the same line of business that might be expected to have about the same degree of systematic or market risk as the business unit. After establishing the cost of equity and cost of debt, the analyst can calculate a weighted-average cost of capital for the business unit in the same fashion as for the company.

7. This section is adapted from Michael L. Blyth, Elizabeth A. Friskey, and Alfred Rappaport, "Implementing the Shareholder Value Approach," *Journal of Business Strategy*, Winter 1986, pp. 48–58.

8. Don Collier, "How to Implement Strategic Plans," *Journal of Business Strategy*, Winter 1984, p. 92.

9. *Ibid.*, p. 93.

10. *Ibid.*, p. 95.

Chapter 6: Financial Feasibility of Strategies

1. The Boston Consulting Group, *Growth and Financial Strategies*, Boston: The Boston Consulting Group, 1968, p. 10.
2. Deferred income taxes result from timing differences in the recognition of some revenue and expense items for book purposes versus tax purposes. As a result of these timing differences, the total tax expense reported on the income statement may not equal the income tax actually paid during the year or payable within one year. Deferred taxes may arise, for example, from taking accelerated depreciation for tax purposes and straight-line depreciation on the company books.
3. Sales growth rather than the asset growth standard of the sustainable growth rate approach discussed in the last section was chosen for testing financial feasibility. This choice is based on the fact that asset growth is almost invariably dictated by sales growth expectations. The reverse, asset growth determining sales growth, would be rarely the case.
4. This case was adapted from Alfred Rappaport, "Do You Know the Value of Your Company?" *Merger & Acquisitions*, Spring 1979, pp. 12–17.
5. The company is assumed to be currently at its target capital structure. Of the $5.708 million in incremental investment, $1.317 million will be financed by debt and the remaining $4.391 million by equity. Note that debt financing constitutes the target 30 percent of the amount financed by equity.
6. The affordable dividend is discussed in two of my articles, "Inflation Accounting and Corporate Dividends," *Financial Executive*, February 1981, pp. 20–22 and "Selecting Strategies That Create Shareholder Value," *Harvard Business Review*, May-June 1981, p. 146.

Chapter 7: Stock Market Signals to Management

1. A 15 percent operating profit margin on next year's sales of $120 is equal to $18 in pretax operating profit and $9 after taxes. With fixed and working capital investment of $8.4 cash flow amounts to $0.6. To this amount add the capitalized (at 14 percent) value of the $9 sustainable cash flow stream of $64.3. The total value at the end of the year of $64.9 represents a 14 percent return on the initial stock price of $57 per share.
2. For a particularly lucid explanation of how elasticity of expectations partially determines the firm's systematic risk see Malcolm S. Salter

and Wolf A. Weinhold, *Diversification Through Acquisition* (New York: Free Press, 1979), pp. 97–99.

3. As discussed in note 1, the capitalized value at the end of the year is $64.3. A 14 percent margin means that cash flow in the first year is zero., Thus, a $64.3 price at the end of the year represents a 12.8 percent return on the initial $57 investment.
4. In my June 27, 1983 *Wall Street Journal* column, "Don't Sell Stock Market Horizons Short," I reported on the proportion of the current stock price assignable to dividends beyond five years. I termed this proportion the long-term value index or LVI. It is a broad index of market confidence in management's ability to implement a sustainable long-term value-creating strategy. Using Value Line dividend projections and recent stock prices, I calculated LVIs for over 1200 companies and a broad cross-section of industries. I found a large clustering around 80 percent. The lowest LVIs in the range of 60 to 70 percent were for the major public utilities—electric, natural gas, and telephone. The highest were for industries such as electronic components (93 percent), medical instruments (89 percent), retail drug stores (89 percent), radio-TV transmitting equipment (88 percent) and electronic computers (86 percent).
5. Lawrence J. Gitman and Vincent A. Mercurio, "Cost of Capital Techniques Used by Major U.S. Firms: Survey and Analysis of Fortune's 1000," *Financial Management*, Winter 1982, pp. 21–29.
6. "Companies Feel Underrated by the Street," *Business Week*, February 20, 1984, p. 14.
7. The efficient-market theory has come under attack as more recent research uncovers some market anomalies. The so-called "small-firm effect", for example, evolves from research that shows that small-capitalization stocks have outperformed large capitalization stocks over long periods of time. Even these findings are however controversial because others contend that the problem lies not with the efficient-market theory but with beta as a measure of risk. These critics assert if the risk of small-capitalization stocks were measured in other ways, they would not outperform the market consistently. Despite the uncovering of several anomalies, according to figures compiled by SEI Funds Evaluation Services, in the fifteen-year period to 1984 over two thirds of the professionals who manage common stock portfolios were outperformed by the unmanaged Standard & Poor's stock index.
8. Allen H. Seed, III, "Winning Strategies for Shareholder Value Creation," *The Journal of Business Strategy*, Fall 1985, p. 51.

Chapter 8: Performance Evaluation and Executive Compensation

1. "Top Executives Pay Peeves the Public," *Business Week*, June 25, 1984. p. 15.
2. Peter F. Drucker, "Reform Executive Pay or Congress Will," *Wall Street Journal*, April 24, 1984.
3. Graef Crystal, "Congress Thinks It Knows Best About Executive Compensation," *Wall Street Journal*, July 30, 1984.
4. Louis J. Brindisi, Jr., "Why Executive Compensation Programs Go Wrong," *Wall Street Journal*, Manager's Journal, June 14, 1982. The disparity between growth in executive compensation and shareholder return does not provide unambiguous evidence that incentives are misdirected. Instead it may reflect a policy that rewards executives for relative rather than absolute performance, particularly during difficult times such as the inflationary 1970s. Shareholders in a given company who realized no real return from 1971 to 1981 may well have done worse were it not for decisions made by management during the period. An alternative but more speculative hypothesis is that the market expectations reflected in 1981 prices were in the judgment of management unduly pessimistic and had they been at more "realistic" levels investors would also have achieved a positive real rate of return for the 1971–1981 period.
5. Lawrence C. Bickford, "Long-Term Incentives for Management, Part 6: Performance Attainment Plans," *Compensation Review*, Third Quarter 1981, p. 14.
6. Richard A. Lambert and David F. Larcker, "Executive Compensation, Corporate Decision-Making and Shareholder Wealth: A Review of the Evidence," *Midland Corporate Finance Journal*, Winter 1985, pp. 7–8.
7. *Creating Shareholder Value: A New Mission for Executive Compensation*, Booz Allen and Hamilton, Inc., 1983, p. 8.
8. Mark C. Ubelhart, "A New Look at Executive Compensation Plans," *Cashflow*, May 1981, p. 1.
9. Arthur M. Louis, "Business is Bungling Long-Term Compensation," *Fortune*, July 23, 1984, p. 65.
10. Johnson Controls, Inc., 1984 Proxy Statement, p. 8.
11. As a reflection of the increasing scrutiny under which executive compensation has come, the popular business publications such as *Fortune* and *Business Week* have begun to publish compensation surveys that examine the correlation between the executives' pay and how well their companies have performed based on several measures—

including returns to shareholders. For example, *Business Week*'s executive compensation scoreboard now includes a "pay-performance index" for 255 companies in 36 industries. The index shows how well the top two executives in each company were paid relative to how shareholders fared. The index is the ratio of the executive's three-year total pay as a percent of the industry average and the shareholders' total three-year return as a percent of the industry average.

If an executive's pay and shareholders' return are both at the industry average, the index is 100. The lower the index, the better shareholders fared. The broad range in the pay-performance index, even within industries, has further fueled the interest in achieving shareholder value.

12. Louis, *op. cit.*, p. 65.
13. "Walton Wriston and the S&P 500," Callard Madden & Associates, Inc., July 24, 1984.
14. This section is adapted from Alfred Rappaport, "How to Design Value-Contributing Executive Incentives," *The Journal of Business Strategy*, Fall 1983, pp 49–59.
15. For expositional purposes only, Alpha is assumed to be an all-equity company. If debt were introduced, it would have to be deducted from the value of the company to arrive at the value of the equity.
16. Another possibility is to introduce a "Soviet incentive scheme," which provides rewards based on the relationship among established targets, the manager's forecast, and actual results. For a given level of actual results, the closer the forecast is to the target, the larger the performance award. This scheme thus motivates the manager to forecast more accurately. For an application, see Jacob Gonik, "Tie Salesmen's Bonuses to Their Forecasts," *Harvard Business Review*, May–June 1978.
17. James G. March, "Executive Decision Making: Some Implications for Executive Compensation," in *Executive Compensation in the 1980's*, David J. McLaughlin, ed. (San Francisco: Pentacle Press, 1980), p. 133.

Chapter 9: Mergers and Acquisitions

1. Malcolm S. Salter and Wolf A. Weinhold, *Diversification Through Acquisition* (New York: Free Press, 1979), p. 117.
2. Stewart Myers sees these strategic growth opportunities as having many of the qualities of options. Myers acknowledges the difficulty of valuing these "options" with our current tools and suggests that in the final analysis the *strategic* case for the merger will have to be made to justify the price. See "The Evaluation of an Acquisition Target," *Mid-*

land Corporate Finance Journal, Winter 1983, pp. 45–46.

3. For a review of some of the major factors to consider in a collaborative venture, see *Collaborate Ventures: An Emerging Phenomenon in the Information Industry* (New York: Coopers & Lybrand, 1984)
4. Salter and Weinhold, *op.cit.*, pp. 136–138.
5. Another example of when a takeover causes assets to be shifted to higher valued uses is presented in the *Economic Report of the President—1985*, Chapter 6, "The Market for Corporate Control," p. 198: "A retail chain may, for example, possess real estate that is more valuable as office sites than retail outlets. Although the retail chain may be well managed, if the company announces it will not sell its real estate or put it to any other use than retailing, then the market has little incentive to value the firm's real estate at its current market price. Even if the market believes that it is inevitable that the firm's real estate will eventually be put to higher valued use, the stock market will substantially discount the property's current market value because of uncertainty over when the transaction will occur and the price that the real estate will bring when sold. The announcement of a takeover attempt at a firm price eliminates much of this uncertainty and can account for a significant portion of the gains resulting from mergers and acquisitions."
6. Many companies have initiated asset restructuring, principally the divestiture of underperforming assets and businesses, and have had favorable market response. Examples include Greyhound, Gulf & Western, Litton, Arco, Allied, ITT, Teledyne, and Whittaker.
7. Julian R. Franks, John E. Broyles, and Willard T. Carleton, *Corporate Finance* (Boston: Kent Publishing Company, 1985), p. 378.
8. Shareholder value may be viewed as corporate value minus value of debt plus the value of a put on corporate value with an exercise price equal to the value of the debt. If the value of the assets or corporate value falls below the value of the debt, shareholders have a right to put the assets to bondholders by defaulting on the outstanding debt. The limited liability of shareholders is precisely this option to default. When mergers increase bond value, the value of shareholders' option to default is correspondingly reduced. For example, the value of the default option for the combined company's debt of $500 million is less than the combined values of the default options on the buyer's $400 million and the seller's $100 million premerger debt. For a particularly useful discussion of the linkage between options and the valuation of risky debt and equity see Richard Brealey and Stewart Myers, *Principles of Corporate Finance*, second edition (New York: McGraw-Hill, 1984), Chapters 20 and 21.
9. Thomas R. Piper and Wolf A. Weinhold, "How Much Debt Is Right

for Your Company?" *Harvard Business Review*, July-August 1982, p. 114.

10. For an overview of recent empirical studies see Michael C. Jensen, "Takeovers: Folklore and Science," *Harvard Business Review*, November-December 1984, pp. 109-121 and Peter Dodd, "The Market for Corporate Control: A Review of the Evidence," *Midland Corporate Finance Journal*. Summer 1983, pp. 6–20. For an illustration of how to compute abnormal returns see Richard S. Ruback, "The Conoco Takeover and Stockholder Returns," *Sloan Management Review*, Winter 1982, pp. 13–33.
11. Because the buyer is on average four to five times larger than the seller, the percentage change in value for the buyer will appear small when compared to the percentage change calculated for the seller.
12. David Larcker, "Managerial Incentives in Mergers and Their Effect on Shareholder Wealth, *Midland Corporate Finance Journal*, Winter 1983, p. 32.
13. Milton L. Rock, "New Focus on Share Prices," *Mergers & Acquisitions*, Spring 1984, p. 4.
14. Michael G. Allen, Alexander R. Oliver, and Edward H. Schwallie, "The Key to Successful Acquisitions," *The Journal of Business Strategy*, Fall 1981, p. 20.
15. Michael Porter, *Competitive Advantage* (New York: Free Press, 1985). For a full discussion of interrelationships among business units and horizontal strategy see Chapters 9 and 10.
16. For more detailed discussions of acquisition search and screen systems see Salter and Weinhold, *op. cit.*, Chapter 9 and James W. Bradley and Donald H. Korn, *Acquisition and Corporate Development* (Lexington, Mass.: Lexington Books, 1981), pp. 85–118.
17. For overviews of some of the cultural issues in mergers see Lawrence A. Bennigson, "Merging Corporate Cultures," *Journal for Corporate Growth*, Volume 1, Number 1, 1985, pp. 73–88 and Myron Magnet, "Acquiring Without Smothering," *Fortune*, November 12, 1984, pp. 22–30.
18. The approach was introduced in my "Strategic Analysis for Profitable Acquisition," *Harvard Business Review*, July-August 1979, pp. 99–110.
19. For a detailed analysis see my "Capital Budgeting Approach to an Exchange-of-Shares Acquisition," *Mergers & Acquisitions*, Fall 1975, pp. 27–29.
20. This case analysis is adapted from Elizabeth A. Friskey and Alfred Rappaport, "Quaker Oats and Stokely–Van Camp," *Mergers & Acquisitions*, Winter 1986. An early version of the case was developed as

a class project by Jim Huston and Laura Thomas and subsequently revised by Jeffrey F. Miller and Robert C. Statius Muller, both of The Alcar Group Inc. For additional case studies illustrating the shareholder value approach to mergers and acquisitions, see "United Technologies and Mostek: After the Acquisition," *Mergers & Acquisitions*, Spring 1982, pp. 49–54 and "American Hospital Supply and Bentley Labs," *Mergers & Acquisitions*, Spring 1984, pp. 50–58.

Index